Catch the Stage
to Phoenix

By Leland J. Hanchett, Jr.

Pine Rim Publishing

Phoenix, Arizona

Cover

Unlike the Hollywood versions, most stage robberies took place where the stage was nearly stopped. Most highway men were not mounted, at least not at the time of the robbery. Liz Hutton, who lives, teaches and paints wildlife in Pleasant Valley did a masterful job of depicting a stage robbery just as it would have occurred on the road to Phoenix. Her husband modeled for each figure.

About the Author

Lee Hanchett is a semi-retired engineer and inventor who enjoys Arizona History so much that he has written four books on the subject. No day is complete without an excursion to some remote spot, which represents, even in a small way, all that was Arizona. There are, he figures, enough such places to keep him going for the next 100 years. By then, he may have to completely retire and take up some new hobby, but for now life couldn't be better.

About the Researcher

Walt Jayroe is a Phoenix freelance writer and researcher. His historical work has appeared in magazines such as *Wild West* and *New Mexico*. In the late 1980s, he began a selective index of the old *Arizona Miner*. The project soon began to mushroom in scope and consume hundreds of hours. The result is "The Miner Index," a history of Arizona Territory, 1864–1880, scribbled on a jillion 3 × 5 cards and kept in shoeboxes in a closet.

Line Drawings by Kris Karalius using CAD 14

Typeset in Century Old Style by Graphic Edge, Phoenix, Arizona

Color Separations by Digital Industries, Phoenix, Arizona

Printed by Graphic Edge, Phoenix, Arizona

Bound by Central Bindery Company and Roswell Bookbinders, Phoenix, Arizona.

Copyright 1998 by Leland J. Hanchett, Jr.

First Edition—First Printing

All Rights Reserved

Library of Congress Catalog Number 98-092193

Printed and Bound in the United States of America

Dedicated to the brave men who drove the stages and the equally valiant men and women who tended the stations.

Contents

Introduction

The importance of the stagecoach is often lost amidst its legend and romance. It was in fact Arizona's first, and for a long while, only means of public transportation. If you wanted to travel to or within the Territory in the early days, you had better own a horse or a horse and buggy, or be willing to do a lot of walking. With the advent of stage travel in the late 1860s, all that changed, at least for those well off enough to pay the stagecoach fare.

Travel by stage between Prescott and Phoenix, both located in Central Arizona, began as a very long trip of some 200 miles. First you would exit Prescott heading north to circumvent Granite Mountain. A turn to the south in Mint Valley would eventually bring you to Skull Valley. Kirkland Valley was next followed by a harrowing trek west through Bell's Canyon and on to Camp Date Creek. There the road turned south again and the next stop was Wickenburg on the Hassayampa.

The sands of that famous upside down river, sand on top—water below, formed the road to a spot near present day Morristown where the stages took to the hard ground paralleling Grand Avenue on into downtown Phoenix. After Smiths Mill came into being, the route went past Vulture Mine and then through Smiths Mill or even later through Seymour, several miles above Smiths Mill on the Hassayampa. The trip took about two days, but why would anyone want to go to Phoenix?

In those days, the capital of the Territory was located in Prescott, and Phoenix was nothing but a small farming community. The pioneers were not lacking in foresight. Many saw Phoenix as the bread basket of Arizona and it didn't take too long before that vision came true. Phoenix from the first was a city blessed with good fortune. It had water, climate, and by the late 1870s, a railroad less than fifty miles away at Maricopa. Additionally, it happened to be about midway between Prescott and Tucson, the first two territorial capitals.

As time went on, shortening the route from Prescott to Phoenix, and thus to Tucson, was of paramount importance. First, the loop around Granite Mountain was removed as a new road went directly from Prescott to Skull Valley, generally following Millers Valley road. Close on the heels of that event, Bell's Canyon and Camp Date Creek were out of the picture as a new cutoff was built through Peeples Valley, along the south slope of Antelope Peak, to Stanton, and on to Wickenburg.

About five years after the shortening of the Wickenburg route, the Black Canyon road was opened and the trip to Phoenix dropped to less than 100 miles and took only a day's travel. Some freighters still preferred the longer but flatter route through Wickenburg. Stage travelers usually wanted the quickest route, so most of them ended up on the Black Canyon Road.

The stories of these two roads and the stages that traveled them form some of the most exciting history of Central Arizona. Today they can only be traced by foot, horseback, or four wheel drive vehicles. Personally, the author prefers the latter and often wonders what our pioneer ancestors would have thought, riding in such luxury.

Catch the Stage to Phoenix

Book One

The Wickenburg Road

Preface to Book One

Travel in the Arizona Territory during the early 1860s did not include transport by stage coach. There simply were none running in the Territory at that time. To get from one location to another, you would have to supply your own means of transportation—horseback, buggy, or walking. The reasons for the deficiency included: lack of good roads, the threat of Indians, and the fact that no companies were organized within the Territory to supply such a service.

In the year 1869, James Grant, a hardy pioneer, who was willing to take inordinate risks, began carrying passengers, mail, and express from La Paz, on the Colorado River, to Wickenburg and Prescott, Arizona. Within a few months, that line was extended to Phoenix and Maricopa Wells. It would be another ten years before similar service was offered between Prescott and Phoenix, on the shorter route through the Black Canyon.

Stage coaches were rarely attacked by Indians, but the threat of such attacks persisted until 1873 when the Indians of Central Arizona were placed on Reservations. Some early trips featured military escorts, but troops were not always available for such duty. In 1871, a particularly despicable ambush of the Wickenburg–La Paz stage resulted in such an outcry from whites, from Arizona to the East Coast, that the U.S. Military was finally set in motion to punish the attackers and ultimately end the Indian menace in Central Arizona.

Close on the heels of the termination of Indian attacks, white robbers endangered the stage lines to such an extent that the U.S. War Department was brought in once again to handle the situation. To help solve the problem, Territorial Governors, Postmasters, and Wells Fargo Express Company owners offered irresistibly lucrative rewards for the capture or killing of "Knights of the Road."

Stage station keepers were always at risk from attacks by Indians, Sonoran bandits, or drunken travelers. Men and women alike survived in isolated places just for the chance to make a few bucks from the stage lines and the passengers they carried. Many paid the price for their courage.

Most stage stops would be remembered as sanctuaries where a weary traveler could get a little rest from what must have been the hell of travel in the nineteenth century. The bumping, swaying stage coach filled with foul smells, drunken passengers, and whatever the weather had to offer can only be imagined in this day of comfortable travel.

One particular stop carries only memories of hate and violence as it shares the record, with Pleasant Valley, for the most white men murdered in Arizona Territory during a decade. Antelope Creek, later called Stanton, stands as a prime example of how low men can stoop when they covet their neighbors possessions, meager as they were.

Another stop was never more than a vision in a few mens minds, yet it too became a synonym for murder and mayhem. Nigger Wells became a place of ambush and death instead of a place of rest and refreshment.

Let's journey back to the 1800s and take a ride on the Wickenburg Stage Road. Be sure to bring all those things necessary for creature comfort. It won't be an easy trip.

Courtesy Arizona Historical Foundation

Leave From..... Prescott, Arizona Territory

Courtesy Arizona Historical Foundation

Arrive.....Commercial Hotel, Phoenix, Arizona Territory

Photo L. J. Hanchett Jr.

Rich Hill from Antelope Creek Crossing

Photo L. J. Hanchett Jr.

The Hassayampa at the Preserve

A mile or so beyond we found stuck on a tree a note addressed to the commanding officer of our escort which we at once opened. It was dated Depot at Canyon Springs, January 1864, and signed by Lieut. Pomeroy of the very company of our little escort. It informed us briefly that the road ahead was nearly impassable, that the Tonto Apaches had stolen forty of his mules and were in open hostilities; that twenty miles on, the road passed through dense woods where the greatest watchfulness would be necessary.

Letter from Joseph Pratt Allyn, pioneer judge, to the *Hartford Evening Press*, dated January 18, 1864, Fort Whipple, Arizona.

Chapter One
From Blazing Trails to Building Roads

Judge Allyn was traveling with the newly appointed Governor of the Arizona Territory and a military escort made up of California Volunteers. Their mission was to set up the territorial government at Fort Whipple, north of present day Prescott.

ALLYN   DUFFIELD   GOODWIN   GAGE   Courtesy Sharlot Hall Museum
First Officials of the Arizona Territory-1863

Allyn continued his story of the home stretch:

> Our soldiers were in good spirits and wanted to go on. Just as the sun was setting we struck the thick timber Lieut. Pomeroy had spoken of. On we went, the road fearfully rough. Fortunately, the moon was very bright. There was no place to camp, and we must go through the wood. Just then someone cried "light." Sure enough, there was a fire off to the right. "Hush," passed along the line. We all gathered in a group, and with a night glass examined the fire. It was unmistakably an Indian one. Our Californians were for going across to it and trying to surprise it. More prudent council prevailed, and we went on. It was pretty certain that the Indians had not seen us, or they would not have built a fire. On we went, slowly toiling over the rough, sharp, rolling lava, up hills and down, watching every fitful shadow of a bush.

Finally, they came to rest on an open plain, but were afraid to build a fire. Cold and supperless, they rolled up in their blankets to sleep.

The next morning they could see smoke in every direction, but no one knew which might be Fort Whipple. Bets were made as to which one could be the Fort and they started off once again.

> About ten o'clock we got under way and an hour brought us to the most infernal canyon for wagons I have seen yet. It was about 300 feet deep and the sides were nearly perpendicular, and covered with rolling stones. I doubt if wagons can get down except by letting them down with ropes. However, we led our horses down and up, and from therein we had a good road to the post, which we reached in time to get dinner. Here we learned that the smokes seen in the morning were Indian signals, telegraphing our movements.

The establishment of territorial government was an important step, but the first officials were several years behind the real pioneers of Arizona. In fact, those officials had two locations to choose from for establishing the seat of government. The more obvious choice would have been Tucson, but strong Southern sympathy there ruled out that option. A sight near Fort Whipple was the other possibility, and discovery of gold nearby made that the best choice.

Early Trail Blazers

Before the 1860s, and the advent of territorial government and mining in Arizona, most white men traveling in the Territory were creating or following trails. Their purpose was to trap beaver, fight the Mexicans, get to the gold mines in California, survey the land added by the Gadsden Purchase, or search for railroad, wagon, and steamship routes. They didn't have roads, they just took the easiest route to get from one point to another. Of course, there were exceptions.

In 1846, the Mormon Battalion broke the first wagon road across Southern Arizona under the command of Lieutenant Colonel Cooke with Pauline Weaver as guide. Lieutenant Edward Beale crossed Arizona following the 35th parallel in 1857 to establish a wagon road across Northern Arizona. By the late 1850s, the Butterfield Overland stage was traversing Arizona, stopping at the only towns of importance, Tucson and Yuma. The stage connected points back east with Southern California but served little purpose for the few inhabitants of Arizona. There weren't a lot of reasons to go to Arizona before 1863, but it was a threatening obstacle in the path of those who wanted to cross it. When gold was discovered in Central Arizona, all that changed.

By 1863, gold had been found in abundance at several sites along the Colorado River. Surely, the mountains of Central Arizona had as much or more to offer. Two parties of men headed into Central Arizona with hopes as high as the lofty mountains they found there.

The Walker Party Exploration

One party was headed by Captain Joseph Walker and his son, Joseph Jr. Included in this group were well known pioneers such as the Millers, of Miller Valley, J. H. Dickson, of Skull Valley, and Jack Swilling, founder of Phoenix.

For a guide, they had Chief Irataba of the Apache Mohave tribe. Dan Conner compiled his manuscript from memory many years later and fortunately, for later generations, those memoirs have survived.

In those days it made sense to follow a stream bed to the source of its water and hopefully its gold. This party picked the Hasayampa, entering its bed where the "creek emptied its high waters upon this desert." Traveling in the summer, the little band found only a, "dry sandy bed to follow quite a distance into the hills." They traveled on through the gorge of the Hassayampa until they reached damp sand, probably near the present day Hasayampa River Preserve. There, Conner learned that the river flowed in daylight but slowly ceased to flow at night.

As they passed the location of the yet undiscovered Vulture mine all they saw was, "the croppings of the mine standing several feet high out of the ground, within plain view of our party, who only observed it as we did any other ledge of rock." Writing years later, Conner no doubt felt the pangs of having come so close to discovering one of Arizona's richest lodes. Conner went on:

> Day by day we continued our journey up this stream, which I thought in my soul was the roughest country, to be composed of ordinary mountains and hills, that I had yet seen in all my Rocky Mountain experience. The creek was a narrow, gorge-like canyon, that can not be traced, either direction, with any degree of certainty, as to its general course, and it wound its crooked way amongst the mountains, apparently, down deep beneath the level of the balance of the country. Numerous obstacles in its bed, such as falls, accumulated boulders, etc., over which it was impossible to take the mules, frequently turned us out of the steep banks, where our route would become either up or down, continuously, on account of the numberless arroyos, gulches and gorge-like hollows found to be pitching down the mountain into the main creek. This kept us in continual search for places to get up, down or across these precipitous barriers.

Having found ample evidence of gold along the river bed, the group stopped for the night at a point determined by Irataba, where the water was submerged below the sand. Here they waited while Irataba summoned his tribesmen to reinforce his desire that no white man should proceed closer to the headwaters of the stream. After the arrival of thirty to forty black, nearly naked Indians, Irataba hastened to tell the whites that one other party had attempted to ascend the mountain and had perished. Captain Walker's now famous response was, "we came to hunt gold of which they knew nothing and for which they cared nothing, and that we wanted to be friends and would not hurt them, but if they begin to steal our mules and shoot our men we will quit hunting gold and go to hunting Indians."

Then, Irataba dismissed his Indians who scattered off in the rocks as mysteriously as they had come. The old chief tried to make the group believe that there was no water above that point and that they would perish if they went on. He even offered his services to guide them back to the Colorado River, an offer which they respectfully declined. Irataba then took leave of the party, absconding with all the tobacco the group possessed.

After discovering and naming Walnut Grove and Copper Creek, the band made a more permanent camp. Conner related: "We considered our long journey at an end, for we were at last in the unexplored regions of Central Arizona, the place of our destination, and located in the finest and largest woodland country by far to be found within the extensive limits of the whole Territory."

The first mining district for Arizona was established in 1863 and its secretary, Mr. Wheelhouse, named the river Hassayampa giving the creek a Spanish pronunciation, unlike the word "Hasyamp" used by Irataba. From there, the Walker Party members spread out to settle other mining districts near what would become Prescott.

Peeples-Weaver Party

Starting from Yuma in April of 1863, this group first traveled to Maricopa Wells where they met some of the Walker Party who had returned for provisions. From there they traveled up the Colorado River to its junction with the Bill Williams River. Placer mining was good, but not enough gold was produce, so on they went into the area now known as Peeples Valley.

Eventually, they arrived at Antelope Creek and by accident discovered Rich Hill. No one would have imagined the wealth in gold nuggets lying on the ground at its summit. Pickings were so good that some only worked until noon in fairness to the others.

Some of this group, including Peeples and Weaver, settled in the area. Others took their wealth back to California.

After 1863, early officials of the newly formed territory used what few roads there were while blazing many trails in traveling to their constituency. Judges of the three district courts, early Governors, and Indian Affairs Superintendents spent countless days moving around the Territory in service of their offices.

Roads Become Important

Only after the capital of the Territory was firmly entrenched in Prescott and the mines of Central Arizona began their remarkable production, did the need arise for major road building. Freight wagons needed roads to bring materials and supplies for the towns and mines. California was the closest source for those goods, so the earliest roads were built to connect Prescott to supply points on the Colorado River. Those supply points were in turn connected by river-boat to the Sea of Cortez below Yuma and from there to San Francisco by steamer.

Places such as Yuma, La Paz, and Hardyville became the jumping off points for settlers and goods headed for Central Arizona. The goods moved slowly across the Arizona desert in freight wagons pulled by twenty mule teams. In fact, most routes from the Colorado River to Prescott were turned from trails to substantial roads by the pounding hooves and rolling wheels of the loaded freight trains. Freighters in search of water along the way located many of the future station sites.

Freight Trains Crossing the Desert

Immigrants, responding to the lure of precious metals flooded into Arizona to settle at Prescott, Wickenburg, Vulture City, or the Vulture Mine itself.

Immigrants Arriving in Prescott

They needed good roads for their travel as well. Of course, some wanted to go on to Maricopa Wells, the Pima Villages, or as far as Tucson and Tubac. Phoenix wouldn't be established for another five years. More roads were developed for these destinations.

Roads became important not only for freighting but also for the swift dispatch of military units to combat the ever present Indians. Maps drawn in the 1870s show connecting roads between the towns and military camps. Soldiers as well as citizens needed supplies, and good roads were the lifelines for all these early pioneers.

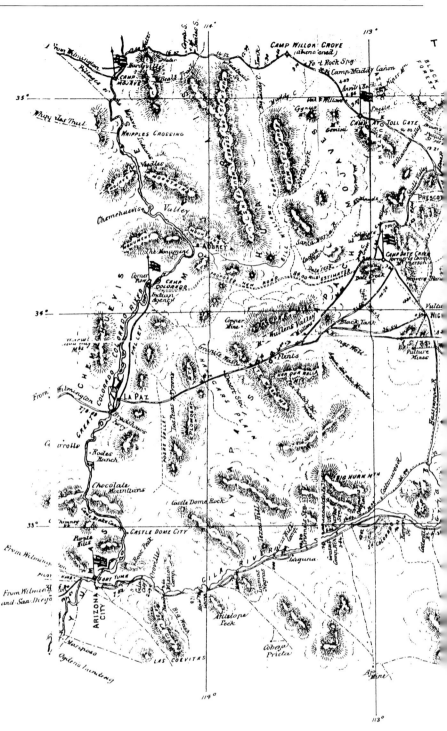

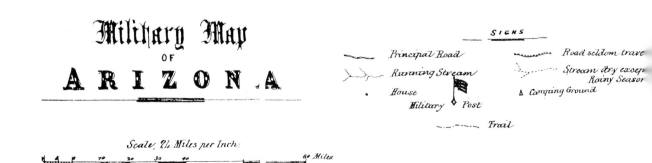

1870 Military Map of Arizona

The Cost of Poor Roads

In his address to the Third Territorial Legislature in the fall of 1866, Governor Richard McCormick lamented the lack of public transportation but praised the roads of the Territory.

> I am ashamed to say that to this day there is not a stage coach running in Arizona, although the Territory has been organized nearly three years. Lines from Wilmington and San Diego to Fort Yuma, and from San Bernardino to Hardyville have lately been established. Connecting lines to Tucson, La Paz, Prescott and the Rio Grande should be provided by some of our enterprising citizens without delay. They might not prove profitable at the start, but would soon become so; and as I suggested to the second Assembly, thousands of persons both in the East and the West, eager to visit our mines, and to examine our country are prevented doing so by the great cost of private transportation. Until well conducted lines of coaches are established, we cannot look for a great increase of population, however tempting our mineral wealth.

> A large portion of our roads are already fitted for easy and rapid travel, and for the outlay necessary to make others so, where private or territorial means are insufficient, it cannot be wrong to petition Congress, inasmuch as no appropriation for such purposes has ever been made to Arizona; while the other territories (I think without exception) have received liberal aid.

What constituted a road "fitted for easy and rapid travel" would be a shock to anyone living at the close of the twentieth century. There was no pavement, ruts were prevalent, the grades were steep, and worst of all, the routes followed the natural contour of the land. Washes were not bridged until after the turn of the century. Instead of bridges, the banks were simply broken down to minimize the jolt from crossing the wash. Typically, the road might be two to three times as long as the straight line distance from point to point.

While a nineteenth century road might be ideal for a man riding on horseback, and not too bad for a light buggy, stage coaches or freight wagons would find it nearly impossible to maneuver over the rough, hilly terrain. When

coupled with the enormous distances involved, it is a wonder anyone or any goods got anywhere.

By 1866, citizens in Prescott were beginning to complain of the long roads to California and the resulting high costs for inbound freighting. An article in the *Miner* dated June 27, 1866 depicts one such problem area.

> **Direct Road to Skull Valley** ... One of the improvements most needed in this county is the opening of a direct wagon road from Prescott to Skull Valley. The present road, around Mint Valley and the Granite Mountain, is a good one, but is from fifteen to twenty miles longer than a direct road would be. The trails to Skull Valley are not over fifteen to sixteen miles, and Messrs. Short, Miller, and Ehle, appointed a committee by the Board of Supervisors, have looked out a way between them which is said to be as short and over which a good wagon road may be made at a small outlay of money, say the work of ten men for thirty days. Their report has been submitted to the Supervisors and will we trust be promptly acted upon at the next meeting of that body. The settlers in Skull Valley, and many persons in Prescott are willing to give their time or to subscribe for the immediate opening of this road, so that the expense to the county will be light, although if it were heavy we believe the people would cheerfully pay the tax for such a road is greatly desired, and must be a great benefit for the county. It will reduce the time of travel by trains [wagon] from Wickenburg and La Paz at least a day, if not two.

It would be five years before such a road was even started. In the mean time, the capital of the Territory had been moved to Tucson some 311 miles away by roads of that day.

Serious Road Construction

In January of 1871, the *Miner* announced the formation of a company to build a toll road from Prescott to Skull Valley.

> We learn that a company has been formed in this place, for the construction of a toll road from Prescott to Skull Valley, via Miller's cutoff. This is an enterprise which has been urged by the *Miner* for years past, and is a matter of no little importance to the community. It will lessen the distance between the two points some fifteen

miles and will, when completed, tend greatly to reduce freights on our staples. And when the road is further extended through Peeples Valley, and across the Black Tanks, avoiding the circuitous route by Bell's Canyon and Date Creek, the distance to the Colorado River will be shortened by about forty miles.

Eighteen months later, under the title "A Good Move," the *Miner* noted the intent to organize a company to construct and operate a toll road passing through Peeples Valley and wished success to the organizers. By then, of course, Phoenix had been founded and road improvement was taking place in newly formed Maricopa County as well.

The *Miner* of July 22, 1872 advised its readers of a "New Road."

Mr. Copeland, arrived here recently from Maricopa County and informed us that a new road had been laid off between Wickenburg and Phoenix, which besides being shorter was a better road than the old one. The new road crosses the Aqua Fria six miles below the old crossing and where it crosses there is plenty of water and a station.

It was 1873 before an official announcement was made concerning the Wickenburg and Prescott Toll-Road. The President was to be C. P. Head, Prescott merchant, while the Secretary was Dr. John H. Pierson and the Treasurer was listed as W. B. Hellings. Charlie Genung of Peeples Valley was the general superintendent. All of these men had more than a casual interest in the creation of such a road. Head needed goods in Prescott, and Pierson ran a stage line, while Genung and Hellings had crops and flour to move to Prescott.

By August of 1872 the *Miner* noted that Charlie Genung had twenty men at work building a road around Antelope Peak and that another fifteen or twenty would start within a few days. Many of these were Mohave Apache Indians. Known as the Peeples Valley cutoff, the road would save twenty-five miles on the trip between Prescott and Wickenburg.

Later that year, toll rates were published in the *Miner*:

For each wagon drawn by two horses, mules, or burden cattle $1.50
For each additional span of horses, mules, or burden cattle 1.00
For each horse/other animal and rider 1.00
For each pack animal, horse, mule, ass, or burden cattle 50
For every sheep, goat, or hog 10
Liberal discounts on the above rates will be made for regular freighters.

Toll roads then, just as today, were a viable alternative when the governing entity could not or would not pay for decent roads. The main difference then was that right-of-ways and other authorizations were usually not necessary. As long as the road contractor spent his money for the construction of the road he could charge users pretty much as he saw fit.

New roads had their supporters as well as their critics. On January 25, 1873, the *Miner* noted:

Loren S. Jenks who recently traveled over the new road made by C. B. Genung, over Antelope Hill [actually around Antelope Peak], says it is now a first rate road for light wagons, and that a little more labor will make it alright for large freight wagons.

Military Roads in Arizona

The military had a lot to do with road building in Arizona. Unfortunately, they weren't always interested in building to places where the general public wanted to travel. An example of one of these roads, although not on the Prescott–Wickenburg–Phoenix route, demonstrates how bad roads could really be in that era.

Martha Summerhayes, wife of Lt. Jack Summerhayes, traveled with her husband and a military escort from Fort Whipple to Fort Apache in the fall of 1874. Describing their ascent of the Mogollon Mountains east of the Tonto Basin, Martha noted:

The roads had now become so difficult that our wagon-train could not move as fast as the lighter vehicles or the troops. Sometimes at a critical place in the road, where the ascent was not only dangerous, but doubtful, or there was, perhaps, a sharp turn, the ambulances waited to see the wagons safely over the pass. Each wagon had its six mules; each ambulance had also its quota of six.

At the foot of one of these steep places, the wagons would halt, the teamsters would inspect the road, and calculate the possibilities of reaching the top; then furiously cracking their whips, and pouring forth volley upon volley of oaths, they would start the team. Each mule got its share of dreadful curses. I had never heard or conceived of any oaths like those. They made my blood fairly curdle, and I am not speaking figuratively. The shivers ran up and down my back, and I half expected to see those teamsters struck down by the hand of the Almighty. ...

This swearing and lashing went on until the heavily-loaded prairie schooner, swaying, swinging, and swerving to the edge of the cut, and back again to the perpendicular wall of the mountain, would finally reach the top, and pass on around the bend; then another would do the same. Each teamster had his own particular variety of oaths, each mule had a feminine name, and this brought swearing down to a personal basis. I remonstrated with Jack, but he said: teamsters always swore; "the mules wouldn't even stir to go up a hill, if they weren't sworn at like that."

By the time we had crossed the great Mogollon Mesa, I had become quite accustomed to those dreadful oaths, and learned to admire the skill, persistency and endurance shown by those rough teamsters. I actually got so far as to believe what Jack had told me about the swearing being necessary, for I saw impossible feats performed by the combination.

On March 11, 1875, the Senate and House of Representatives approved a bill to construct roads in Arizona under the direction of the Secretary of War. The sum of $15,000 was set aside for the purpose of building military roads from Fort Whipple to Camp McDowell with a branch to Camp Verde. Additionally, a road was to be constructed from Fort Whipple to Skull Valley "direct." Within two months, Lt. Thomas was reported to be surveying the road from Fort Whipple to Skull Valley, as requested by Congress.

The *Miner* of October 1, 1875, carried a letter from one of the men working on that road.

The Graders

On the Military Road, September 29, 1875

Editor *Miner*: I have been thinking that a correspondence from our camp might be of interest to readers of the *Miner*, and suiting action to the thought, I take up my quill to dot you a few items.

Our camp is at present about ten miles from Prescott. Our water is brought on pack mules from Mountain Spring, where we were camped for several days; about two miles from us in the direction of Prescott. Mr. Fairchild, a citizen of Prescott, has located this spring and intends building a station for the accommodation of travelers. We are quite well provided with tents, having three large ones, one in which we eat and the other two are used for sleeping apartments. Besides these there are a number of private tents which together with the blacksmith shop, officer's and foreman's quarters, make quite a canvas city.

We are pushing our way through these rough hills quite rapidly, leaving behind us a good road, which speaks well for the engineering abilities of Lieut. Thomas, who viewed it out and is superintending its construction. Our force consists of eighty-five muscle warriors, armed with picks, shovels, axes and other necessary instruments, and the rocks, hills, and trees confess their inability to resist our determined advance, and prostrate themselves or retreat into the canyons below us.

The road will be finished by or before the 1st of November. The distance from Prescott to Bower's Ranch is hereby reduced one half. Quite a number of ranches have been taken up along the road, and the farmers' beginning can be seen on every clearing.

Rolyan

The winter of 1875-1876 found the military road to Skull Valley in use, but not equally appreciated by all users. No doubt, snow in the pass at nearly 6,000 feet elevation didn't help.

The *Miner* of February 11, 1876 reported:

The A & NM Express Co., has taken its stock off the new road between here and Skull Valley, finding it impracticable, and having put a team at Jake Miller's place in Skull and another at Phillip Hall's in Mint Valley. So that hereafter they will run the old road. The driver, Geo. Gange, informs us that one hundred yards on the new road will injure a team worse than any ten miles on the old road.

By the 3rd of March the story had changed considerably:

The A & NM Express Co. have returned to the new road over the Granite range and are now running direct across the mountain. This gives them back their six horse teams, which being cut up in order to make another station or two on the Mint Valley route has only allowed them four horses stock. They hope now that the worst storms are over, and that they will not again be interrupted by snow on the military road.

Apparently the problem was more than just snow. A traveler in August of that year noted in the *Miner* of August 18th:

Without desiring to criticize or find fault, I must in truth say, that though the appropriation was without doubt honestly expended, the road itself is practically a failure. We met Charlie Genung's six horse team ascending the summit from the west, with a load of 2,000 pounds, and it was all the six large animals could do to make the ascent a few feet at a time. It is all that four good horses can do to make the ascent without a load. To be of practical use, the road must be rebuilt around the mountain peaks instead of over them.

By November, 1876, the *Miner* noted that the Miller brothers were building a toll road on the Dixon Trail from Prescott to Skull Valley. They expected it to be ready for use by the stages that next summer. It took three tries, but private enterprise prevailed!

No sooner than the road had become a success, the County of Yavapai wanted to purchase it to make it a free road once again. The Miller brothers finally accepted a $10,000 bond in payment for their efforts.

Courtesy Sharlot Hall Museum

Sam Miller

Road Work by the Stage Companies

The year 1877 saw the capital of the Arizona Territory return to Prescott. Road building activities stepped up to meet the demands of the traveling public. Interestingly, even the stage companies took an active role in road construction.

On June 22, 1877 the *Miner* carried an article declaring that the C & A Stage Company was busy repairing the road between Wickenburg and Antelope and that the traveling public would be most appreciative.

The *Miner* of July 6, 1877 noted:

J. H. Pierson [of the C & A Stage Co.] received the contract from the road commissioner of Maricopa county for the construction of a road from Smith's Mill to Wickenburg, on the west side of the Hassayampa, and is to be paid $1,500 for the work.

New roads to new locations were important, but improvements to the most traveled road between Prescott and Phoenix, through Wickenburg, demanded a majority of the road builders attention. Even the stage companies were getting into the act, maintaining roads they had been using since 1868.

Road construction crews, made up of many workers, had little to fear from the Indians, but travelers along those roads were under constant threat of attack.

Bell's Canyon

WICKENBURG
MASSACRE
IN THIS VICINITY NOV 5, 1871
WICKENBURG — EHRENBURG
STAGE AMBUSHED BY APACHE
MOHAVE INDIANS
JOHN LANZ — FRED W LORING
P.M HAMEL — — W.G. SALMON
FREDERICK SHOHOLM AND
C.S. ADAMS WERE MURDERED
MOLLIE SHEPPARD DIED OF
WOUNDS
ARIZONA HIGHWAY
DEPARTMENT 1937

Photo L. J. Hanchett Jr.

Marker Near the Wickenburg Massacre Site

*Perhaps you may be inclined to think that in the presence of such scenes
[as the cultivated fields of Kirkland Valley] we became oblivious of the
existence along the route of ye noble "reds," but such is not the case.*

Weekly Miner, May 18, 1872

Chapter Two
The Indian Menace

In a letter from Los Angeles to the editor of the *Miner*, the stage traveler goes on to say:

> Anticipating the possibility of sickness on the way, we took aboard, before leaving Prescott, a large stock of medicine, technically termed spiritus fermenti. You will understand that one of the effects of this medicine on the system is to induce the belief within the bosom of a white man that he is equal in prowess to about a score of Indians. It is a delightful sensation, and thus pervaded Mr. B. and the writer as we immerged into Bell's Canyon.

The settlers of the Arizona Territory were confronted with the "Indian Menace" from the start. At first the Federal government wanted to help but the Civil War took precedence over protection of its Western citizens. Reconstruction in the South proved to be the next hurdle. When troops finally arrived in Arizona in sufficient quantity to be of some help, Indian sympathizers persuaded the government to try treaties instead of force.

Between the passing of the "Organic Act of 1863" which created the Arizona Territory and General George Crook's campaign of the winter of 1872-1873 against the Tonto Apaches and Mohave Apaches, or Yavapais, Arizona lost nearly 1,000 of her citizens to the "Indian Menace."

The Indians felt justified in their attacks on the whites. Hadn't the land been free for anyone to use since time began? How could the whites honestly believe that a few well placed stakes gave them exclusive use to the land where Indians had hunted for ages?

The white men on the other hand considered the land as spoils of battle. Why should the conquered ones have any say in what the white men did or where they went? There could only be one winner and the whites had all the aces in this game.

Rarely did Indians attack the stages. A stage coach had little to offer but the horses or mules, a favorite food in the Indian diet. Nevertheless, the Indians of Central Arizona were one of several factors in delaying the implementation of stage routes.

Freight wagons or herds of stock were more frequently targeted. Outnumbered settlers living or traveling in remote locations were always vulnerable.

Citizen Preparedness

William Hardy in his *Early Reminisances*, recorded in the *Arizona Journal—Miner* of February 3, 1897, tells a fascinating story of how the pioneer citizens of Arizona coped with the Indian problems of that day.

Hardy happened to be staying in early day Prescott when Chief Justice Turner ordered the Sheriff to summon a Grand Jury. On the day set for the term, he and many of the townsmen, out of curiosity, went to a little building called the court house.

At 10 a.m., the jurymen began arriving. Each came with his rifle and, as they entered, set it against the wall. Each had a revolver in his scabbard and leather pouches full of cartridges. The judge took his seat in a rough chair, and as the roll was called, each juror took his seat with his revolver at his side. The judge hesitated as he administered the oath. Then he remarked that it was near noon and court would stand at recess until 1 p.m.

As each juror left, he took his rifle and went to his dinner. When they were out of the court the Judge went to Captain Hardy remarking that it was unusual for a jury to carry arms and would it be in order to ask that they lay them aside while acting. Hardy answered: "No, you know Judge that the Apaches have been very lively. I would advise you charge the jury as if they had no weapons."

The next day, Indians attacked the town herd. Without asking leave, the jury rushed out, returning in about an hour as though nothing had happened. After that, the judge carried his rifle and kept his revolver strapped on him, ready for action.

Perilous Bell's Canyon

Bell's Canyon, just west of Kirkland Valley, was a favorite ambush spot for Indians en route between the reservations on the Colorado River and their mountain haunts of Central Arizona. Being part of a trail used in common by both the white and red man, encounters were bound to happen. On the 3rd of May, 1865, three men lost their lives to the marauding Indians within the boulder strewn walls of Bell's Canyon. Cunningham, Sage, and Bell were all murdered, probably by the same group of Indians.

Although copies of the *Miner* are missing for much of that period, an article in the *Los Angeles Tri-City News* dated May 20, 1865, recounts the incident.

More Murders By The Apaches.

From a private letter received by Mr. W.G. Sill, Postmaster of this city, on Thursday last, from Mr. S. J. Poston, dated at La Paz May 11th, we learn that Mr. Charles O. Cunningham (formerly of the Monte) of La Paz, was shot and instantly killed on the 3rd instant by Indians at Willow Springs about forty miles this side of Prescott. Richard Bell and Cornelius Sage were killed the same day on that route within a few miles of the same place. There are three [other] men missing, supposed to have been killed. The Indians stole about thirty head of mules from Date Creek Ranch. Other accounts say that eleven bodies were discovered between La Paz and Prescott, that the murdered men were scalped with the single exception of Cunningham, whose clothing, pistol, etc., were untouched. The Indians, it is supposed, did not intend to kill Mr. Cunningham. The whites were shot from ambuscade. Carleton's war of extermination does not seem to be progressing against these murderous wretches. It is hoped Gen. Mason will prosecute a vigorous war of extermination against these cowardly Apaches.

Freight Wagon Attacks

Scarcely more than a year later, on August 11, 1866, freight wagons led by Mr. Freeman were brought to a sudden halt by a combination of La Paz and Tonto Apaches in Skull Valley. The Indians expectations were simple. They merely demanded the wagons, freight and mules in return for safe passage of the teamsters. It was a sort of toll to be paid by all whites using the Indian's right-of-way through Skull Valley. Freeman wisely opted to return to the camp of Lieutenant Oscar Hutton located some eight miles to the west.

Starting out again the next day and escorted by some of Lt. Hutton's men, Freeman once again was detained by the Indians with essentially the same demands as before. Hutton, unsure of how to proceed, sent a messenger to Ft. Whipple near Prescott. Word came back at 3 a.m. on the 13th that since the

Indians had demonstrated hostile intentions toward the wagon train and were over forty miles east of the safety line for their reservation, they should be dealt with harshly but that the issue should not be forced. Conversations with the Indians revealed that Mr. Leihy, the Indian Agent, wanted fifty buckskins and had told them that they might wander around as they pleased to get them.

The following morning, Mr. Freeman was becoming anxious to proceed on to Prescott with his train. Lt. Hutton sent four soldiers as escort while he and the rest of his party stayed back to parlay with the Indians. After traveling only a mile and one half, Freeman was again surrounded by Indians anxious to approach the train. Hutton started after the train with only twelve men. On arriving at the place where the train had stopped, Hutton and Freeman allowed about eighty bucks to approach the train, but only after convincing them to leave their bows and arrows behind.

Secretly, each Indian had concealed a knife on his person and finally two made threatening gestures towards Mr. Freeman. A sentry Hutton had posted on the hill warned the soldiers and teamsters that several Indians armed with rifles were concealed behind rocks on the hillside. An old squaw yelled out for the braves to attack with their knives. Finally, one who claimed to be a chief thrust his knife at Mr. Freeman. Another Indian made a thrust at one of Hutton's men who caught the blade with his hand suffering a terrible wound. The injured soldier then shot the Indian and the battle was on.

Lasting only forty-five minutes, the encounter resulted in twenty-three Indians killed and double that number wounded. Hutton lost one man killed and one man wounded. Twenty-nine whites had, using superior weaponry, soundly defeated over one hundred Indians. Hutton complained vehemently in his report of the laxness of the Indian Agents on the Colorado River reservations. Richard McCormick, Territorial Governor, commended Hutton and his men for their gallantry and decisiveness.

The Murder of George Leihy

Just three months later, a band of Tonto Apaches turned on the very man who had given them passes to leave the Colorado reservations. Superintendent of Indian Affairs, George W. Leihy and his clerk, Mr. Everets were traveling from Prescott to La Paz on the Colorado River. With them were a friendly Mohave and a Mohave Apache for whom Leihy had obtained a release from the Fort Whipple guard house. The latter had been part of the band which attacked Freeman's train.

Upon reaching Bell's Canyon, the Indians decided to proceed on to Fort Whipple near Prescott for supplies thinking their passes would protect them. Just then they noticed Leihy and Everets approaching the canyon from the East. They decided to kill Mr. Leihy whom they thought to be the great chief of the whites. They thought this would sufficiently alarm the whites and restore the country to the red man.

When the alarmed citizens and soldiers arrived at the scene, having been alerted by the return of Everet's mule, stuck full of arrows, to Bell's ranch, what met their eyes was almost too sickening to describe. Everet's beheaded body was full of arrows. Leihy was dreadfully mutilated. His head had been smashed with stones until it was literally flattened, the arms and legs broken in many places, while the heart was gone, replaced by two bullet molds.

The Mohave Apache Indian was also killed while the other Indian, taken to be a Maricopa, was dragged off to the mountains and tortured to death in the manner prescribed by Apaches for their enemies to the South.

Citizens of Prescott concluded that many of the worst atrocities were committed by Indians from the Colorado River area, or those in the habit of resorting there. Most felt that the issuance of passes should be discontinued.

More Treachery Near Bell's Canyon

In August of 1867, Indians claimed two more victims on the road near Bell's Canyon. Two soldiers coming from recently established Camp McPherson to Fort Whipple were ambushed at Willow Spring. Their bodies were found stripped and the Indians made off with two animals and two guns. The *Miner* of August 10 reported: "It is not surprising that these outrages and the sign of Indians in every locality have alarmed our citizens and prompted them to call a meeting to seek better protection."

Protection came from only two places in those days, either you got help from the troops sent by Washington, or you did it yourself. Travelers along the road from Prescott to the Colorado River were under constant threat of Indian attack. The California and New Mexico volunteers who manned Fort Whipple were assigned responsibility for the Tonto Apaches to the east and the Mohave Apaches or Yavapais to the west. In spite of their efforts to guard the mail and destroy whatever rancherias they found, little progress was made in controlling the Indians.

Establishing Camp McPherson

Located along Date Creek since 1864, two infantry companies of volunteers gave some protection to settlers and wagon trains on the Prescott–La Paz road. Further to the north and east, travelers and farmers in the fertile Skull Valley area were plagued by Indian attacks. In early 1866, regulars replaced the volunteers who in turn moved up to Skull Valley. By the end of the year, regulars had also moved into Skull Valley and all Arizona volunteer troops had been disbanded, much to the disgust of local citizens. Volunteers were better armed, mounted, and experienced than their youthful replacements.

Even with the regular troops now available, they weren't always in the right spot to prevent or avenge Indian attacks. On March 2, 1867, three teamsters were killed when their freight train was attacked eight miles west of the camp at Date Creek. The Yavapais ran off with eighteen mules and four horses with no calvary in pursuit. It seems that all of the troops from Date Creek were in Skull Valley on that particular day.

On January 23, 1867, Camp McPherson was established sixty miles from Prescott and thirty miles from Wickenburg on the main stage and freight line from Prescott to La Paz. Its strategic location in the heart of Yavapai country was solely to subdue the local hostile Indians.

On March 11, 1867, four companies of calvary led by Brevet Brigadier General John Gregg arrived at Prescott, Arizona Territory. That should have been the beginning of the end for the Indian problem in that area. Unfortunately, politics once more prevailed and Gregg was overridden in his hard line by Indian Affairs Superintendent, George Dent, son-in-law of General U.S. Grant.

A week later, The Arizona *Miner* declared, "General Gregg has we think made a hit in locating this new post at the Willow Spring three miles from Bell's Canyon on the Wickenburg, Date Creek, and La Paz road. The canyon is notoriously the worst Indian hole in this part of Arizona, and has long been the terror of travelers." To this it added, "The post at Date Creek and that at Skull Valley were not near enough to be of service and moreover they were never strong. Camp McPherson will have two companies and so much scouting will be done from it that the whole La Paz road will soon be made safe."

On that same date, under a title of "Gen. Gregg's Orders," the *Miner* noted, "Now that $50,000 has been appropriated for the great Colorado River Reservation, we hope Superintendent Dent will get it in order and have a clear understanding with his red children that if they leave it they will be the prey of Gen. Gregg and his dashing cavalrymen. Reservations are useless unless the Indians are kept on them." By November, 1868, the Camp McPherson had been renamed Camp Date Creek.

Attacks Near the Vulture Mine

Bell's Canyon wasn't the only ambush point for the wandering Apaches of Central Arizona. A narrow canyon on the road connecting the Vulture gold mine with the mill located north of Wickenburg was another favorite haunt. The mine, discovered by Henry Wickenburg in 1863, was fifteen miles south of Wickenburg. By 1866, wagons full of ore moved slowly over the connecting road and were ideal targets for Apache arrows and bullets.

A letter to the Arizona *Miner* from Wickenburg, dated November 16, 1868, described a recent Indian attack and the thoughts of the citizens of the area:

> Indians and Indian sign are thick around us. On the 12th inst., one of our oldest and best citizens, Francis Pouget, was killed by Indians at a place about nine miles from here while on his way to the Vulture Mine. It is too hard on us to be left without protection. Why are other places in the Territory protected by the Government and not this place? We have more at stake here than have the people of any other town in the Territory. We have about 1000 head of stock and twenty wagons engaged daily in hauling rock from the mine to the mills a distance of fourteen miles. Our population numbers about four hundred and night and day all are in danger of losing their lives and property by the Indians. Our mills are doing as well as ever. People are continually arriving here from Texas, California and other states. Farmers have a ready sale for their grain at eight cents per pound, gold, but what security have we for life and property? The Indians can come here at night and kill us. We cannot watch them at night as every man here works during the day and needs rest at night. Now, the Government should do something for us. Cannot the military commander at Fort Whipple spare us twenty men?

Courtesy Desert Caballeros Museum

Braking the Ore Wagons

Occasional Revenge

Sometimes, citizens were sufficiently angered by the Indian outrages to pursue them without help from the military. King S. Woolsey, farmer, rancher, miner, and Indian fighter, was one such citizen. Between 1864 and 1867, Woolsey led groups of settlers on three raids against the Apaches.

As a member of the Walker party, Woolsey, moved from his home at Aqua Caliente, west of Maricopa Wells, to the Aqua Fria just east of Prescott. Being located near a trail often used by the Apache Indians, Woolsey soon became exasperated by the constant loss of stock in his area.

The famous "Battle of Bloody Tanks" near present day Globe was the result of his first endeavor to rid the Territory of Apaches. Confronted with several hundred Indians, the small band of thirty to forty settlers opted to talk rather than fight, or at least that's what they told the Indians. The real plan was to have each one of the five settlers in the parlay kill an Indian counterpart on que from Woolsey. Two dozen Indians were killed in that fight, including five Apache leaders. Only one settler lost his life.

Woolsey's second foray was ostensibly for the purpose of prospecting as well as Indian killing. Little was accomplished other than a decision to meet again a few months later for another outing.

The third expedition saw Woolsey and about one-hundred miners fail once again, as far as killing Indians was concerned. Having traveled to the eastern border of the Territory, they at least proved that the settlers could fend for themselves without the U.S. Army. Neither did the party find any gold to speak of, but many of the group still felt that vast mines would someday be discovered in Eastern Arizona. This was not the end of citizen armies responding to the threat of Indians.

Courtesy Sharlot Hall Museum

King S. Woolsey

A few years later, on August 21, 1869, at the mining town of Weaver, between Wickenburg and Prescott, Indians were seen prowling around. Finally, they shot the bell-mare of a pack train belonging to a Mexican. John Garner, a mail rider between Prescott and Wickenburg, described what followed.

As soon as it became dark, the people of the place met and under the leadership of Joaquin Barbe, well known around Wickenburg, took up the trail of the Indians, which they followed with great difficulty to the head of Antelope Creek, where they discovered their rancherias containing about one hundred and forty huts and some two hundred and seventy-five Indians. The little force of pursuers, about twenty, posted themselves at various advantageous points around the camp and at five o'clock in the morning opened fire upon it, driving the occupants who were not killed or wounded into the surrounding rocks. The attacking party then charged upon the rancheria and, succeeded in entering it, commenced to destroy everything within reach. They had to abandon this task, however, almost as soon as commenced, for the Indians, upon seeing the small force that had driven them from their camp, charged back with great fury, and the little band of attackers, unable to stem the fierce rush of the enraged savages, were forced to retreat. In attempting to resist the onslaught of the Indians, three of the men of the party were wounded, one, a Frenchman named Portola, being shot through the arm, and a Mexican receiving three separate wounds. The party then started for Wickenburg, where, upon their arrival, the people raised a large sum of money in token of their appreciation for the daring attack they had made on the savages.

A Petition for Aid

By 1867, the capitol of the Territory had been moved from Prescott to Tucson. In early 1871, the Sixth Legislative Assembly of Arizona, meeting there, passed a resolution to establish a committee to take sworn testimonies in regards to the Indian hostilities in Arizona between 1869 and 1871. The *Memorial*, asking protection from hostile Indians, was prefaced by the following:

Your memorialist are aware that occupying a geographical position on the southwestern border of the United States, with no telegraph facilities and limited political influence, the suffering and deaths which have attended the settlement of this Territory, in consequence of the hostility of the Apache Indians, are but little known or appreciated beyond our borders. Your memorialist have therefore compiled testimony, by a large number of reliable citizens and officers of the army, with the view of fairly and more forcibly making known the conditions of affairs in this Territory, which shows that a savage war still exists herein, causing the murder of hundreds of our citizens and the loss of a vast amount of property; and that in no period since the settlement of the Territory has the loss of life and property been greater than during the year 1870; and that the hostility of the Apache Indians, and want of protection, have led to the abandonment of many valuable mines; and that large farming settlements have been and are being abandoned for like causes. Your memorialist would further state, that the people of this Territory are attached to it, and find its climate, pastoral, agricultural and mineral resources, all the elements necessary to make it a populous and desirable country in which to live; that they have endured the hardships and braved the dangers

incident to a pioneer life, with a fortitude that should command the admiration of a brave people; and though hundreds have fallen beneath the scalping knife and tomahawk, or suffered torture at the burning stake, the survivors fill the broken ranks, and continue the contest. Our people have made their homes here, and have no other, but unless protection be given them, the constant decimation that is made will soon sweep from the country all traces of civilization, except deserted fields and broken walls.

Although the preface may have been a little overdone, the testimonies of the individuals are certainly compelling.

John H. Fitzgerald. *sworn*: Resides at Wickenburg, A.T.; is a member of the present Legislature; that the train of E. Ariola was attacked, five miles from the Vulture mine by the Apache Indians, in the month of June, 1869, killing three men and capturing eighty mules, valued at $7,000.

In September, 1869, the Apaches attacked the men herding the mules of E. Ariola; they captured eighty-six mules and ten horses, while feeding in sight of the Vulture quartz mill.

In March, 1870, he went to the house of one McWilliams on the river Hassayampa, and found Horace Greely, his partner, murdered by Indians and lying on the floor.

In July, 1870, the Apache Indians took from Joseph Tye and myself, while in camp near the town of Phoenix (Salt River), twelve head of work oxen; considers life and property unsafe in nearly all parts of the Territory.

Another citizen of Yavapai County gave the following information:

John L. Taylor, *sworn*: Residence, Prescott, A.T.; was formerly Sheriff of Yavapai County; is presently a member of the Legislature; that in the fall of 1869, a man by the name of Osborn was murdered, about two miles north of Prescott by Indians.

That in the fall of 1870 he assisted in burying the body of William Dennison; and about two weeks thereafter Thomas Rutlidge was murdered, about two miles from Prescott, the Indians taking from him two horses and one pistol.

Considers the Apache Indians more hostile and bold at the present time than heretofore.

Fort Whipple, Arizona Territory

Wm. J. O'Neil, added his observations of the Indian problem.

Resides in Kirkland Valley, Yavapai County. In January, 1869, John T. Howell was attacked by fifty Indians, murdered, and two mules captured.

In July, 1869, four soldiers and one citizen, carrying the United States mail, between Prescott and Date Creek, were attacked by Indians. Two soldiers were killed and the citizen wounded, and the mail and five horses captured.

In November, 1869, Wesley White was killed by Indians while watching his corn crib, within fifty yards of his house.

In June, 1870, Alfred L. Johnson and "Kentuck" were murdered by Indians about twelve miles above Camp Date Creek, on the road to Prescott.

Considers the Indians more hostile and dangerous now than since his residence in the Territory.

The Governor of the Territory, A.P.K. Safford, added a good overview of the situation.

He is the present Governor of the Territory and has traveled extensively through the same and does not consider that any portion of it is safe from depredations by the Apache Indians, except along and a few miles east of the Colorado River; and since his residence there is scarcely a road or trail east of that point that has not been the scene of Indian hostilities; that at this time scarcely a day passes without murders and robberies reported to him; and that he has never known the Indians more active and successful than now; that the Apache Indians depend principally for their support upon theft and robbery, and do not desire nor will they accept any terms of peace until they are thoroughly subjugated by military power; that they are cruel in the extreme, witness having seen, in August, the charred remains of a white man who had evidently been burned alive-also a scalp tied to a pole.

Apparently, the message did not fall on deaf ears, as General George Crook, with Safford's pleading, was sent in 1871 to the Territory as commander of the Department of Arizona. Crook replaced General Stoneman, first commander of the newly created department, who had been dubbed "economy" as a result of his attempt to close numerous posts and supply depots, to the disgust of settlers throughout the Territory. Stoneman was probably following the lead of the Board of Indian Commissioners who felt that peaceful settlement by the Indians on the reservations was the right course to pursue.

Governor Safford understood that only by the proper application of military force would peace be forthcoming. General Crook was quick to take action. After meeting with Safford and several field commanders, Crook embarked on a six hundred seventy-five mile reconnaissance of the Department. Having spread the word that all Indians must come to and stay on a reservation, Crook made preparations for his first campaign in Arizona.

To the dismay of the settlers, Vincent Colyer, Secretary of the Board of Indian Commissioners arrived in Arizona with a special appointment from President Grant. Crook deferred to Colyer's wish to handle the Indians with Kid Gloves.

Crook did, however, establish a temporary reservation at Camp Date Creek where the Yavapais were promised, and actually received, rations. Control was minimal as long as the Indians kept the peace. Some small bands did however drift away attacking wagon trains and settlements in the area.

An Attack on Kirkland Valley

The *Miner* of October 21, 1871, gave the story of settlers defending their homes in Kirkland Valley.

> The readiness with which the Apache Indians will submit to circumstances when force instead of entreaty is the power employed to influence his actions, was never better exemplified than in the case of those thieving scoundrels who, two weeks hence, made an attack on the settlers of Kirkland Valley. They put in an appearance at the homes of the settlers, declaring their determination to murder and

pillage all before them—evidently believing that the comparably small force of the settlers would flee in dismay at their approach—but they were mistaken; for the settlers instead of abandoning their homes, defended them in a manner worthy of their profession as architects of a new commonwealth of the Southwest, and put the savages to flight. Not supposing that the latter could be thus equally vanquished the settlers kept a close watch upon their movements, expecting every moment to see a hundred or two hundred armed warriors descending upon them; but they were agreeably disappointed to learn, on the day following that upon which the attack was made, that Lo [a generic term for Indian] was satisfied to consider the account settled and had returned to Camp Date Creek to have his wounds properly dressed. Thanks to their intrepidity in defending their homes against overwhelming numbers of their savage foes, these settlers will probably enjoy a respite from the open hostility on the part of Apache Mohaves, in the future; and it is pretty safe to conclude that whatever depredation these Indians will hereafter commit will be done upon the old, safe system, viz; shoot in the back and steal under cover of night.

Unfortunately, the respite was short lived and the next attack was, as the *Miner* predicted, from ambush.

The Wickenburg Stage Massacre

On November 5, 1871 a band of Braves under Chief Ochocama did the unthinkable by attacking the west bound stage in a wash outside of Wickenburg, killing the driver and five passengers including the popular, young New England journalist, Fred W. Loring. Two passengers, a man and a woman, escaped, bringing news of the attack back to Wickenburg where a group of citizens promptly took up the tracks of the murderers.

Many wanted to believe that someone other than Indians had performed the heinous deed. Some said it was Mexicans, others insisted it was white men dressed as Indians. A few, such as Peeples Valley resident Charles Genung, used the confusion as an excuse to, "run some greasers into the ground." Of course, Genung had Indians clearing a new road through Peeples Valley to Wickenburg. Who would do that job if the Indians were found guilty and run out of the area?

General George Crook

Courtesy Desert Caballeros Museum

Fredrick W. Loring

A Coroners Inquest provided the following verdict.

We, the undersigned, summoned as a jury to hold an inquest on the bodies of the following named persons, found murdered in the stage coach, about six miles from the town of Wickenburg, on the La Paz road, on the morning of the 5th of November, 1871, from all the evidence obtained from the two surviving passengers, do find that C. S. Adams, John Lanz, Fred W. Loring, Fred W. Shoholm, W. G. Salmon and P. M. Hamel, (found scalped), came to their death by gunshot wounds, received at the hands of Indians trailed to the Date Creek Reservation.

Popular notion had it that only the brave men who fought fearlessly against their Indian attackers would be scalped. Furthermore, scalping of only one man, even when many were killed, was a characteristic of Western Apache raids. P. M. Hamel must have been the only heroic man on the stage that day or he was just lucky enough to have been that special victim.

Testimony by the survivors, Mr. Kruger and Mollie Sheppard, revealed that the attackers wore the blue pants of the Reservation Indians and displayed the gait, appearance, and bearing of Apaches. In a letter written for the *Army and Navy Journal*, dated January 6, 1872, Kruger describes the events of that day.

Ehrenberg, A.T., December 9th, 1871.

William G. Peckham, Esq.
Trinity Building, New York

Dear Sir:

In acknowledging the receipt of your letter of November 16th, 1871, I am pleased to be able to give you an account of the death of my friend Loring, who was well known to me and whose untimely death is deeply regretted by me. We left Fort Whipple, near Prescott, Arizona Territory, on Saturday, November 4th, in the best of health and spirits. To be sure, the stage was rather crowded, but being all of such good temper we had a real nice time, Loring being the most lively of us all, anticipating a speedy return to his friends East. Well he retained his inside seat until we reached Wickenburg, on Sunday morning, November 5th, 1871, when, after leaving there, he preferred to have an outside seat, to which I most decidedly objected; but he insisted on being outside for a short time. I had two revolvers and he had none; in fact, no arms whatever. He rejected my offer of a revolver, saying at the same time, "My dear Kruger, we are now comparatively safe. I have traveled with Lieutenant Wheeler for nearly eight months, and have never seen an Indian." Well, we rolled on until about 11 a.m., when the fatal attack was made The first warning I had was the warning of the driver, who cried "Apaches! Apaches!" At the same moment the Indians, who lay concealed, fired the first volley, killing poor Loring, the driver, and the other outside passenger, a Mr. Adams. They killed also the off lead horse and wounded the other lead horse. The horses very much frightened, then ran forward about twenty yards, when they came to a sudden stop. At the same time Loring fell off the stage and so the other passenger. At the same moment the Indians fired the second volley from three sides—the both sides and rear—not more than four or five yards from the stage, killing Mr. Shoholm, one of the inside passengers, and wounding Miss Sheppard, myself and a Mr. Salmon, of Lieutenant Wheeler's party. The latter one was mortally wounded and fell out of the stage, and crawled away, but was finally captured by the Indians, scalped and otherwise mutilated. The only one not then wounded was Mr. Hamel, of Lieutenant Wheeler's party. Both he and myself commenced immediately firing. Each one fired six shots. Not having any more ammunition I ceased firing. The Indians then disappeared behind the bushes.

But what a terrible spectacle it was to see the six dead bodies in plain sight! Loring was lying right under my very eyes, not yet dead, but suffering, apparently, terribly. He was shot through his left temple, his right eye, and his lungs. He suffered for about four minutes, but I am positive that he died before I made my escape. Knowing that it would be useless to attempt to escape until the Indians would come back to plunder the stage, I remained perfectly quiet, having in the mean time ascertained that Miss Sheppard was yet alive, but badly wounded. She succeeded in getting a loaded revolver from one of the killed passengers, which she gave to me. I then told her to keep cool and be ready to run as soon as I would give the signal. Well, in about six minutes of terrible suspense I saw the Indians slowly creeping toward the stage. I counted and saw plainly fifteen Indians all dressed in blue soldiers' trousers. When they came within five yards of the stage I jumped up, yelled and fired at them. The woman, at the same time, yelled also, and we succeeded admirably in driving them off for the time being, and got time to leave the stage. Before I left the stage I cried out as loud as I possibly could if any one was left alive, but only Mr. Adams answered; but he was mortally wounded and could not even move his hands or feet, so I had to leave him to his fate. He was afterward found with his throat cut and otherwise mutilated. The Indians afterward followed me for about five miles, and I had a running fight with them until I fell in with the "buck-board." I had to carry the wounded woman for over two miles in my left arm. I myself received one shot through the right armpit, coming out on the shoulder, and two shots in my back. The woman also had three shots, one dangerous.

How I could escape with my life, and be able to save the life of Miss Sheppard, is more than I can account for. That I left my mark with the Indians, there is no doubt, because two Indians died from gun-shot wounds at Camp Date Creek Reservation; but the commanding officer refused to have the thing investigated, for fear he would find sufficient evidence that they were his pets, that is Camp Date Creek Indians. At all events

there is no doubt whatever that the outrage was committed by Indians, and that by Camp Date Creek Indians, those so-called friendly Indians whom Uncle Sam feeds.

Captain Charles Meinhold of the 3rd Cavalry was ordered to proceed to the massacre site from Camp Date Creek and make a thorough determination of what happened and who did it. Meinhold's report on his findings is a classic of military investigation.

First, Meinhold debriefed Miss Sheppard and Mr. Kruger at Wickenburg where they had been brought after the incident. He learned that the stage had been attacked at a point eight miles west of Wickenburg at 8 am on the 5th of November. The attackers, they said, were a party of Indians about ten to twelve in number.

The stage was fired on from both sides with the first volley killing a lead horse and all passengers except themselves and Mr. Salmon. Kruger and Sheppard got out of the coach and hid in some bushes on the left side of the road. After being pursued for a short distance by the attackers, they were able to proceed west down the stage road until they met a mail coach coming from Ehrenburg on the Colorado River.

Meinhold found Kruger to be, "positive in his assertion that the attacking party were Indians." Sheppard would have a slightly different viewpoint.

On the following morning, Meinhold went to the attack site which he described as:

> A point where the road turns down a little hill into a dry arroyo. On the right side of the road and close to it is a large mesquite bush under which I discovered three or four moccasin tracks, of the pattern used by the Mohave Apaches. On the left side and at a distance of 20-30 paces from the road and on an eminence which commands the view for a long distance of the road from Wickenburg, I found as many more tracks of the same description, also two tin cans (butter cans apparently) thrown away at some military post, picked up and used by the attackers to carry water, a pack of Spanish cards, rounded on the corners, in a manner I have seen cards in the hands of Indians at this Post.

Meinhold also noticed that some of the attacking party had left excrement indicating that their diet consisted of melons and mesquite beans.

From there, Meinhold attempted to follow the attackers and found, at a point one-half mile from the scene, that the tracks divided with three tracks leading direct to Camp Date Creek and four towards the Hassayampa. At a distance of about three miles both tracks joined pointing towards the Hassayampa. Meinhold measured one noticeably larger track and followed it with the others for a distance of twenty-two miles until he was next to the Hassayampa Canyon where so many tracks appeared that he could no longer follow the original seven attackers.

Meinhold then tried to locate any trail of the attackers along the Wickenburg–Camp Date Creek road which might have been made as the group traveled from Camp Date Creek to the attack site. This approach was without success so he returned to Camp Date Creek to write his report.

At the end of his report he added impressions he obtained from talking to people at Wickenburg when he first arrived there. Many thought that the ambush was done by Mexicans who had been planning to rob the gold shipment from the Vulture Mine. Typically, the shipment was sent to the coast shortly after the first of the month. If indeed the attackers were Mexican, it would have been the only time a group so large as that got together to commit a crime. Typically, Mexicans would only work in groups of two to four to commit nefarious schemes against stage coaches. On the other hand, Indians would only attack when they outnumbered their victims.

Mollie Sheppard was somewhat paranoid concerning some white men who had been inquiring about where she had gone after selling her brothel in Prescott. According to Meinhold, this was her only reason for thinking that some whites might have been involved in the ambush.

The minority of those asked by Meinhold felt that the act was perpetrated by Indians. Judging by responses from well known citizens of Wickenburg, Meinhold didn't ask the right people.

A letter to the editor of the *Miner*, dated November 11, 1871, from a number of prominent citizens of Wickenburg, revealed the following:

• The murderers were on foot, were wearing Indian moccasins, and left many Indian articles along the trail.
• Within four or five miles of the scene of the ambush, the various trails of the murderers combined into one large trail leading to the Date Creek Reservation.
• The trail showed them to be a large party of Indians, some forty or fifty in number.
• With Captain Meinhold, George Monroe and Mr. Frink took the trail again and followed it until soldiers and citizens were convinced that the perpetrators were Indians.

Meinhold never mentioned that he was with anyone during his tracking of the perpetrators.

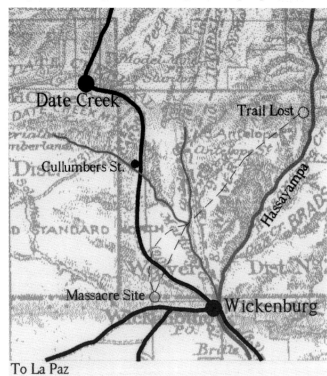

**Map of the Area of the
Wickenburg Massacre**

General Crook was enraged and took to the field in March of 1872 to determine exactly who the murderers were. Once again, his plans were foiled by a special peace commissioner. This time it was General Oliver Howard who again delayed Crook from going on the white man's version of the warpath.

The Goldwater Ambush

Following an unsuccessful bid to supply the army posts of Arizona with corn and barley, the Goldwater brothers, Michael and Joseph, left Prescott with partner Dr. Jones on a sunny summer day in 1872 bound for Ehrenburg on the Colorado River. Their course took them over the wagon road through Mint Valley on the way to Date Creek.

Possibly their anger at the loss of the contract preoccupied their minds. Certainly no one was looking for Indians. Suddenly, out from behind the rocks and trees thirty Mohave Apaches attacked the two buggies. Michael and Dr. Jones were in the lead with Joseph following close behind. Bullets crashed into men and rigs with Joseph taking the most hits. Wounded in his back and shoulder, Joseph could barely retain consciousness as his wagon raced ahead with one of his horses shot in the neck. The *Miner* of June 22, 1872, told the rest of the story:

> Open ground was soon reached and better still, white friends, in the persons of L. R. Stephenson, George Jackson and Jas. O'Leary of Walnut Grove, who were coming to Prescott in a wagon. Upon meeting them the Goldwater party had to come to a halt, as the frightened horses could not pass their wagon, and it was then discovered that Jos. Goldwater was dangerously wounded. But the hellish Indians were advancing, and the whites must either fight them or get away from them. Jones, Stephenson and others were for staying and fighting the savages who numbered about forty. But, upon reflecting how Jos. Goldwater was suffering, retreat was the word, and retreat they did, followed by the Indians. Skull Valley was soon reached. The party stopped at E. F. Bowers' place, which gentleman got two soldiers of the mail escort to ride to town and Fort Whipple, over the trail, which feat was very quickly performed. Dr. Baily, Medical Director of the Department, sent

down surgical instruments as per request of Dr. Jones; the balls were probed for; the wounded man was relieved, and is now, we believe in the hospital at Camp Date Creek, where, it is hoped, he will speedily recover.

> Stephenson and party came to town the next day, when Steve informed us that, to the best of his knowledge and belief, the attacking savages were Indians belonging to Camp Date Creek ...

Joseph Goldwater did survive, recuperating at his home in San Francisco.

An Indian raid on Culling's stage station, west of Camp Date Creek, on the 4th of September, 1872, which netted all of the horses and stock, finally turned the tide and enabled Crook to commence his now famous winter campaign of 1872–1873.

General Crook Settles the Issue

General Crook wisely felt that the starting point for curtailing the outrageous behavior of the Mohave Apaches would be the arrest of the perpetrators of the Wickenburg stage massacre. Crook had been collecting hard evidence for nearly a year and felt confident that he knew who was to blame.

Crook issued a report to the assistant Adjutant General at the Military Division of the Pacific, San Francisco, California, dated September 18, 1872.

> Sir:
> I have the honor to report that for some time I have been satisfied who the parties were who committed the massacre of the stage passengers near Wickenburg last November, in which Mr. Loring and others lost their lives, and have been keeping as quiet about it as possible while using every endeavor to get the individual Indians into position so as to capture them.

> Having completed my arrangements, I left here on the 6th instant to meet Irataba, the Chief of the Mojaves, with an interpretor at Date Creek. The Chief was conversant of the massacre and the parties who committed it, and was to identify such as were present at the council at Date Creek so that the arrest could be made.

On arriving at Date Creek, I found that at least two thirds of the Indians belonging on the reservation were absent from there and that the band had left in a defiant manner stating that they were not coming back, while others had left with the permission of the Agent to go to a certain place with the promise to come in whenever he sent for them, both of which promises they had failed to keep, and in addition, several bands of stock were stolen from parties on the road from Date Creek to Ehrenberg, the trails leading to the country over which the Indians were roaming.

The Indians who were at Date Creek seemed uneasy and suspicious, and in very bad temper, appearing with their arms and warpaint. Some of the parties who had participated in the stage massacre were there, but very uneasy, and when the Indians were assembled I had some men detailed to make the arrests as soon as the Indians were identified. As they were designated, the soldiers stepped up to arrest them, when one of the Indian's friends, standing back of the soldiers, stabbed one of them in the back. A shot was fired, by whom I could hardly say, but I think it was by the soldier stabbed, and in an instant firing began on both sides, the Indians making for the hills. I made every effort, as did all of the Officers present, to stop the firing but it was all over in an instant.

Several local citizens watched the affray including Charlie Genung. He of course felt the Yavapais should not be treated in such a high handed manner, but he needed them to help build a toll road through Peeples Valley. Crook went on:

I returned to Prescott on the 9th and on the 10th instant received a dispatch from the Commanding Officer of Camp Date Creek stating that the Indians wanted to talk with me and I went at once.

The Indians came in again and I promised them that I would grant amnesty to all the assassins who were still at large as I had one in the guard house and two others were killed. Upon this, nearly all the Indians I had met the first time came in again and said if I would allow them to remain, they would be responsible for all the Indians who should come in. They did not deny their complicity with the stage massacre, but said there were a good many bad Indians among them, and that heretofore they had been afraid to tell on each other when depredations

were committed. They promised that hereafter, they would not only tell me when any depredations were committed but they would go out with the troops, if necessary, to punish the offenders.

Ochocama, Crook's Prisoner, later escaped but only after receiving a bayonet wound which ultimately caused his death. Crook concluded:

As much as I regret that the arrests could not have been made without trouble, I am well satisfied that, as it now happens, the affair will now be productive of good, as it is upon this basis and no other that you can rely upon Indians who come in upon our reservations.

The application must come from them and not from us, they must sue to come in, and not feel all the time that they confer a favor upon us by doing so.

Crook's campaign that winter resulted in the decimation of the renegade Apaches in Tonto Basin and Northern Arizona. By December, 1872, Date Creek Reservation was bursting at the seams with Yavapais. Crook declared that section of the country safe from marauding Indians. No longer could they murder white men under the guise of being peaceful reservation Indians. Crook, sadly, was premature in his assertion as another outrage was about to happen.

A Final Act of Horror

In issues of March 15 and 22, 1873, the *Miner* carried three articles on the brutal murders of Gus Swain, John McDonald, and young George Taylor. The notice dated March 22 paints the picture most vividly.

On Tuesday night, March 11th, the Salt River stage with five passengers, passed a wagon by the wayside, three miles south of Lamley's station. The driver and passengers saw a man stretched out by the wagon, but feeling that the Indian question, at least hereabouts, was at rest, they believed it to be a camp for the night. But the early break of day revealed the deadly work of the savage foe—an old pioneer, August C. Swain, lay dead by the side of his muleless wagon, mutilated. By his side lay a young man, John McDonald, who, the day before, arrived at

Smith's Mill, rose early and was en route to Wickenburg, and, who, on arriving at the place also met the fate of his dead companion. They were found side by side.

But our tale of sorrow does not end here; P. W. Smith and Geo. Taylor, son of Peter Taylor, drove from Smith's Mill to Lamly Station the same afternoon; Mr. Smith remained for the night and young Taylor, feeling every security, at 5 o'clock started for home, some five miles distant, on foot. His not returning that night caused but little excitement, but on the return of Mr. Smith, Wednesday morning, nothing was talked of except the sad affair of Mr. Swain and the young man, supposing young Taylor was about the camp. Soon, however, came from an anxious mother's lips, "where is George?" The almost certainty of his fate was felt as the words came from the fond mother. A party at once started, but no success attended their efforts, until Thursday morning, the 13th, a little distance from the ill fated spot where Swain and McDonald fell, on a hill, not distant, they came upon a scene too horrible to report, fully, in your journal. Suffice it to say that the sight caused the stout heart of the old pioneer to quiver. Here lay young Taylor. Evidently the savage foe had done all he could to put out the candle of life by procrastinating, and every invention of his hellish and barbarous ingenuity. Fifty odd arrows were taken from his naked body. One of the mules taken had been slaughtered and remains of fires were visible; and the feast had been taken and the war dance performed. The appearances are that he fought desperately against great odds. The trail is a new one, coming from the west and going to the east. And the number, judging from the well beaten trail, would indicate hundreds. Young Taylor was a strong, fine young man, favorite of all who knew him; and a favorite, if I may so speak, of fond and loving parents.

The remains were at once sent to Vulture City for burial, arriving Thursday night at 10 o'clock. To the large number of citizens present, the solemnity of the occasion seemed to pervade all hearts. Mr. B. Sexton committed the body to its last resting place by reading a portion of the solemn and appropriated service of the Episcopal church for the dead.

The editor then added the following: "It is thought that they were eastern Apaches returning homeward from a trading trip among the Indians of the Colorado. But, speculation aside, they were Indians, and murderous ones at that, and it is to be hoped that Lieutenant Rice's command will find, surprise and kill the last devil of them." Possibly, these Indians were on their way to the peace talks at Camp Verde and this would be their last "outing."

The settlers were no doubt satisfied to learn that not only Rice's command, but also those of Wessendorf, Woodsen, and Randall were successful in running them to the earth in their stronghold on the summit of Turret Butte, in Tonto Basin, where they fancied no enemy would dare follow!

Peace Comes at Last

Editor John Marion, under the title of "Peace At Last," describes, in the April 12, 1873 issue of the *Miner*, his first hand impressions of the signing of the peace treaty at Camp Verde.

It was on Sunday, April 6, 1873, at Camp Verde, that the key-stone was set in Crook's arch of peace, to the great joy and gratitude of all who witnessed this crowning act of glory in the career of the conqueror of more than twenty tribes of Indians, whose horses stretch from far off Green River to our own Gila. Yes, Sunday, the blessed Sabbath, was the auspicious day; and as the "better the day, the better the deed," we believe that the peace will be lasting: more lasting than any canting, miscalled "peace" commissioner has ever made, or ever can make.

On May 1, 1873, eight hundred Yavapais set out for the Verde Reservation. Thus ended the Indian Menace in Central Arizona and for the most part, peace was brought to the settlers throughout the Territory.

By 1875, these same Yavapais were on their way to the reservation at San Carlos. General Crook said they could always stay at the Verde River Reservation, but then he too had been moved to the Department of the Platte to fight the Sioux.

Photo L. J. Hanchett Jr.

Wickenburg, Arizona

The Historical Society's Concord Stage

James Grant, the pioneer stage man of this section arrived here Tuesday afternoon last, from California, in a brand new Concord wagon, drawn by six mules, in which, also came the mail and six passengers, whose names are as follows: Wm. H. Buffum of Campbell and Buffum; Miss M. Wilburn; Mrs. Jennie Wells; M. Shonesen; Lt. Ledgewood; and Mr. Saunders.

The *Miner* October 2, 1869

Chapter Three
Establishing the Stage Lines

The arrival of a Concord stage coach in Prescott seems insignificant except when one realizes that a scant three years before there was not a single passenger stage running in the Territory. Vehicles called stages previously carried mail and express to and through the Territory, but passengers required a little more delicate handling than those items. A swing station with a single attendant, corrals and a supply of feed would satisfy the needs of the team of horses or mules pulling the stage. Human passengers demanded food and rest along the way.

The discovery of gold along the Colorado River sent streams of miners, merchants and freighters to La Paz near present day Ehrenburg. James Grant and John R. Frink, seizing the opportunity, began a mail stage from San Bernardino to La Paz in 1863, but they were only the third partnership to undertake such an endeavor. The other two lines ran all the way from Los Angeles to La Paz.

It wasn't until February, 1864, that a mail contract was actually let by the Federal Government to serve gold towns along the Colorado River. Grant and Frink got the contract and the competition disappeared. Shortly thereafter Frink sold out, leaving Grant to go it alone. A better man couldn't have been

found. For the next eleven years Grant was praised by the whole Arizona Territory for his ability to deliver the mail.

Courtesy Judi McLeod

James Grant

A new mail route was established by 1865, to get the mail between Santa Fe, New Mexico, and Los Angeles, via La Paz and Prescott. The contract holder was Sanford J. Poston of Arizona, and soon he had James Grant working for him on the La Paz–Prescott run. The *Los Angles News* of March 21, 1865, noted:

> The new line of mail stages to run between San Bernardino, California and Albuquerque, New Mexico, is now fairly under way; the route includes La Paz and Prescott. Mr. James Grant, formerly express man between Los Angeles and Prescott, as we learn, has contracted for and will carry the mail between La Paz and Prescott.

James Grant's Story as told by his daughter Louisa

James Grant left Canada, and his wife, daughter, and son, in 1852 heading for Northern California. Once there, he opened a mercantile business in Maryville having discovered that the real winners in a gold rush were the men who sold the shovels, not the ones who dug for gold!

In 1860, Grant moved to Southern California, but the lure of uncharted lands was just too much to pass up, so he bought a Pony Express Service, carrying the mail from Los Angeles to Prescott. Grant was no slacker, he carried the mail himself on the route.

In Louisa's words:

> As he traveled along he saw a vision of the stage line he hoped to operate and mapped out the route and located water where he could build stations and corrals where stock could be cared for, passengers accommodated and meals provided. It was a huge proposition.
>
> In 1867 or '68 he was awarded the contracts in Washington, D.C. to carry the U.S. mail from San Bernardino, California to Prescott, Arizona via Lapas on the Colorado River to Wickenburg and Camp Date Creek, Skull Valley, etc., and also from Wickenburg to Tucson via camp McDowell, Florence, Camp Grant, etc., passing through what is now the city of Phoenix, where the stage station and corrals were located.

Another man, Phinneas Banning, is credited with running the finest stage line in Southern California. Unfortunately, his routes only covered Los Angeles to San Bernardino and on to Yuma.

According to Francis Johnston in his book *The Bradshaw Trail*, Banning's stages were painted bright reds, yellows, greens, and blues and adorned with the finest appointments including leather interiors. Each coach held thirteen passengers and was equipped with lights and horns to signal their arrival at the stage stations. Drivers were well mannered men who wore tailored suits, fine shirts, cravats, polished boots, gauntlets, and wide brimmed, cream colored hats.

Arizona would never experience such luxury travel at the stagecoach level. By April of 1867, Banning withdrew his romantic stages.

The mail route now shifted North through the Mojave Desert, entering Arizona at Hardyville on the Colorado River. Grant continued his mail stages traveling from that point to Prescott. By May 1868, the toll road to Hardyville had been abandoned and the mail service reverted to the southern route. Grant then ran his mail stages from La Paz to Wickenburg with W. N. Ballard's line connecting at La Paz for travel into California.

Within a month Grant had a connecting route in place between Wickenburg and Maricopa Wells, south of today's Phoenix. This line tied in to Capron's stage from Los Angeles to Tucson.

By August, 1868, James Grant, Arizona's pioneer stage man and one time Territorial Auditor, had sold the stock of goods at his store in Prescott and was intending to devote his full time to overseeing his stage routes in Arizona.

In November of 1868, Grant was having problems obtaining military escorts, a must in the Arizona Territory because of the Indians. Grant hired his own guards and the mail still got through. In 1869 Grant settled his difficulties with the Army and was once again benefitting from regular escort service. Grant was lauded as the man who could ride more hours without sleep than any other man in Arizona.

Courtesy Arizona Historical Society/Tucson

Maricopa Wells

Although the first to have mail stages in Central Arizona, Grant was slower than the competition to start passenger service. *Miner* of July 17, 1869:

> New Enterprise—A coach, owned and driven by B. L. Reese, arrived here from Wickenburg Wednesday evening last, with three passengers, E. J. Cook, Captain Barrett and another gentleman. Mr. Reese requests us to inform the public that it is his intention to run his coach, regularly, once a week, between Wickenburg and Prescott, and that he has fixed the rate of fares as follows: From Wickenburg to Prescott, $30. From Prescott to Wickenburg, $20. Passengers can make the round trip for $40.

Passenger service on Grant's line began in earnest by September of 1869. Using the Concord stages Grant simply put himself head and shoulders above the competition. The Concord was the Mercedes of wagons. Nothing could touch it for passenger luxury, and baggage capacity.

The Concord Stage

The brainchild of Lewis Downing and J. Stephen Abbot, the Concord coach had its beginning in the New Hampshire town of that name in 1827. Each coach cost $1050 and weighed in at 2000 lbs. Fortunately, James Grant was probably able to buy several at sale prices following the advent of the railroad in Southern California.

Down to the wheels, the Concords were works of art. With spokes made of seasoned white pine and hubs of elm or black cherry, the wheels could easily withstand the rigors of Southwestern temperature extremes.

The bodies were solidly built and further reinforced with iron straps. Three inch thick leather through-braces cradled the coach as it hung between the front and back ends of the chassis. Their purpose was to protect the horses from sudden stops, not to comfort passengers who deemed the devices part of the cruel and unusual punishment of stagecoach travel.

The adjustable leather curtains did little to protect the passengers from dust, wind, snow or rain. With interior seats just over four feet wide, and head room less than five feet high, passenger discomfort was a given.

Possibly the other appointments such as padded leather seats, bright paint, exquisite landscape on the doors or interior gold leaf scrollwork, made up in some way for the horribly rough ride ahead.

Picnicking with the Military Escort

Ehrenburg, Arizona Territory 1871

Nevertheless, nothing else came close to the Concord through all the years of stagecoach travel. The arrival of a Concord stage always brought out the crowds much as the landing of a Concorde jet does today.

In addition to the Concords, Grant had another distinct advantage. He held the mail contracts, and by 1870, the three most important routes north of the Gila River were his alone. New contracts let by the Post Office to James Grant were:

Hardyville to Yuma, $7,448
Hardyville to St. George, Utah, $6,815
San Bernardino to Prescott, $16,448

The contracts were to extend from July 1, 1870, to July 1, 1874.

Passengers alone could not support a stage line, and competitors soon learned that vital lesson. Lucrative Government mail contracts were the key to success. Carrying a Wells Fargo box helped too, but once stage robbing became a Territorial pastime, many stages were dispatched without the "Treasure Box." There were no stages in Arizona owned by Wells Fargo.

The *Miner* for January 1, 1870, noted that James Grant's family had arrived at Wickenburg from Canada. Grant had not seen them for seventeen or eighteen years! Letters home during the early years of his absence sounded much like that of other pioneer men who left their families to seek fortunes on the frontier.

Grant would tell them over and over of how much he missed them and how soon he planned to return home for a visit. It must have taken a special love to keep those hopes alive for eighteen years, but somehow James and Alta Grant managed it. In the years to come, Alta would work side by side with her husband caring for passengers at the Wickenburg station.

On December 17, 1870, the *Miner* editorialized on the status of stage lines in Central Arizona.

Our Stage Lines

It is gratifying to be able to state that travel, by stage, is increasing. Grant's line from San Bernardino to Prescott, via Ehrenberg, La Paz and Wickenburg, is now, we learn, well patronized, and the accommodations along the line are better than ever before, especially on this side of the Colorado river. Not long ago, it was common to hear passengers growl at the accommodations upon this line; now while they assert that there is big room for improvement, they do not complain as of yore, so we take it that Mr. Grant and the station keepers are doing better than formerly. This is right, Central Arizona needs people, and they should not be deterred from coming here by poor stages, sickly teams, and bad fare.

In early 1874, James Grant had taken Dr. John H. Pierson into the fold of the Arizona Stage Company. Pierson had become his son-in-law in December of 1870 when he married Louisa A. Grant in Prescott. By March of 1874, a man named Van Duzan had successfully bid for the new mail contract between San Bernadino and Prescott. Pierson had stages but Van Duzan now had the mail contract. Naturally, they planned to go into business together to deliver the mail, express, and passengers.

James Grant was, at least on the surface, intending to bow out of the business. He and his wife had moved to San Bernardino, and it was rumored that he would be starting up the National Bank of San Bernardino while son-in-law Pierson took over the stage line. On September 22, 1874, James Grant and his wife, Alta, sold one third of the real property held by the stage company to James Stewart, a resident of California, for three thousand dollars. That property consisted of lots twenty-one and twenty-three, block nineteen, in Prescott and, "The land, houses, blacksmith shop, wagon shop, and corral known as the 'Home Station' in Wickenburg." The other two thirds interest was divided between Grant and Pierson.

Stage Poster for Grant's Stage Line

James Stewart

James Stewart began his stagecoach career in his early twenties, as driver on the St. Joseph, Missouri to Idaho route. While there he worked his way up to Superintendent and Paymaster of the Northern Overland Stage Line. When the railroad came through, Stewart moved on to Los Angeles and soon was driving stages for James Grant from San Bernardino to Prescott. By 1871, Stewart had a horse ranch at San Bernardino and was superintendent of Grant's stage line.

On May 21, 1875, James Grant died. Death supposedly came while he was investigating a shorter route across the desert to San Bernardino. The *Miner* of June 4, 1875, ran a lengthy article on his demise.

Another Pioneer Gone

Died—At San Bernardino, Cal. On Saturday, 21st ultimo, James Grant, in the fifty-fifth year of his age.

Mr. Grant came to California at an early day, and engaged in mercantile pursuits at Maryville, in that state. Came to Arizona about the year 1862; was one of the first white men to cross the great Colorado desert from San Bernardino to La Paz, Arizona.

In 1863 or '64 he established an express between what is now Prescott and San Bernardino, carrying it himself. He was afterwards engaged in merchandising at Prescott, and built up a thrifty business; at the same time holding the position of Territorial Auditor, until the removal of the capital to Tucson in 1867.

Upon the establishment of regular mail communication between Northern Arizona and California, Mr. Grant brought the first United States mail to Prescott, and has ever since been engaged in the transportation of the mails-first as the carrier, then as the contractor and manager; and at the time of his death was president of the California and Arizona stage Company, an institution built up by his indomitable energy.

The immediate cause of his death is attributed to the hardship and exposure that he underwent in an endeavor to search out a new and shorter route across the desert. He was a man of liberal views, possessed of a kind and generous heart, true to his friends, and if he had enemies he was not bitter against them. He may have had his failings; who has not? But there is no "old time," Arizonan who can say that he ever came to Grant for assistance and was denied, if it was in his power to render it. He has left his mark on Arizona, and may the clods of the beautiful valley of San Bernardino rest lightly on his grave.

Within a month and a half John Pierson and James Stewart were given all of Grant's interest in the same real property belonging to the California and Arizona Stage Company, plus the land and stage station in Phoenix. Grant's heirs, wife, Alta, son, Edward, and daughter, Louisa were the donors.

Dr. Pierson was, by the start of the following year, Secretary of the company. James Stewart was styled Superintendent in September of that year but was elevated to President by December. Apparently, the stage line was then using buckboards as stage vehicles, even on the runs to California.

Courtesy Judi McLeod

John H. Pierson

John Henry Pierson

Dr. John Pierson was one of many controversial characters in that part of the Territory. Some, including Governors Safford and Hoyt, trusted him enough to appoint him as Notary Public for Wickenburg. Others such as Charlie Genung, early pioneer and later scribe for the area's history, felt confident that he was, at best, a murderer.

Born in Vermont and probably educated abroad, Pierson had been brought to the Territory by Thomas B. Sexton, Superintendent of the Vulture mine, around 1868. Setting himself up as mine physician, he built a fine house for himself near the mine hospital just north of Wickenburg at Vulture City. The census for 1870 shows him as a single man, occupation physician. Charlie Genung felt that Pierson conspired with Sexton to bilk miners out of their share of the mine's profits, and the mine company out of its revenues.

In addition to the fraud conspiracy, Genung felt certain that Pierson had poisoned another doctor who also practiced in Wickenburg. Supposedly, Pierson had administered an overdose of morphine to young Dr. Miller when he complained of a stomach disorder. Why Miller, a doctor himself, did not realize he was being given an overdose is another mystery.

At the time of his father-in-law's death, June, 1875, Pierson was running the stage station at Wickenburg for the California and Arizona Stage Company. His was singled out as one of the few prosperous businesses in Wickenburg after the closing of the Vulture Mine in May of 1872.

The California and Arizona Stage Company was temporarily threatened by a potentially large competitor, the Arizona and New Mexico Express Company. The nominal head of Wells Fargo, Henry Wells, had sent his son, Charles

H. Wells, to superintend the fledgling operation headquartered in Tucson. The first stage left Tucson on January 30, 1876, arriving at Prescott the evening of January 31. The next day that same stage departed for Whitewater, California. Cost per passenger was $60 to the railhead and $93 to San Francisco.

The C & A immediately countered with a reduced fare of $50 to the railhead through San Gorgonio Pass and San Bernardino. In spite of cheaper fares with the C & A, the *Miner* on May 12, 1876 reported activity on the A & NM

> Judge Tweed arrived from Phoenix by A and NM Stage, on Monday morning, and opened the District Court in the afternoon. His wife, who is in delicate health, accompanied him as far as Wickenburg and from there went to California, in hopes to find relief in a change of climate.

The summer heat brought an end to the C & A's concerns as its competitor was starting to collapse by the first of July of that year, according to the *Citizen* of Tucson. By July 15, the *Miner* reported that the Wells Fargo express contract had been turned over to the C & A Stage Company which was by then delivering passengers to a closer railhead at Indian Wells near Caliente, California. Money and name didn't always win out over experience and determination.

By March of 1877, the California and Arizona Stage Company was running between Prescott and Ehrenberg as well as between Prescott, Phoenix, and Florence. Apparently, James Grant's son, Edward O. Grant, did not follow in his father's footsteps as far as stages were concerned, but chose instead to become a merchant in Prescott. He even moved into the same building previously occupied by his father's store.

Charles P. Stanton, of Antelope Creek, talked about his friend Pierson in a letter to the *Miner* dated March 30, 1877.

> Our indomitable friend, Dr. Pierson. Is the veritable *rara arias* of this section, far more remarkable than anything, feathered, biped or

quadrupedal, to be met with in either ancient or modern history. On Sunday morning I visited the headquarters of the California and Arizona Stage Company, and there standing on the esplanade in front of the office, stood Dr. Pierson with a massive equipoised head, firmly secured between a solid pair of shoulders. Stages were arriving from every point of the compass.

On July 25, 1878, Stewart and Pierson sold the California and Arizona Stage Line's property to Jack Gilmer, of the Gilmer and Salisbury Stage Company, for the sum of $3,960. Gilmer and Salisbury were well known for their competence in running stages, with over 5,000 miles of routes in Utah, Nevada, Colorado, Montana, and Idaho.

Headquartered in Utah, Gilmer and Salisbury were destined to become the largest stage operators in the west. That title would have to wait for the downfall of the Wells Fargo stage empire and Gilmer's acquisition of its most profitable lines in Utah.

Courtesy Sharlot Hall Museum

Prescott Stage Station

James Stewart became Arizona superintendent for the new owners, running large stages between Prescott and the railroad terminal at Maricopa. Their Arizona operations expanded quickly to include most of the Territory's major markets.

An inventory, based on the Tax Rolls for the holdings of the C & A Stage Company just before the sale to Gilmer and Salisbury provides insight into the operation of a stage line. In Yavapai County, C & A was assessed for lots 21 and 23, with improvements, in block nineteen at Prescott, Weaver Hill Station, eighteen head of horses, sixteen sets of harnesses, two coaches, 2300 lbs of grains, and five tons of hay. In Maricopa County they had station corrals, and blacksmith and wagon shops at Wickenburg along with lots 7 and 11, block 21 in the town of Phoenix.

Dr. Pierson Moves Again

Soon after the sale of the stage line, Dr. Pierson moved to Peeples Valley where, coincidently, Charlie Genung had been a long time resident. Using his influence, Pierson promptly gained appointments as road overseer for Yavapai county and postmaster at "Antelope Valley." Trouble fomented almost immediately.

It seems that Pierson hired a body guard by the name of Oscar Baer, and after a couple of run ins with Genung, Baer supposedly threatened Genung's life. In November of 1879, Genung and his brother-in-law, Carl Smith, left by wagon for Wickenburg. At a point on the Antelope Hill route, Genung discovered Baer at work on the road. Genung reported that Baer, having seen him, jumped to one side of the road for his six shooter. Genung opened up with both barrels of his shot-gun killing Baer instantly. Genung, of course, claimed self defense.

The *Miner* of November 21, 1879, reported the results of the coroner's inquest.

Dr. Warren E. Day, who went to Antelope Saturday to hold an inquest and make a post-mortem examination of the remains of Oscar Baer, shot on the 14th instant has returned. We are informed of the following facts, which are reliable. Baer had twelve wounds on his body, as follows: one shot wound through the head, one in neck over right carotid artery, one passing below "Adam's apple," and lodging in spinal cord, two wounds through right shoulder fracturing the bone, two right side penetrating the stomach, two through right hand, shot wound breaking left shoulder, one graze wound right hip, and one wound carrying away portion of his chin. He evidently died instantly of cerebral hemorrhage.

The deceased was brought to Peeples Valley yesterday, and interred by friend's in a very praiseworthy and Christian manner.

It seems incredible to read a coroner's report where such extreme damage is done only to the supposed aggressive party. Twelve wounds on Baer's body and Charlie Genung's Bill of Indictment was "ignored!" One would think that Baer's gun would have been in his hand if he were planning to ambush Genung.

Pierson and his friend Charles Stanton pulled a fast one on a man by the name of Barney Martin in November of 1880. It seems that Stanton had pointed a gun at Martin in a threatening way and Martin took him before the Justice of the Peace for it. Of course, Pierson happened to be that Justice. Pierson not only let Stanton off, but also made Martin pay a twenty-eight dollar fee to the court.

Martin then filed a complaint of extortion against Pierson which resulted in a Grand Jury indictment. When the case came to trial before the Third Judicial District, Pierson hired the highly competent team of Rush and Wells, attorneys. Martin of course lost and the case against Pierson was dismissed. The event was nevertheless a precursor of more trouble to come between Martin and Stanton.

Sometime after June, 1881, John Pierson packed up and headed back to San Bernardino California. According to Genung, he left a lot of debts and victims, both alive and dead, behind him.

Pierson and family would reside in San Bernardino, California until March 5, 1898, at which time John Pierson was committed to the Southern California State Hospital at Highland. Mary A. Peterson applied for the commitment and she and Miss Pierson were witnesses. Drs. Hazelett and Stiles, State Medical Examiners in Lunacy, certified that John Pierson was insane.

Seven years later he would die from a drug overdose which may have accounted for his earlier diagnosis of insanity. On December 14, 1905, J. H. Pierson was interred at the Hillside Cemetery in Redlands, California. Louisa then moved back to Toronto, Ontario, Canada.

The stage line name reverted back to Arizona Stage Company in the early 1880s and was sold by Jack Gilmer to Kate Salisbury of Oakland, California on October 20, 1886. A new line entitled the Prescott and Phoenix Stage surfaced in 1886. By 1895 a rail line had been completed between Phoenix and Prescott. From that time until trucks and autos came in style, stages were only used as adjuncts to the railroad.

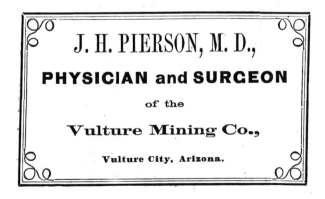

J. H. PIERSON, M. D.,

PHYSICIAN and SURGEON

of the

Vulture Mining Co.,

Vulture City, Arizona.

Photo L. J. Hanchett Jr.

Assayer's Office at the Vulture Mine

Mill Site at Vulture City, North of Wickenburg

Soon after the subjugation of the Indians, some of the old "boys" used to predict that as soon as our mines would commence to pan out, white robbers would take the place of Indians.

Miner, December 22, 1876.

Chapter Four
A New Breed of Stage Robbers

Courtesy Arizona Department of Library, Archives and Public Records

A "Staged" Holdup

Under the title "A New Industry," the *Miner* goes on to say, with tongue in cheek;

> We thought so, too, and sinful as it was, used to pine for a chance to record such a maneuver in these columns because in those days, times were dull and money scarce, and, as it was our duty to record "progress" of all kinds, we reasoned that it would be a lively card for our section if it could only boast its ability to give white road agents an occasional job. We do not exactly look at it in this light, now that we have reached a paying point, and have something to lose. Besides the class of road agents which California, Nevada, and other States have sent us are not real "gentlemen of the road," but blood-thirsty fellows, who regardless of all etiquette and orthodox road agent's breeding, signaled their first attempt to carry out their little communistic plan by conduct unbecoming brave "knights of the road."

California and Nevada may have been sending stage robbers to Arizona due to the introduction of railroads in those states. Trains were certainly more difficult to stop and rob, so Arizona, with only stage lines, must have looked like greener pastures to the highwaymen of those states.

Only a few weeks had passed before the *Miner* started devoting significant space to reports of stage robberies. Lightheartedness was giving way to concern and frustration.

The *Miner* of January 12, 1877 revealed that the California and Arizona Stage had been robbed. Fortunately, the supposed robbers had been caught. Unfortunately, one or both turned out to be far more intelligent than the average "knight of the road," or possibly, far more ignorant. The strange progression of events could have been bad luck or just plain stupidity.

Milton Alexander Vance and his sidekick, Thomas Berry, were ostensibly looking for a spring in the area near Woolsey Canyon, northwest of Prescott, on the night of January 4, 1877. Coincidently, the California and Arizona stage was being robbed between Prescott and Skull Valley that same evening. J. H. Evans, a mail guard on the stage told how it happened.

> On the night of Thursday I was going from Prescott to Wickenburg: while going around Woolsey hill somebody said "halt." They each hallowed "halt" several times: just after they hallowed "halt," the leaders came in contact with a rope stretched across the road, which threw them: the stage then came to a dead halt; at the same time one of the parties said "Throw up your hands!" One of the parties said "How many passengers are on?" The driver said "Two." I was then ordered to get down off of the stage and to go to the side of the leaders: I walked there and was again ordered to halt; Jesus, the driver, was then ordered off the coach and to stand where I was; the man with the gun stood in a line with Jesus and myself; the man on the right hand side of the stage came around and searched each one of us for arms; finding nothing, he proceeded to the front boot and threw the mail and express off, and commenced to cut the mail sacks; he asked for a hatchet; the driver told him we didn't have any; he then took the king bolt and tried to open the express box with it; failing to do so he struck it violently several times, against the hind wheel, and finally succeeded in shaking it open; he then rifled it of its contents; after remaining there about an hour, he ordered the driver to hitch up and go down the road a mile or a mile and a half, and return in one hour and get the mail and box; we returned and found the mail scattered over the ground; there was nothing remaining of the express box but the way packet; after picking up and putting the letters in the bag, we proceeded to Skull Valley; I left the coach there and procured a saddle horse and came to Prescott; went to the Sheriff's office and told Standefer what had occurred and we went in search of the men; about a mile and a half from here on the road to Skull Valley we saw two men coming down the road with three animals ...

Standefer, U.S. Marshall for the Territory, and Evans found in the two mens' possession, and in their saddle bags, a chunk of gold addressed to Mr. Fisher at Ehrenberg, two packages of bullion, and a registered letter, all of which had previously been on the stage. Vance's explanation was simple, the articles had been given to them by a passerby whom they did not know and could not identify. Vance offered these details:

> When we were ready to start on, a man rode up to me as I was fixing my saddle, he was within about ten feet of me before I saw him. He asked if I was going to town, I replied that I was. He

requested me to do him favor and I consented. He then stated that he had some articles he wished taken to the express office, and handed me the small package, found on me when arrested and I put it in my pocket, he then spoke of a letter and handed me two other packages; I handed them back to him and told him they were too heavy for my pocket; he asked if I had no way of carrying them on my saddle. I told him of my saddle pockets, he said he would put them in there and did so; I saw no more of the letter, but supposed he had put it in the pocket; he said nothing of what they contained: immediately after this he said goodnight and went away. I had expected an explanation from him about the matter, but supposed the articles would explain themselves; up to that time we had not worn the blankets. He having a blanket on him induced us to think of doing the same and we were arrested with them around our shoulders.

Of course, Evans, the mail guard, had noticed that the two bandits had blankets wrapped around them as the stage was robbed. Prisoner Vance then went on at length to explain why he had originally told Marshal Standefer that he and his partner had not been on the Ehrenberg road. It seems that Vance was not familiar enough with the area to know which route was called the Ehrenberg road.

Justice Cartter was not buying the rather obvious explanations Vance had cooked up and proceeded to advise him that he and Berry would be held to answer before the next Grand Jury. Their bail was set at ten thousand dollars each and they were remanded to jail. On September 7th of that year the *Miner* noted the results of Vance's trial.

> Milton Alexander Vance, the sharpest, cunningest and most dangerous stage robber, because the smartest, that has ever operated in Arizona, this morning received his sentence for robbing the mail in Woolsey Canyon, in March last, which was that he be confined at hard labor in the penitentiary for and during the term of his natural life.

Just over a year later, Vance's partner, Thomas Berry, wrote a letter to the editor of the *Miner* describing his and Vance's captivity and subsequent escape. The letter was published in the *Miner* issue of February 6, 1878.

After a few days wandering amid the waving forests, and over the green-decked valleys, enjoying nature's sublime beauties, I find myself once more within the old bastille of Yavapai County, with its unattractive, unenticing surroundings, the aroma from which presents a striking contrast with that of the flower-beds and the abundant vegetation I found everywhere between Prescott and the Eden of Arizona–Salt River, where my bright hopes were blasted, and I again made to feel that my lot is indeed a sad one. As your readers are aware, I was in company with Milton A. Vance, arrested January 5, 1877, on a charge of having robbed the United States mail. We were tried during the summer of 1877, found guilty and sentenced to imprisonment for life. A serious sentence for men who did not commit the crime, but made to appear as such through the treachery of others. After our trial, etc., we were conducted by Ex-U.S. Marshal Standefer to Fort Whipple, and there confined in the guard-house for safe keeping—where we remained until the night of the 18th of July. About eight months of this time our confinement was solitary, accompanied by a slow process of starvation. Our food consisting of half boiled bacon, bread and soldier's coffee double diluted with an occasional change of parboiled beef in pieces that would not have scared a hungry dog or coyote to have tackled them on account of their extraordinary size. To complain of our food was only to make bad worse. As for clothing, we had to depend upon the private soldiers entirely; and in this connection allow me to say, that they at all times were most kind to us. Four months since we made complaint to the doctors that the close confinement was injurious to our health, when an order was given that we should have exercise. It was dosed out to us in abundance. Under a close guard, ironed down with 16-pound shackles, we were put to policing around officer's quarters, digging ditches, laying water pipe, making roads, tearing down old buildings, putting up stables, white-washing, etc.; to do all of which we necessarily got to handle tools, and whenever opportunity presented itself, we concealed such as would assist us in making good our escape. Our assortment was finally complete; we tried them and they proved to be everything desired. We were about thirty days making good our liberty. The cell we occupied was 2 ft. 6 in. wide and 7 ft. long. The floor is laid on sleepers 4 × 6 inches, and raised about 5 inches off the ground. We worked our way to the west end of the building under the floor where we found the same about 18 inches off the ground, which gave us ample room to work and a place to throw the dirt and rock from the hole we were excavating.

The wall runs beneath the surface 2½ feet, and is about three feet thick. When we had about completed the tedious undertaking of digging our way out, we procured some hard-tack and bacon, rolling it up separately, and then bid adieu to the unattractive quarters we had been so generously furnished, and were soon standing out in free-space. Here Vance and myself separated, agreeing that we would separate, never to meet again. I took to the west of Fort Whipple, went up a gulch that led me to Mr. Hudson's ranch. Finding that I was unable to travel on foot, from effects of rheumatism, I decided to take Mr. H.'s horse, which I espied grazing, and which finally led to my arrest and return to Prescott.

Allow me to state that, had I known Mr. H. as I now know him, his horse would have remained unmolested by me. After mounting the unlucky horse, I took a southerly direction, which led me into heavy timber, where fine grass and plenty of water met my ever watchful gaze.

After leaving Prescott a respectable distance, I set up housekeeping on my own hook and tried cooking Uncle Sam's bacon, in a style I had not been in the habit of seeing while sojourning in the temporary quarters furnished by Marshal Standefer. I had a splendid view of the surrounding country from an elevated peak to the south-east of Prescott. The next day after my escape 'the noble animal' threw one of his shoes and me also, the shoe going in one direction and me in another. The day following I luckily found an old horseshoe, with some stubs of nails in it which I sharpened with two smooth stones, and placed the shoe on the foot of my [Hudson's] horse, in a style that would have made the son of the Vulcan art wonder. My route was south of Agua Fria, through the rough mountains until I struck the old road over the black mesa from Phoenix to Prescott. I proceeded on my journey south, leaving the road at Swilling's old ranch, and taking across the hills to New River station or near there, where I struck a nice spring. I formed the acquaintance of three men at the New River mansion, one being a black whiskered Don, the same who finally gave me away. I told these parties that I was looking up astray mules. I remained in the vicinity of this station ten days. During the time I was camped there, the men at the station passed my camp going out to cut hay; I went to their hay camp; they returned to camp with me. I was the possessor of a pair of scissors and one of the gentlemen enquired if I understood cutting hair, to which I responded in the affirmative and proceeded to relieve him of a fine fleece for which any tonsorial artist would have charged him double price. At last Mr. Hudson came to the camp at New River station en route to Salt River, related his loss and "black whiskers" gave me away for $100. I saw Mr. Hudson arrive in the evening, as I was on watch from the top of the mountain above my camp, where I had enjoyed myself for several days hunting, etc., killing a fine, fat goat which gave me plenty of food. The next morning, from my elevated state, I saw the wagon take the route in my direction. I went down from my roost of the night previous, procured my camp outfit, such as it was, and left for Salt River by a rather circuitous route. When within ten miles of Salt River Valley I halted to rest my charger and aching bones from a long ride without saddle, when I noticed a hero riding along the road. I mounted and went out to meet him, thinking he had seen me. I had a pistol ready for him in case of emergency. It was "black whiskers" from New River station. I accompanied him to the outer settlements of Salt River. He told me he was going for clothes and money belonging to him in Phoenix. We camped near a house; he went in to purchase some barley, I went in with him. By some means he whispered and the man knew who I was. We went back to our camp, made down our pallets where I directed, and the man at the house slipped away to Phoenix and soon returned with Deputy Sheriff Phy. It was my intention to have left this place soon, and with me I should have taken "black whiskers" until I reached the desert south of Salt River, where I intended to bid him good-bye. Sheriff Phy inquired of me the name of the man living in the house nearby; but I told him to go and inquire. He started for the house and called out to someone for the trail heading to the point of the mountain, then turned back to my camp remarking that his saddle-girth was out of fix and dismounted to repair it; entirely throwing me off my guard, when I found myself covered with two six-shooters. I could have killed one or two of the party if I had felt so disposed but such was not my wish. I went to Phoenix, was ironed and here I am in my cell.

Thomas Berry

Truly an amazing story, told by the captive instead of the captors. Vance apparently made good his escape and was not heard from again in those parts.

While Vance and Berry were still imprisoned, other robberies were taking place. According to the *Miner*:

Wickenburg, April 10

Stage arriving here this morning from Prescott was attacked by robbers, five miles this side of Prescott, and express box taken. Mail was not touched. Robbers after possessing themselves of box, ordered stage to drive on. No clue to the robbers as they were masked closely.

Stage Robbed

As will be seen by our dispatch from Wickenburg, the C. And A. Stage which left here last evening was robbed, five miles out, of the express box. We have learned that the express box contained less than fifty dollars. Marshal Standefer and John Brickwood have gone out in search of the robbers, and it is to be hoped they may capture them.

No Clue to the Robbers

United States Marshal Standefer went out yesterday to the scene of the stage robbery of the night before but got no trace of the robbers. He found the express box, broken open and entirely empty, and near it a package of brass couplings for a water pipe addressed to Mr. Peralta, Wickenburg. This package which weighed fifteen pounds or more, together with the fifty-eight dollars in money, we understand was all the box contained, and when the robbers found what sort of treasure they had captured they no doubt felt that they had made a bad speculation and turned their attention to making their escape. There is no encouragement in this country for men of genius in that line. Several first class robberies have been perpetrated within the last few months, and in every case something has occurred to deprive the enterprising operators of their expected profits. We are no advocate of lawlessness in any shape, and especially that of redressing wrongs outside of the Courts and officers of the law, but as sure as these annoyances continue, the people are not going to submit to it quietly, and the time is not far distant when a few of these gentry will be strung up to limbs, or shot down like sheep killing dogs. We must be permitted to come and go in peace even though it costs the lives of a hundred of these robbers.

The Plundered Stage

It is said by those who met the outgoing stage beyond the scene of the robbery, on Monday night, and heard an account of it from the passengers, that it was very amusing even to themselves, after it was over, to witness the industry with which they stowed away the small amount of change that each one carried to defray traveling expenses. Of course, no sensible man travels with any considerable amount of available means on his person, but even a few dollars to buy grub in a strange country, becomes of such importance as a much larger sum would be under other circumstances, and it behooved them to take care of what they had. Some threw their wallets under the seats, some stuffed them in their boots, some in their bosoms, etc. W. M. Lent who is never known to have more than ten dollars about him, seemed to be the most unconcerned of the lot, and thought of offering them his pocket-book and contents as a ransom so as not to be detained any longer.

Four articles in one *Miner* issue dated April 13, 1877, but no suspects to show for the effort. Just a month later, Marshal Standefer would take to the road again in pursuit of more stage robbers. This time the story had two plots.

Wickenburg, May 14

Robbers took in the stage three miles out from here night-before-last. The mail bags were cut, the treasure box cleaned out, and the passengers robbed.

The last mail robbed contained $534 in money order funds from here, and checks in the amount of $400 belonging to D. Dietrich.

The *Miner* edition of May 18, 1877 gave the details of the robbery:

The stage which left this place on Saturday morning, carrying mails, treasure box and several passengers, arrived at Wickenburg in due time and after leaving that place and when about two miles out was stopped by four masked robbers, well armed, who demanded the treasure box, mail bags, and loose change on the person of the passengers.

Our Sheriff, Ed. F. Bowers, who was aboard taking Mary Sawyer, an insane woman to Stockton was robbed of a fine gold watch and $450 in gold coin.

Frank Luke who was also a passenger, had on his person $340 in gold and sixty-five in currency. When demanded to hand over he gave them his pocket book containing the currency and also an order on parties in San Francisco for $250 more. Supposing this to be all he had they handed him back his order, it being valueless to them, and did not search farther. Thus he escaped from being compelled to yield up $340 which would have materially interfered with his trip to West Point.

We have not learned the amount or whether any money was lost from the treasure box which the robbers took. The mail bags were cut open and the mail matter mutilated. At last accounts a party was out in search of the robbers and it is to be hoped that these highwaymen may be caught and not sent to Yuma for safe keeping. We understand the mutilated mail will be returned to this place and fixed up for a new start. Stage robberies in Arizona are becoming as frequent as Indian murders were a few years since and it is to be hoped that something may turn up that will make these low breed curs desist from going on the highway and resort to something honorable whereby they may exist.

Frank Luke was followed in his military career by his son, Frank Luke Jr. of World War I fame, but the most unique aspect of this robbery was that it was performed by an employee of the Post Office Department acting undercover. The *Miner* of June 1, 1877 attempted to explain what really happened.

As much comment has recently been made by citizens of Prescott, and elsewhere, in regard to the late stage robbery, near Wickenburg, we have interviewed U.S. Marshal Standefer on the matter, and elicited from him the following facts, which are substantially as follows:

Owing to the numerous robberies of our stages, Special Agent Alexander, of the P.O. Department, conceived the very excellent idea of employing a man who would ferret out the highwaymen, in fact, go in with them, and then give information which would assure their arrest. This was done with John Mantle who, a short time since, gave information that led to the arrest of the stage robbers who robbed the stage near Indian Wells, and the recovery of the money. After having been used as a detective in California, he was sent to Arizona for the same purpose. He came here, hunted up Johnson and Sutton, alias Brophy, went in with them and

robbed the stage near Wickenburg, and delivered the bullion into the hands of the stage agent at Ehrenberg, at the same time giving agent Evans information which led to the arrest, of which our readers know. That this man Mantle acted entirely in good faith in the recent robbery near Wickenburg, the Marshal is not prepared to say, and rather has his doubts that he did not, on account of the money delivered over, which leaves quite a discrepancy between the amount delivered over to the agent and that claimed to have been lost.

That any sensible person should, for a moment, entertain or harbor a thought, that the Stage Company have not in this as in all former occurances of a similar nature, acted on the square is really preposterous and does the Company great injustice who have always been active and went to great trouble and expense in ferreting out stage robbers and causing their arrest. That they knew Mantle was here for the purpose of trying to find out the highwaymen who infested this section of our Territory, we have no doubt, and that they should try and assist in making the discoveries is perfectly natural and right. Marshal Standefer arrested John Mantle, and took him to the Yuma prison, entered a complaint against him as a highway man and he is held to answer at the next term of the Grand Jury for the Second Judicial District in the sum of $10,000, when if it is found that Mr. Mantle did not act in good faith and has committed a crime, he will be dealt with according to the extent of his offense.

What a dilemma! Everyone was acting in "good faith" but the bottom line was that the Sheriff got robbed at gunpoint by a man in the employ of the Post Office, and aided by the stage line. Furthermore, Mantle didn't even return all the stolen money. In today's system this would be a real exercise in jurisprudence.

A letter to the *Miner* dated December 1, 1877, described the proceedings in Yuma.

The case of the supposed mail robbers, Sutton and Brophy, has become already notorious, not only throughout this Territory, but from the Occident to the rising sun. Sutton was tried by a jury and ably prosecuted by E. B. Pomeroy, H. N. Alexander, and Col. D. O. Whiting of Los Angeles, and defended by C. W. C. Rowell of San Bernardino and an attorney from Prescott. The trial and consideration lasted four days, and the jury was discharged—standing six and six. The defendants, Brophy and Sutton, under the advice of Rowell, and against the solemn protest of their other attorney, pleaded guilty to the lowest crime known to the law under the indictment, and were sentenced to five years in the Territorial Prison, where they are now under the charge of Mr. Geo. Thurlow, who will make them believe before the expiration of their time, that when they go hence they had better sin no more. Thurlow ought to have been a preacher; he has a warm heart, pleasant countenance, and a tongue which seems to have been soaked in the oil of eloquence for a week. He talks to the prisoners but somehow they don't talk back.

Now, Mr. Editor, here is what the United States Grand Jury of the 2nd Judicial District of our Territory says:

"In the examination of the robbery cases of the United States mail, a state of facts was brought to light which in the opinion of the Grand Jury is deplorable in the extreme. We find one John Mantle, while in the service and under the authority of the Postal Service Department of the United States, planning and executing a robbery of a stage and of the U.S. mail.

We find that he was sent to this Territory and appointed Director to work up the facts concerning stage robberies and bring to justice the perpetrators of any stage robberies which might occur within the Territory. Mr. Mantle came here heralded by secret letters to two or three stage agents, but without notice to a single U.S. Official within the Territory, and no officer, either of the United States or the Territory was ever informed of his intentions.

We find that in the town of Prescott he, with others, planned to rob the stage-passengers and mail traveling from Prescott to Ehrenberg. That his plan was put into execution whereby passengers were robed and placed in jeopardy of their lives and the mail was broken into and robbed.

The different stage agents along the road of the contemplated robbery were notified, but neither the passengers or the driver knew what was coming. Ed. F. Bowers was one of the passengers.

The robbing was committed a few miles from Wickenburg, and the stage agent—Pierson—of that place, knew at the time the stage reached his office what was to happen, yet neither Mr. Bowers nor the others were told a word so that they might have provided for what was coming, and to save their effects and perhaps to secure the robbers.

The robbery was committed under cover of guns and pistols, and the least motion of resistance by any of the passengers might have led to loss of life of one or more of the passengers. As it was, all the money had by the passengers was taken from them—some four hundred and fifty dollars from Sheriff Bowers, and valuable letters mutilated and destroyed. The money taken has never been returned by Postal authorities or anyone else.

The Grand Jury cannot too severely condemn this light-handed experiment of the Detective branch of the Postal Service, and its execution showed, in the opinion of the Grand Jury, an almost criminal lack of common sense.

It is the belief of the Grand Jury that in this instance, the robbery was instigated by the influence of John Mantle who led the party, instead of merely participating in it. There are many unfortunate people in the world, who, through poverty and destitution, might be led by a stronger will to the commission of crime, and who, untampered with, would honestly struggle on. It is to be hoped that it is not within the province of the Postal Department, to continue furnishing leaders for such people. If there had been lives lost, who would have been responsible? Probably the same parties responsible for the money lost by the passengers.

The Grand Jury cannot too much condemn the actions of Pierson, stage agent at Wickenburg, in not notifying the passengers of the contemplated robbery. He knew Mr. Bowers, and he knew from his position as Sheriff of Yavapai County, that he could be depended on, and yet he let the passengers, ignorantly go on to a certain loss of money and perhaps cruel death.

In the opinion of the Grand Jury, this detective experiment has been a useless one, with no other good result than a public caution to the world at large, of the possibilities within the reach of the detectives peculiar intellect."

Signed John W. Dorrington, Foreman

In the trial of defendant Sutton, Sheriff Bowers who was called for the defense, was asked by Goodwin, this question, "Had you been informed at the time the stage passed Wickenburg, on the evening of May 12th, that an attempt would be made to rob the stage on which you were a passenger, having in custody an insane woman, on route to Stockton, California, and that John Mantle, one of the trio who would attempt to rob the stage was an employee in the Postal Service of the United States, and could be relied on as such, could you not have captured or taken the other parties who are charged with having been present at the time when, and the place where, the alleged robbery is said to have taken place?" Mr. Bowers firmly answered "I could."

On motion of the prosecution, the question and answer were stricken out by Judge Porter, and the defendant had the exception noted.

The Grand Jury who indicted Mantle, Sutton and Brophy for United States mail robbery, were twenty-three in number, and are regarded as representative citizens of Yuma. They did their duty faultlessly—no shadow of suspicion can by any possibility be cast upon their action. They concluded that if the stage was robbed at the time and place set forth that John Mantle, Alexander, Adams and others were equally guilty with the unfortunate wretches who note time by heart throb on "yonder hill" near where to the city of the dead, and no more guilty than some who have the freedom of the earth.

The Grand Jury of Yuma, in their report, gave credit to U.S. Marshal Standefer for his actions in the matter of the stage robbery above referred to, and for his attention to the duties of his office.

On April 19, 1878 the stage out of Wickenburg, bound for Ehrenberg, was robbed by three masked men. Within a few months this robbery would become well known throughout the Territory as the supposed outlaws were three well known men. Official bungling of the case would lead to the totally unnecessary death of one of the men and the delay in capture and conviction of the real perpetrators.

Potential rewards, as suggested by the *Miner*, no doubt gave added zeal to those pursuing the supposed outlaws. The *Miner* of April 26, 1878, gave the details.

Stage Robbed
U.S. Mails and Wells, Fargo & Co.'s
Treasure Box Taken!!!

Our dispatch from Wickenburg tells of the robbing of the stage last night by three masked men, four miles west of that place en route to California, passengers, mail and express robbed. It is not stated whether the silver bullion was taken or not, though it is hardly probable that they attempted to get away with so great a weight. There were two bars of Peck bullion from this place worth $3,372.61 and $1,512 in gold bullion from the Crook mill. Wells Fargo & Co. offer a standing reward of $300 each for the arrest of express robbers besides a portion of the treasure recovered as salvage.

The Governor will no doubt offer a liberal reward, and it is usual for the Postal department to do likewise. So that the capture of the three will be apt to yield the captor or captors between two and three thousand dollars, to say nothing of pay for recovery of the treasure stolen.

We have no account , as yet, of the amount shipped from Phoenix by that stage, nor of what is supposed to have been in the mails. Two passengers left here by stage yesterday morning, viz.: A. Angles and W. Linchan, who are supposed to be the ones robbed.

Rewards of that size brought out the worst in people. On the frontier, some men would turn in their mother for an amount less than two to three thousand dollars. Unfortunately, the justice system had not kept pace with the rewards possible in the case of grand larceny.

Mexicans Take Up Stage Robbing

In an almost prophetic piece of writing, the *Miner* of October 4, 1878 tried to make the population aware of the threat from Mexican stage bandits and what actions the government would take.

The Department of Justice at Washington, the War Department, Secret Service Bureau and Wells Fargo & Co., as well as others of note, are co-operating to bring about a cessation of mail-stage robberies. We are not authorized to say what the action of the Government will be in the direction of repelling Mexicans who may cross the international boundary line and after raiding on the mail-bullion-stages, and robbing the passengers, return to their mountain vastness in Sonora or Chihuahua; but enough is known to make it certain they will be treated with even less consideration than the bandits who have made some "stretches" on the line of the Rio Grande in Texas almost uninhabitable. There is no desire on the part of the War Department, to take the "pursuit and capture" of "road agents," in any disguise, out of the hands of the civil authorities, as the Department of Justice, acting through United States marshals, and they, in their turn, through their own exertions and those of their Deputies, have accomplished a great deal more lately than the public is yet aware of; and as the Post Office Department is constantly in receipt of telegrams from its agents, and the agents sent out under other authority are also acting promptly, the situation "along the line" is thoroughly understood at Washington and will be dealt with as public security demands and to the fullest extent that existing law will permit; and perhaps we may say in this connection the legal basis for action is ample.

Within a day, the Wickenburg to Yuma stage was robbed by a pair of Mexicans, according to an article in the October 11, 1878 issue of the *Miner.*

Stage Robbed Near Date Creek
Three hundred Pounds of Bullion Taken,
Lieut. Wood Robbed, Parties in Pursuit,
Etc., Etc.

F. W. Blake, Agt., W.F. & Co., Prescott.

Stage robbed by two road agents eight miles south of Date Creek, en route to Yuma. Three bars of bullion and sixty dollars taken. Passenger robbed of his money and watch.

E. O. Grant, Agt. W.F. & Co.

The passenger mentioned was Lieutenant P. G. Wood who is known to have had with him $580 and a good watch. The three bars of bullion were from the Peck mine and mill, weighed about three hundred pounds and worth $5,116.20. This is the first instance where silver bullion has been taken by robbers on this road, and, we believe, the second in the Territory.

Eugene Whitcomb, who drives from here to Date Creek left there after the news of the robbery had come to the station, and reached here last evening. He brings word that Henry Adams, with three men, and Wm. Gilson, with

two men, started from Date Creek on good horses and well armed immediately on receipt of the news, intending to pursue and capture the robbers if possible. From the great weight of the bullion it is thought that it will hardly be possible for the rascals to get away with it and elude their pursuers.

We hope by tonight's stage to hear that the bullion and money have been recovered and the robbers killed or captured. Should they be killed, the news will be more welcome than to hear of their arrest. If Bill Gilson comes up with them and they resist, they will be apt to fall.

A further notice in the same *Miner* issue stated:

The stage robbing business is now assuming a more serious aspect than heretofore. Silver bullion, the principal product of Arizona, has heretofore been considered safe from the attacks of robbers owing to the weight of the bars and small worth as compared with good old greenbacks, but on two recent occasions, at least, the freebooters have commenced to try the experiment of getting away with silver bullion, and so far as appears, at least, with temporary success. What the final result will be, of course, remains to be seen

The Order from the War Department allowing the Department Commander to use troops to assist the Civil officers, did not come a minute too soon, and Col. Wilcox will exercise all the authority the Order gives him to overtake and bring all robbers to punishment. The recent robbery near Date Creek seems to have been of the most daring yet perpetrated, and is perhaps but a forecast of what may be expected unless the most vigorous measures are adopted to catch and kill the guilty.

Two weeks later, the *Miner* gave notice of one of the suspected robbers.

A Mexican who has been hanging around William Gilson's, and other places near Camp Date Creek, for the last two years, is suspected of having a hand in the stage robbery near that place.

By March of 1879, nearly six months later, Wells Fargo & Company's detectives had identified one of the suspects as Jesus Molino and were attempting to track him down. The search included a trek to the eastern extremes of the Territory, with round trip mileage in excess of 800 miles, for Deputies Walker and Pierce. Meanwhile, the other suspect, Juan Rubal had been captured by Deputy U.S. Marshal, R. H. Walker at the town of Signal in Mohave County on February 24, 1879.

Juan Rubal and Jesus Molino were indicted by the Grand Jury for the Third District Court in Yavapai county for robbery at the June Term. On June 20th, both men were to be tried, but each pleaded "guilty as charged" and were each sentenced to ten years in prison.

The Politics of Stage Robbery

Certainly, the object of most stage robberies was money or other valuables. On one occasion the word "valuable" took on a new meaning. The *Arizona Journal-Miner* dated September 11, 1894, obviously took pride in publishing this dubious account.

Elevated Hands!

The First Gun of the Campaign is Pulled.

The Republican Delegates are Held Up
Near Congress Last Night.

By a Populist or Democratic Highwayman
Who Makes a Clean Sweep of Everything.

Major Vaughn today received a dispatch from R. N. Coleman, in Kirkland Valley, saying that the stage which had just arrived there from Congress brought the information that last night as the southbound stage for Phoenix reached the big gulch two miles below Congress a lone highwayman gracefully stepped out from behind his cover and commanded a halt. It was obeyed instantly. He then asked the occupants to step out, which they obeyed likewise with alacrity, and one by one, J. C. Martin, Editor Funston, Dr. Vickers, A. J. Doran and two others answered with trembling voices "Here!" "Gentlemen, I will examine your credentials, and in the meantime you may elevate," was the salutation. Of course this also was obeyed, and the robber commenced to cast a vote on a dead sure thing, singling out Doran as the first victim. With the probable councilman he made short work, and after taking his gold watch, pocket book and other wares, asked him if he had any proxies. He answered,

nay. Vickers was No. 2, and the way he went after the doctor was really ludicrous. He knew the doctor was loaded, and to make sure thing the latter was permitted to lower his hands so as to take off his boots, in order that nothing could be concealed. The doctor obeyed with a grunt, and on mentioning Murphy's name was told to shut up. "I'm on to you," was the greeting of the highway man to J. C. Martin, "'You roasted me once and now I'll play even. Get out your subscription book, and don't overlook any proxies either." With the boss of the *Journal— Miner* he was particularly severe, going through him twice, and telling him he was a chump to travel on a stage when he had a pocketful of railroad passes. From Mr. M. He got ten silver dollars, which seemed to please him immensely.

When Editor Funston was reached, there was a weakness noticeable in his victim, and telling the skylight journalist to look through the Lowell telescope for a few seconds, he pillaged this poor editor of all he had—a dollar in cash, a corroded watch and seven Republican proxies. Uttering an oath, the highwayman sized up the other two and asked them if they were politicians, to which they answered no. He was merciful, and only made a partial cleanup of the plates on these miners. He asked the driver his politics, and on being informed that he was a Democrat-Populist, was complimented by the political holdup.

After securing five gold watches, $600 in cash and 37 proxies, the procession was told to lock step and move into the barracks. Looking in, the robber spied a "sack" on the seat, which he demanded, but it was so heavy that it took two men to lift it. The bandit almost fainted when he beheld it, as also did the delegates when it vanished.

The driver was told to move, and with echoes filling the air of populism and democracy, the first political holdup of the season ended and successfully too, for the enemy. Today the wires are being burned with messages of condolence and offers of assistance, and a new subscription is being talked of to keep up the dignity of the brethren in a strange land, where even hand outs are unknown and where no ray of sunshine is ever extended to a body of busted delegates.

Stage coach robberies continued until trains took the place of stages for the transportation of people and goods. Yet another new breed of thief, in some ways more daring, but certainly less of a gentleman, became the scourge of the railroads.

Depot Museum at Skull Valley

Photo L. J. Hanchett Jr.

Goldwater Store at Seymour

A Good Station—Persons traveling from Prescott to Maricopaville will find the Wickenburg Station kept by A. Hamilton and his excellent lady, a good place to stop off and rest. We can recommend them.

Arizona *Miner* May 9, 1879

Chapter Five
Stations Along the Wickenburg Road

Stages were running from Prescott to Wickenburg and on to La Paz by July, 1868. A month later a line was started from Wickenburg to Maricopa Wells southwest of Phoenix. Over the thirty or so years that stages lumbered up and down that somewhat circuitous route, stage stations sprung up and disappeared with great frequency. A few prevailed over most of the life of the stage lines.

A good reason for the emergence or disappearance of stations was the constant improvement to the roads by shortening the distance between points traveled. New stations would pop up on a new stretch of road just as old stations would be abandoned when sections of roadway were no longer used.

Stage stations were a requirement on the line as horses and passengers needed to be refreshed at least once every thirty miles. Most passengers would revive with a little rest, food,

and beverage. Horses had to be replaced with fresh stock capable of pulling the load another thirty miles through who knew what.

Three of the stations were located in the towns of Prescott, Wickenburg, and Phoenix. Others were found in locations as remote as Antelope Creek, Date Creek, or Skull Valley. Isolation brought perils from the Indians, Sonoran bandits, and nature herself. The men and women who maintained those outlying stations under such adverse conditions can only be admired for their courage.

Of the stations that prevailed, a few had stories so unique as to warrant a special place in Arizona's history, thus, we give them a full chapter on their own. Others, still important to the stage lines story, will be highlighted in the vignettes to follow. One station never quite reached existence, but its stories are some of the best to be found on the Wickenburg Road.

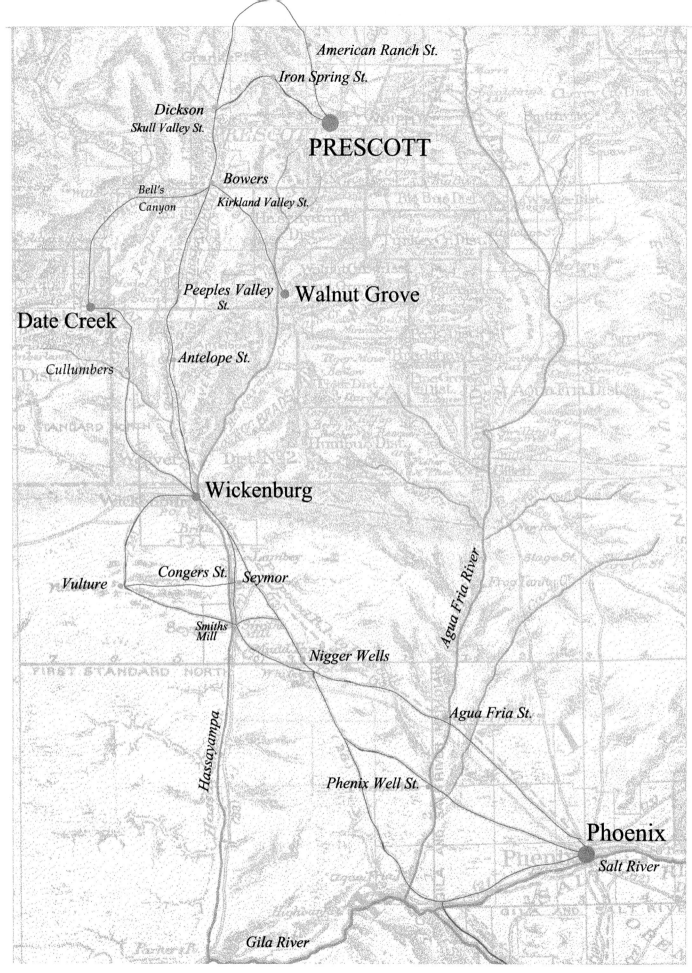

American Ranch St.

Iron Spring St.

Dickson
Skull Valley St.

PRESCOTT

Bowers

Bell's
Canyon

Kirkland Valley St.

Peeples Valley
St.

Walnut Grove

Date Creek

Cullumbers

Antelope St.

Wickenburg

Congers St.

Seymor

Vulture

Smiths
Mill

Nigger Wells

Agua Fria River

Agua Fria St.

Hassayampa

Phenix Well St.

Phoenix

Salt River

Gila River

To Maricopa Wells
The Wickenburg Road from Prescott to Phoenix

Courtesy Sharlot Hall Museum

American Ranch

The tract of land where American Ranch was situated originally had been homesteaded by Dan Conner of the Walker Party. According to William Hardy, the founder of Hardyville, Jefferson H. Lee traded Conner a gun and a few shells for rights to the property.

Lee built an adobe house in the late 1860s to accommodate his family as well as travelers on the road from Prescott to Wickenburg or Hardyville on the Colorado River. By early 1876, a new road was completed from Prescott

through Millers Valley direct to Skull Valley. Soon the stage heading south for Wickenburg and Phoenix would bypass American Ranch.

Lee, possibly with the hope that the new road would be a flop, built a beautiful two story house and stage stop in 1876. Downstairs it boasted a barroom, kitchen, dining room, and two store rooms. Upstairs there was a parlor, four bedrooms, and a large room for meetings or dances.

Iron Springs

Bob Atkinson came to Arizona with the army. When his enlistment expired he went to the Iron Springs District to prospect. There he located a claim or two and a squatter's right to Iron Springs and some acreage. Soon after that, he moved cattle into the area and built a large two story house near the Spring around 1874.

As the road was completed from Prescott direct to Skull Valley, he saw an opportunity and took advantage of it by opening a stage station for meals, change of horses, and lodging for those desiring to stay over. Of course, a bar and grocery store completed the setup.

Bob brought his wife and family there, planted an orchard below the spring, and put in an iron pipe from the spring to a large watering trough. From the latter emerged the name Iron Springs. With growth and notoriety, Atkinson's place became one of the favorite gathering spots for celebrating the Fourth of July. The *Arizona Enterprise* July, 1878, carried an article entitled "Preparation at Iron Spring."

For comfort and convenience at the coming celebration, Mr. Atkinson has already put up a splendid building, 25 × 50 feet, with a stand for the Orator of the Day, and the orchestra in the evening. To this structure, on the side, is a room, full length of the building, intended as a comfortable place for the ball supper, and at the end are two neat dressing rooms. The main building is so arranged that during the day a large portion of one side can be left open for ventilation, and conveniently closed at night. It would rather seem to us that Mr. A. had overdone the thing in the enormous expense he has put himself to, but we are assured that he does nothing by halves and that everything else is to be in proportion. While the day part of the business is to be a "basket party," every arrangement has been made to meet the wants of those who cannot conveniently carry a basket-meals to be provided at all hours of the day and prepared by the best of caterers, which we look upon as an improvement altogether upon the basket system. In fact we saw or learned of nothing left undone that would add to the pleasure of people who are confined to the town during the year and need the change and recreation this opportunity affords. The care and expense Mr. A. is undergoing to make this affair a pleasant one is certainly deserving of patronage, and not alone for this, but the ceremonies of the day, the grand scenery, etc. will repay everyone who can get there, and we doubt not but our livery men will provide transportation for all who have none of their own.

The managers have assured us that good order will be preserved throughout the day and that it is their intention to make this Fourth of July memorable with the visitors, for its pleasant recollections and good cheer. Messrs. Hathaway, Clark, Hussey and Palmer will all have large teams, leaving Prescott during the day, and we are informed that the fare for the round trip is $2. Private teams will be out in force and everything gives promise of a large and harmonious attendance. Elsewhere see programme of the day.

Certainly, one would not expect this kind of activity in a "Wild West" territory less than fifteen years old, but such celebrations of holidays were common throughout the West.

A year later, following attendance at another spectacular Fourth of July celebration put on by Bob Atkinson, the *Miner* called the Iron Springs Station "One of the best in the country."

After the railroad from Prescott to Phoenix was completed in 1895, traffic on the stage road nearly ceased and Bob's income was affected greatly. A few years later, about the turn of the century, Atkinson was made an offer by the Iron Springs Outing Club to purchase his possessory right and improvements for $2,000. Atkinson accepted and moved his family to Prescott.

Following a few tours that carried Phoenix business men and their families to Iron Springs by train, enough lots were sold and the Territory's first summer camp area developed.

Skull Valley

Named after the Indian remains found by the first whites to enter the area, Skull Valley soon took on a special importance to the citizens of Prescott. Its elevation and the availability of water encouraged the growth of crops such as corn and other grains. Prescott needed these for its military and civilian population and well appreciated the fact that they could be supplied from this point rather than imported, at higher cost, from California or New Mexico.

Although pioneer, Joseph Ehle had some kind of station in Skull Valley as early as 1865, it is not until well into the 1870s that we find a real stage station located at Bowers' ranch. Edward Franklin Bowers had been Sheriff for Yavapai County from 1875 until 1878.

By 1878, John Dickson was running a competing station located about a mile or two north on the Prescott-Wickenburg road. Dickson had married Ehle's daughter, Mary, in 1864. Today nothing remains but some of the cottonwoods where Dickson's station stood.

Ed Bowers ran for Sheriff again in 1878, but was defeated by Joseph Rutherford Walker, nephew of one of the early pioneers to Central Arizona, Joseph Reddeford Walker. In early 1879, Ed Bowers died leaving his wife Olive and their four children to run the station.

Ollie Bowers was listed as station keeper in the census of 1880 and her children at that time were all under ten years of age. Ollie apparently struggled on for some time supporting her family with the proceeds from running the station. This certainly was no job for a woman, and Ollie was one of very few ladies with such an occupation.

No doubt, she hired someone to do the harder work of caring for and changing horses, but just being available twenty-four hours a day to deal with the traveling public must have taken its toll on a woman who was still raising small children. Part of Ollie's home exists today as a ranch house in the southern part of Skull Valley.

Courtesy Sharlot Hall Museum

Kirkland Valley

William Kirkland first entered Kirkland Valley in 1863, without his wife, Missouri Ann, infant son, George, or two year old daughter, Elizabeth. They had been left behind at Aqua Caliente while William went north to find the Walker party and the gold mines whose fame had spread all the way to California.

Stopping at Kirkland Valley, William used a small hut he had built as home base for his searches which eventually led him to Walker at Lynx creek. Kirkland couldn't forget the beautiful little valley cut by a meandering light green line of cottonwood trees, standing by a clear cold stream and bounded by lush grass meadows.

The Territorial Census of 1864 found William Kirkland living at "Kirkland's Ranch of Arizona with his wife and two children." His occupation was given as farmer and miner.

Soon William began construction of a new stone house that could resist Indian attacks and provide the family a good measure of security from nature and the wildlife of the area.

For many early Arizona Pioneers, the grass was always greener somewhere else. By 1865 the Kirklands had moved to Tubac. The story goes that the Kirklands moved so often that their chickens, at seeing William, immediately fell on their backs and stuck their feet up to be tied for wagon travel. The 1870 census has the Kirklands back in Kirkland valley, and, by then, stage coaches regularly wound their way past the clear, cold stream.

The first station keeper of note was Judge Jacob W. Kelsey who moved to Kirkland Valley with his wife and daughter in 1871, after a brief residency in Wickenburg. The *Miner* of January 20, 1872 recalled a trip taken by its editor, John Marion, through the southern portion of the Territory. In it he mentions, under Kirkland Valley, "Mr. Kelsey, who has been in the valley but a short time, has done considerable upon his place at which stages and buck-boards stop."

Apparently, Kelsey ran his station until 1878. On July 19 of that year, the *Miner* noted that Judge Kelsey had died shortly after his return to Kirkland Valley from Prescott. Kelsey had been devoting much of his time to Court business at the current session of the District Court.

A week later the following article appeared in the *Miner*. "A Mr. Hamilton, who has kept the Peeples Valley station for the last year, has rented the Kelsey station at Kirkland Valley, and will open a first-class house for the accommodation of the traveling public."

Hamilton's tenancy didn't last long, however, as noted in the *Miner* of January 3, 1879. "Wm Hamilton and family, who have been keeping the Kirkland Valley station since last August have given up the place and are about to emigrate to the Gila and await there the arrival of the iron horse."

By April 25, 1879, a new station keeper had moved in. According to the *Miner* of that date, "Mr. Henry Brizzee, an old Mexican War veteran and a pioneer of the Pacific Coast, has rented the Kirkland Valley station from Mrs. J. W. Kelsey, and will soon be prepared to take care of the traveling public."

The census of 1880 does not list a station keeper at Kirkland Valley but Ollie Bowers station was far enough south that it could have been used as a stop for Kirkland Valley. The Kirklands had left years before to locate in the Salt River Valley, but they did leave their name there and it remains today.

Cullumbers Near Camp Date Creek

The Crumbling Walls at Camp Date Creek

Sam Cullumber probably thought he was making a good decision when he bought a 460 acre ranch from his father, William, in January, 1871. The ranch was ideally located in Martinez Valley on Martinez Creek. There were mountains on the east and west sides, while to the north the ranch was bounded by Burks Ranch and to the south by the Farnsworth and Stanton Ranch.

Formerly known as the Martinez Ranch, the property was located right on the stage route from Prescott to Wickenburg. James Grant needed one more stop between Kirkland Valley and Wickenburg for his stage coaches to change horses and the passengers to take a short break. What could be more ideal than a stage stop right smack in the middle of this beautiful little valley?

Sam went to work building a two story house, adobe corals, and a well, all the requirements for an excellent stage station. Being only four miles south of Date Creek, Sam wouldn't be completely isolated, and besides,

his friend Tom Harris agreed to help Sam run the station.

Things went well for a little over a year. Then one day calamity struck, just as it had so many other times in the Arizona Territory. A party of bold Tonto Apaches attacked the station murdering both Harris and Cullumber and they ran off livestock belonging to Cullumber and James Grant.

The account reached the *Miner* in a roundabout way, but tells much of Army life on the frontier. On February 24, 1872, the wife of Lieutenant Ebstein, from Camp Date Creek, wrote the newspaper giving all the horrible details. While his wife was at the Camp, expecting the worst, Ebstein was safely located in Prescott.

Have had a great day of excitement here. Cullumber and Harris were killed last night. Jemaspe (a friendly Apache–Mohave Chief) came in this morning and said the Tontos were nearby. Indians sent up a war whoop and forty or fifty went out. Captain Dwyer was down at the ranch [Cullumbers]. This afternoon, an Indian came back; said they had found ten Tontos and wanted the soldiers to go out. Ten or twelve men, with Gilson, went. Have just returned having killed two Tontos. Apache–Mohaves and Tontos were suspected, so we are very glad the real murderers were found.

The *Miner* went on to say:

The driver of the stage, which, owing to this murderous affair, did not arrive here until late yesterday morning, informs us that he examined the station where the men were killed, and found the house plundered; the walls, floors, etc., smeared with blood. He also says the Indians had dared the troops at Camp Date Creek to go out and fight them; that there must have been hundreds of hostile Indians in the mountains around Date Creek; that, in all probability, they are there yet, and that he will not return without a large escort.

In another article from the *Miner* dated March 16, 1872, it was revealed that a letter from Phoenix, dated March 12, told of an attempted arrest of some other men suspected of murdering Cullumber and Harris. It seems that the Maricopa County Sheriff and a posse found two Mexicans believed to be the culprits, but had to kill both of them as they resisted arrest.

We may never know who really killed the two station keepers, but isn't it interesting to note how often Mexicans were determined to be the bad guys even when overwhelming evidence at the scene suggested Indian involvement. Maybe the two Mexicans weren't liked too well in Phoenix anyway.

A sad father, William Allan Cullumber, member of the first Arizona legislature and resident of Walnut Grove, acted as administrator for his son's estate. By mid 1873, the ranch had been sold and Sam's dreams along with it.

Peeples Valley

Abraham H. Peeples, leader of the other well known party to first explore the mountains of Central Arizona, settled on a ranch in what became Peeples Valley soon after leaving the findings at Rich Hill. The first notice of Peeples Ranch occurred in the *Miner* dated April 6, 1864:

> There was a murder at Peoples' [sic] Ranch on Saturday night last. A Mexican attacked Mr. Alexander Hampton with a knife and killed him instantly. The desperado then made off with two horses. A crazy man at the ranch was knocked down and left for dead, but is still living.

By September of that year, Peeples had moved on to help in the settlement of Aubrey on the Colorado River.

One of the best known citizens of Peeples Valley was Charlie Genung who resided there with his family for nearly forty years. In 1872 Genung supervised the construction of the road through the valley and around Antelope Peak, with an ultimate destination of Wickenburg. Peeples Valley was also known as Antelope Valley during the early days of the Territory.

Apparently, the stage station at that location belonged to the C & A Stage Company from at least 1875 to 1878 when the line was sold to Gilmer and Salisbury. By 1878 the station was called the Weaver Hill Station.

By 1881, James Hamilton owned the station. Interestingly, "Baby Hamilton" was buried in the Peeples Valley Pioneer Cemetery in 1883, along with numerous other pioneers. The cemetery also contains two unknown Mexicans and four unknown Indians.

James Hamilton

James Hamilton remained in Peeples Valley until 1895. In January of that year, following an unusually hard rain in central Arizona, Hamilton lost his life while traveling on a stage bound for Wickenburg. The story is told in the *Arizona Republican* for January 22, 1895.

Two fatalities resulting from high waters occurred last Sunday on the Agua Fria and one of the tributaries of the Hassayampa. The first victim was James Hamilton, a well known ranchman in Peeples Valley. He was on his way to Phoenix by stage and was the only passenger. As the stage approached Antelope Creek, a half mile south of Stanton, the crossing seem to be impassable. Hamilton directed the driver to proceed to another point, to reach which it was necessary to pass over a steep declivity. The driver objected, but was urged by Hamilton to attempt it. The vehicle was overturned and rolled down into the creek. The driver escaped from the water unharmed, but Hamilton disappeared in the flood. His body was afterward recovered and it was found he had died a double death. Both arms and his neck were broken. He leaves a wife and three children.

Courtesy Arizona Historical Society/Tucson

Wickenburg

The station at Wickenburg was probably in the hands of the Arizona and then the California and Arizona Stage Company from its inception in 1868, until its sale to Gilmer and Salisbury in 1878. From the sale of one third of that company to James Stewart in 1874 until the Tax Roll of 1878, such was certainly the case. This station was called "Home Station" by James Grant, from the beginning, no doubt due to its strategic location as the hub of Grant's stage operations in Central Arizona.

We also know that Dr. John H. Pierson, Grant's son-in-law, ran the station from at least 1873 to 1878. The *Miner* of May 24, 1873 states under the title "Wickenburg:"

We alighted about 2 o'clock in the morning, cold and dry in our interior department. Nourishment, beds, etc., were produced by Dr. J. H. Pierson, and all hands snored away until the everlasting China man rang for breakfast which was worthy of the ladies of the house, Mrs. Grant, Mrs. Pierson and Miss Crabtree, an interesting and accomplished young lady ...

In a letter from Tucson, addressed to the editor of the *Miner*, dated January 9, 1875, the writer notes:

Leaving Prescott for the Capital [Tucson] the proper route is by the California and Arizona Stage Company's buckboard, which leaves your town at 9 o'clock at night, and bangs you over an uneven road, already familiar to almost everybody in Northern Arizona, and which needs no comment from me, until a night and day have passed and you are landed in the once flourishing village of Wickenburg, but which today exists as the old missions of the southern part of this territory, a wreck of its former self. ... As it is, there is no place of life except at the quarters of the stage company. They have the only good buildings in the town; apparently do most of the business; and the weary traveler finds a satisfactory rest and good treatment which, without a doubt, is equaled by no other place on the post roads of our territory, at least your humble correspondent found it so, in his own experience.

Following the transfer of the Stage Company, complete with the Wickenburg Station, to Gilmer and Salisbury, the new owners maintained possession of the station as long as the line carried their name. Employees or subcontractors actually operated the station during that time.

After 1882, the stage station was run by various people including Henry Wickenburg, founder and namesake for the town. The Tax Rolls of 1884 show him in possession of the stage station and corrals.

Courtesy Desert Caballeros Museum

Henry Wickenburg

Henry Wickenburg

Henry had called Wickenburg home for most of the time since his discovery of the Vulture Mine, south of town, in 1863. A frugal bachelor, Henry owned what was probably the finest farm in the area.

In 1866, he was involved in a dispute with John Willis which nearly cost Henry his life. Shot in the head by Willis on April 19, 1866, Henry took over two months to recover from the wound. Willis was brought before the Grand Jury at the May Term of the 3rd District Court in Prescott.

An indictment was made, but the Special Prosecuting Attorney the next year found himself in a predicament not so unusual for the conditions of the Territory at that time. In a statement dated May 17, 1867 he notes that once the defendant's sureties had surrendered him to the proper County authorities, there was no place found to confine him.

There simply was no public prison at the time! Furthermore, Henry Wickenburg, the injured party, failed to appear against the defendant. The prosecutor had no choice but to enter a nolle prosequi in the cause. Willis was released and the case was struck from the Court Docket.

As if the Town of Wickenburg had not had enough problems, on February 22, 1890 the rock dam at Walnut Grove broke under the pressure of heavy rains. Within two hours, the hopes of hundreds of people were dashed along with many homes located on the river. Even Henry Wickenburg's farm was destroyed. The town itself survived only because of the widening of the river at that place.

It wasn't until 1895 when the railroad connecting Prescott and Phoenix was completed that Wickenburg got a new lease on life. Stability arrived just in time as the Vulture Mine, the Town of Wickenburg's true parent, was gasping its last breath.

Courtesy Sharlot Hall Museum

Vulture Mine

From its beginning in 1863, the Vulture was Arizona's greatest mine located at the terminus of a dead-end road extending sixteen miles south from Vulture City, just north of Wickenburg. By 1872 a new road for hauling ore was completed from Vulture to Smith's Mill on the Hassayampa. From there the road continued east to connect with the old road from Wickenburg to Phoenix.

The stage lines shifted their route almost immediately to accommodate people traveling to the mine and mill. Apparently, due to the existing boarding house located at Vulture, no stage station was ever established there, but the Arizona Stage Company was taxed for a corral and barn by 1884.

A brief history of the Vulture is necessary to understand the mine's role in establishing other stops along the stage route. Certainly, Phoenix as well as Wickenburg would have been considerably delayed in their development without Henry Wickenburg's find of the century.

Whatever the reason for Wickenburg's naming it "Vulture" upon its discovery in 1863, the name was certainly appropriate considering the mines location at the edge of a vast expanse of desert wasteland. Lacking capital and mining experience, Wickenburg sold a share of the mine to New York investors in 1866.

Nothing came easily for Wickenburg and the battle of ownership of the mine was just beginning as he only collected $25,000 of the $75,000 sale price. The Vulture Company went ahead full steam, opening a twenty stamp mill just north of Wickenburg that was supplied ore by freight wagons from the mine itself.

The Vulture Company needed cash to keep the hungry men and animals working day and night extracting, hauling, and grinding the ore filled with precious metal. Thomas B. Sexton and William Seward Pierson of Windsor, Connecticut put together a plan to raise $250,000 of operating capital in the year 1870.

In less than two years, operations came to a roaring halt as a fault in the ore vein was discovered. Sexton, realizing the possibility of financial disaster, according to Charlie Genung, absconded with all the gold available plus the miners hard earned wages and savings. In fact, Sexton hung around Wickenburg for nearly a year after the mine closed. What he took with him at that point is anybody's guess.

Wickenburg lost its main reason for existence and the farmers in Phoenix lost a prime market for their produce. Wickenburg still had its strategic position at the fork in the roads leading to California, but tourist trade wasn't like it is today. A store, one saloon, and the stage station were about all there was to keep the economy going.

In 1879, the Central Arizona Mining Company tried their hand with the Vulture. Erecting a new mill first at Seymour, on the

Hassayampa, and then at the mine itself, importing water by pipeline from the same stream. This eastern based company finally gave up by the mid 1880s.

Horace A. W. Tabor, a Colorado silver magnate, bought the mine in 1887 for $265,000. By 1889 Tabor tried to sell the mine to Kaiser Gold of London, but that deal fell through. Finally, the mine was sold for the last time in the nineteenth century for $15,000 at a Sheriff's sale.

Stages ran through Vulture to Phoenix and Wickenburg from 1872 until the advent of the railroad in 1895. From 1872 until 1878, the route went through Smith's Mill. After that the course was through Seymour and then south to catch the Smith's Mill to Phoenix road.

Seymour

Courtesy Sharlot Hall Museum

The Mill at Seymour, Arizona Territory

James Barney, writing in the April, 1940, issue of *Arizona Municipalities*, provides a clear insight into the development and early demise of Seymour.

Seymour was founded on both the east and west banks of the Hassayampa River in the year 1879, by James M. Seymour of the Central Arizona Mining Company. To raise more capital for the operation of the mine and mill, the Cascade Consolidated Mining Company of Arizona was formed in the year 1880 with Bethel Phelps, William Bond, and Horace Ruggles, all of New York, James M. Seymour, a resident of Chicago, Illinois, and James A. Hunt, of Arizona, as Trustees. The two corporations merged under the laws of the State of New York to operate under the name Central Arizona Mining Corporation with $3,500,000 worth of stock, par value $10 per share.

To the east of the river was the town itself while on the west side was the mill for grinding ore from the Vulture Mine. For about a year, along this dusty, primitive thoroughfare, lined by more than a score of buildings, passed the entire traffic between the Salt River Valley and Wickenburg and points to the west and north.

The twenty stamp mill located just across the river provided much of the employment for the town of Seymour. Following a year's operation, the new mine manager, Shipman, decided that it would be more profitable to process the ore at the mine. The old mill from Seymour was used in the construction of a new eighty stamp mill at the mine.

The only drawback to Shipman's plan was that mills need water and none was available at the mine. At a cost of over $70,000, a pipeline, made from tin at the mine's blacksmith shop, drew water from the Hassayampa near the old mill site and pumped it to the new mill at the mine.

Removal of the mill meant the depletion of most of the population at Seymour. Only a few men were left to operate the pumping station on the west bank. In addition, Dan Conger and his wife Lydia Jane kept a small stage station, corral, and store at his ranch there. The other residents lived in small frame buildings as this became the Seymour as known in the 1880s. As late as 1884, the Arizona Stage Company owned a corral and land at Seymour.

Lydia Jane Conger

Dan Conger's store and station lasted at least through the early 1890s, judging by a story in the *Phoenix Herald* dated February 27, 1890, just days after the Walnut Grove dam disaster.

Tuesday morning the party [rescue] reached Smiths Mill where they found Ed Scarborough and team safe and sound. Proceeding to Seymour, old mother Conger was found naked and starving. Her store and every earthly possession had been swept away, including $1,500 in gold coin, that was hid between her cloth ceiling and the shingles.

Today, an old rock house has been reconstructed at the Seymour Ranch located on the east bank site. This building is thought to have been the original Goldwater store.

Agua Fria

Having assisted Jack Swilling in the settlement of Phoenix, Bryan Phillip Darell Duppa, Lord Duppa to his closest friends, located, in 1870, a claim on the banks of the Agua Fria River near present day Sun City. There he established probably the most dismal stage station on the frontier.

Bryan Phillip Darell Duppa

Duppa came from a struggling "landed" family in England and was in direct line to inherit the family estate at Hollingbourne, Maidstone, Kent after his brother's death in 1873. Duppa's Uncle, George, had already moved in, and being the only family member well heeled enough to afford the place, gave little opportunity for poor Darell to claim his

rightful position as "lord of the manor."

This same Uncle George had been Darell's employer in New Zealand from about 1855 to 1863. While there, George wrote home to the family that Darell was, "amiable, generous and careless to a degree, without purpose or ambition in life." Probably good traits to tough it out on the Arizona frontier, but certainly he was not possessed with the organizational skills and work ethic necessary to have founded and developed Phoenix as some have suggested. The title of "Founding Father" clearly belongs to Jack Swilling.

When asked why he picked that particular spot Duppa replied that while stopping over one night the Apaches tried to run him off. He not only fought back successfully but remained there just to show them his determination.

An early visitor to Duppa's station was Captain John G. Bourke. In his book *On the Border with Crook*, Bourke describes in depth his impressions of Duppa and his station.

> Darrel Duppa was one of the queerest specimens of humanity, as his ranch was one of the queerest examples to be found in Arizona, and I might add in New Mexico and Sonora as well. There was nothing superfluous about Duppa in the way of flesh, neither was there anything about the "station" that could be regarded as superfluous, either in furniture or ornament. Duppa was credited with being the wild, harum-scarum son of an English family of respectability, his father having occupied a position in the diplomatic or consular service of Great Britain and the son having been born in Marseilles. Rumor had it that Duppa spoke several languages—French, Spanish, Italian, German—that he understood the classics, and that, when sober, he used faultless English. I can certify to his employment of excellent French and Spanish, and what had to my ears the sound of pretty good Italian, and I know too that he was hospitable to a fault, and not afraid of man or devil. Three bullet wounds, received in three different fights with the Apaches, attested grit, although they might not be equally conclusive evidence of good judgement. The site of this "location" was in the midst of the most uncompromising piece of desert in a region which boasts of more desert land than any other territory in the Union. The surrounding hills and mesas yielded a perennial crop of cactus, and little of anything else.

> The dwelling itself was nothing but a "ramada," a term which has already been defined as a roof of branches; the walls were of rough unplastered wattle work, of thorny branches of ironwood, no thicker than a man's finger, which were lashed by thongs of raw-hide to horizontal slats of cottonwood; the floor of the bare earth, of course—that almost went without saying in those days—and the furniture rather too simple and meager even for Carthusians. As I recall the place to mind, there appears the long, unpainted table of pine, which served for meals or gambling, or on the rare occasion when anyone took into his head the notion to write a letter. The room constituted the ranch in its entirety. Along the side were scattered piles of blankets, which about midnight were spread out for tired laborers or travelers. At one extremity, a meager array of Dutch ovens, flat-irons, and frying-pans revealed the "kitchen," presided over by a hirsute, husky-voiced gnome, half Vulcan, half Centaur, who, immersed himself for most of the day in the mysteries of the larder, at stated intervals broke the stillness with the hoarse command: "Hash pile! Come a' runnin'!" There is hardly any use to describe the rifles, pistols, belts of ammunition, saddles, spurs, and whips, which lined the walls, and covered the joists and cross-beams; they were just as much part and parcel of the establishment as the dogs and ponies were. To keep out of the sand laden wind, which blew fiercely down from the north when it wasn't blowing with equal fierceness from the south, or the east, or the west, strips of canvas were tacked on the inner side of the cactus branches.

> My first visit to this Elysium was made about midnight, and I remember that the meal served up was unique if not absolutely paralyzing on the score of originality. There was a great plenty of Mexican figs in raw-hide sacks, fairly good tea, which had the one great merit of hotness, and lots and lots of whiskey; but there was no bread, as the supply of flour had run short, and, on account of the appearance of Apaches during the past few days, it had not been considered wise to send a party over to Phoenix for a replenishment. A wounded Mexican, lying down in one corner, was proof that the story was well founded. All the light in the ranch was afforded by a single stable lantern, by the flickering flame from the cook's fire, and the glittering stars. In our saddle-bags we had several slices of bacon and some biscuits so we did not fare half so badly as we might have done.

Duppa stayed on at this station until the flood of February 1873, when the station, and more importantly the well were wiped out by high waters. It may have been just as well, as the road was realigned in 1872 with the new Agua Fria crossing being six miles down stream from the old one.

Duppa Moves Back to Phoenix

Duppa spent most of the rest of his life living with friends in the Phoenix area. As an added inducement, along with his congeniality, suggestions of his possible land holdings in New Zealand and England may have made his friends a little more willing to put up with his drunk and unruly periods. Ultimately, even the beneficiaries of his will received little but his gold watch for their troubles.

With the opening of the new road, D. White started the first station at the lower crossing in 1872. White, like many other station keepers, faced dangerous situations. The *Miner* for July 27, 1872, states:

On Tuesday morning D. White, from Phoenix Wells, on the new road to Wickenburg, came in town and reported the following: A Mexican bought a saddle from John Berger at Wickenburg, and left for Sonora without paying for it. Berger, who had been fooled in the same way before, did not intend to give it up so easily, and struck out after him. On Monday evening the Mexican arrived at Phoenix Wells station and put up for the night. After the boys had lain down, horses were heard approaching. The Mexican, hearing the noise, got up out of bed excitedly and rushed out pistol in hand, when shooting between Berger and him commenced very soon. Nine shots passed between the two, when the thief lay down, exclaiming, "I am shot," and then and there pulled out his money and paid the American for the saddle. The Mexican has since died.

Thomas S. Graves from Wickenburg set up shop as station keeper at the same place in August of 1873. Helping out as "kitchen engineer" was "Old Dud."

Apparently the station changed hands frequently, as an ad in the *Miner* for September 27, 1873 says that Mr. Becker is proprietor of the station at the lower crossing of the Agua Fria now called Phoenix Wells.

The next owner of that station was Joseph Phy, once Deputy Sheriff for Maricopa County. Phy moved there in September of 1876. On June 1, 1877, the *Miner* notes that:

Joe Phy who lives at Agua Fria station lost twenty-nine head of cattle. Believing they had been run off by Mexicans or Indians, Joe came to town and taking one of the Morril lads with him, started for the trail, telling his friends not to be anxious about him. Last Friday, however, his long absence was thought alarming, and a party of three started in search of him. They found his trail following his herd, and returned and on Sunday Phy came in, having recovered twenty-seven head of stock. One of the two missing was killed and eaten by Indians. It is probable that two Mexicans drove off the herd as one of them was offered for sale at Decker's station by a Mexican. Finding themselves pursued they left the band hidden near Gila Bend and made themselves scarce.

By 1879, Captain M. H. Calderwood was in possession of the Agua Fria station where he remained for many years thereafter. Calderwood distinguished himself as Speaker of the Ninth Legislature in 1877, and Sargent at Arms of the Eighteenth Legislature in 1895.

Courtesy Sharlot Hall Museum

M. H. Calderwood

Calderwood started at the northern or old crossing, then had stations at both the old and new crossings, but later settled at the northern location. In 1876, the *Miner* noted:

> The coach makes but one stop between Wickenburg and Phoenix, which is at the Agua Fria, where Capt. Calderwood has a fine stock ranch, excellent water, and who sets a good table giving great satisfaction to his many guests. The Captain is now about building a new and commodious house and hotel, and in a few years will, with his present good management, have a fine, prosperous establishment. Mrs.Calderwood is a daughter of Judge Tweed, and is a most estimable lady.

By 1879, the *Miner* added:

> W. [sic] H. Calderwood, who owns and personally superintends the station at Agua Fria, 18 miles north of Phoenix, is putting up and has nearly completed a fine new residence for his family and the convenience of travelers. This gentleman is also busy opening a new road from the Bradshaw road near New River, direct to Maricopa, by the way of his station, which is several miles shorter than the old route.

Photo L. J. Hanchett Jr.

Leviathan Mine Near Stanton

Photo L. J. Hanchett Jr.

Stanton, Antelope Creek, and Rich Hill

Mr. Nicholas, division agent of C & A Stage Company, will build a station at Wilsons [Antelope Creek] immediately. ... The California and Arizona Stage Company have finished the building of a new stable at Mr. Partridge's place on Antelope Creek. Mr. Partridge is about to erect a new store and hotel for the accommodation of the miners of the district and the traveling public. ...

Arizona *Miner* March 9 and April 13, respectively, 1877.

Chapter Six
Antelope Creek—A Tale of Two Stations

During the early part of the 1870s, passengers riding a stage coach in Arizona were lucky to find anything more than a place to stretch their legs when the stage stopped to change horses or drivers. By late 1877, Antelope Creek would have had two facilities complete with eating places if fate had not changed the course of events.

Possibly, the California and Arizona Stage Company was to blame for not building the corral at Wilson's where the stage stop already existed. Maybe Partridge wouldn't have got those big ideas in his head about making money off the traveling public. Nevertheless, there they were, an existing stage station and store called Wilson's Place and a soon to be competitor named Partridge building, "a large station and store at that place." What started as a little friendly competition between two stage stations, ended in the loss of many lives.

A little background on each of the players would be helpful in this story, known for its pathos. George Wilson, William Partridge, John Timmerman, Barney and Rosa Martin, Charles Stanton, Froilana Lucero, and even Charlie Genung each played a prominent role.

The man who has the dubious distinction of being the central character in this story is Charles P. Stanton, gemologist, assayer, miner, rancher, and station keeper. For many writers he has also earned the title of swindler, gangster, murderer, and all around bad guy.

Charles P. Stanton

Stanton first comes on the scene in this country November 1, 1867, when he filed his intention to be naturalized in New York City. In a letter to the editor of the *Miner* dated June 18, 1879, Stanton states that for eighteen years he had been engaged in mining in the United States and portions of South America. He then goes on to say that before coming to this country he filled important positions in various parts of Europe and that he came to the United States as a political refugee, a fact which he said could be proven by an examination of the Records of the Court of Common Pleas, for New York City. That portion of his naturalization record, if it existed, was not preserved.

Apparently Stanton felt compelled to mention these things because someone had accused him of being an escaped convict. Later, scribes would claim he had been kicked out of the priesthood for stealing church funds. Others mention that an affair with an Irish lass was the root of his downfall. Those, more kindly, suggested he had been educated at the University in Dublin, for he certainly was a learned individual.

Stanton's early adventures abroad are indeed difficult to trace. Neither the Catholic Church of England nor Ireland have any record of a Charles Stanton studying for the priesthood. The University of Dublin records do not show a Charles P. Stanton.

Stanton is first recorded in Arizona as a miner in the Weaver–Antelope Creek area, according to the census of 1870. Supposedly hired as an assayer by Thomas B. Sexton, mine superintendent for the Vulture Mine, Stanton became a prime target for accusations of complicity in the embezzling of mine profits. According to Charlie Genung, he would short his assay of a load of ore so that when it reached the mill it was only worth what Stanton had declared. Of course, along the way others would remove significant amounts of free gold from the load supposedly to share with Sexton and Stanton.

While employed at the Vulture, Stanton purchased an interest in several mines in the Antelope Creek region. Probably his most significant acquisition was portions of the Great Sexton lode, just west of Antelope Creek, from Heyman Mannasse, Wickenburg business man, in March 1871, and (T.) B. Sexton in December 1871. This may have been the reason that Stanton eventually settled in the Antelope Creek area.

Stanton was visiting that region in early 1871 when he submitted a report to the *Miner* concerning an earthquake he experienced on February 7, 1871. *Miner*, February 18, 1871:

> At eight minutes after 3 p.m. On Wednesday the 7th instant the shock of an earthquake took place in the direction of the Weaver or Antelope range of mountains in a due east line from the sink of Martinez creek,

and apparently at a point where said range takes a semicircle from the Wickenburg road towards Antelope creek. At the time, your correspondent was standing on the open plain, about one mile from the base of the mountains, when his attention was suddenly attracted by a noise resembling a tremendous cannonading —the fire apparently commencing at the south, and ranging northerly, accompanied by a slight but perceptible vibration of the earth, concluding with a heavy monotonous noise. At the time the atmosphere was dense and serene, with a few translucent lamellar clouds over the range. The entire space occupied by the shock was 122 seconds, commencing at eight minutes after 3 o'clock p.m., and finishing at ten minutes and two seconds past 3 p.m. The vibration of the earth appeared to be from east to west.

> Very respectfully,
> Charles P. Stanton

His next move, closely following on the heels of the Vulture mine closure in the summer of 1872, was participation in one of the grandest diamond swindles to hit the West. On November 23, 1872, Stanton triumphantly returned to San Francisco on the Overland Train from Denver. He had left San Francisco three months earlier after having been naturalized there on August 26, 1872. In his possession were several pounds of precious stones supposedly valued at $1,000,000. Within the thirty pounds of treasure was a ruby, one of the largest in the world, said to be worth $250,000.

To add credence to the story, Stanton was met at Green River by General David D. Colton, Henry Janin, and John Bost, all prominent California businessmen, who accompanied him to San Francisco. The stones were all found in a "Diamond Region" bordering on the Territories of Arizona, Utah, and Colorado.

Unfortunately, Stanton had taken a little too long in getting back to the coast to announce his find. An agent of the San Francisco and New York Mining and

Commercial Company had returned to San Francisco from the "fields" just after Stanton's arrival and by November 25th the cat was out of the bag. The area said to have been salted and the San Francisco Diamond Market got the word just days after Stanton's return.

For most of that week, the whole city was in a turmoil. Stanton held to his story of this wonderful find while critics continued to cut away at the edges. The final test would be to weigh the ruby and then, most importantly, test it for hardness.

Some well known jewelers sided with Stanton, but later it was learned that they too had a financial stake in the matter. One significant test was reported in the *Alta California* paper:

What Mr. Hanks Thinks

Having given our readers some information concerning sapphires and spinelles, collected with care from some of the best authorities in the public libraries, we propose to tell what Mr. Henry O. Hanks, the expert, thinks of this Stanton ruby which was submitted to him yesterday afternoon. He weighed it carefully and found it to be 22.26 carats and 3.68 specific gravity, which is .32 less than a ruby-sapphire should be. He also found that it could be scratched with a sapphire, which led him irresistibly to the conclusion that it was not a ruby, but a spinelle. He announced his opinion to the owners of the gem, but they do not wish to accept it. It was painful to behold the faces of that little group of owners when Mr. Hanks gave them the results of his tests. They each and every one looked as if a fortune was slipping away from them and they couldn't help it.

STATE OF NEW-YORK

In the COURT OF COMMON PLEAS, for the City and County of New-York.

I, *Charles P Stanton*

do declare on oath, that it is bona fide my intention to become a citizen of the United States, and to renounce forever all allegiance and fidelity to any foreign Prince, Potentate, State or Sovereignty whatever, and particularly to the Queen of the United Kingdom of Great Britain and Ireland, of whom I am a subject.

Sworn this *first* day

of *Nov* 186*7*

CJarvis jr CLERK.

In the final analysis, the "ruby" was valued at only $250. Spinelles were used as jewels in watch movements.

The *Denver Times* was quoted in the *Alta California* of November 28, 1872 concerning a story provided by Dr. R. F. Adams of Chicago. It seems that Adams and his wife arrived at Fort Defiance at about the same time Stanton did in October of that year. Adams recalled that Stanton had hung around the fort for a while then made his "trip" and returned to the fort. Stanton was seen purchasing stones from Indians at about twenty-five cents per handful!

Stanton allegedly told Adams that he did not expect to make any money on the stones, but that he had been sent out by a San Francisco diamond company with fifteen to twenty million in stock and that with the reports he would take back to San Francisco the stock would become very valuable and he personally would make an immense amount of money.

Later, Stanton went to Santa Fe, telegraphing ahead of his wonderful ruby. On his arrival in Denver, he reported that Messrs. Huggins and Justice from Tiffanys and Company, at Santa Fe, had declared his ruby was worth $250,000. The truth was, Tiffanys' had no agents in Santa Fe!

Undaunted by the fact that he was being seen as either an accomplice, or a dupe in the swindle, Stanton announced his plans to return to the "diamond region" the first week of December. Maybe, it was to collect more gems to prove his point, but more likely he thought San Francisco wasn't nearly as safe for him as Arizona would be.

An Arizona *Miner* issue of January, 1873, reported that Stanton's "ruby" was noted in the *Scientific Press* as being worth $6,000 to $7,000. In that day not a bad income for three months effort.

By August of 1873 Stanton was back in Arizona building an arrastra to work ore from the Great Sexton mine. Later that year Stanton returned to San Francisco to purchase a mill for the Great Sexton.

In 1874 Stanton reported that a five-stamp mill was on its way from California. Stanton continued to reside at Antelope Creek during 1875 and 1876, working his mine and prospecting for cinnibar in the area.

George "Yaqui" Wilson

The *Miner* of August 10, 1877 gives the following background on Yaqui.

> Some years ago he lived on the Yaqui river, in Sonora [Mexico], where he was engaged in trade; and being constantly annoyed by first one and then another faction claiming to be the Government of Mexico, sandwiched in between bands of guerillas, who claimed no allegiance nor rendered obedience to any authority, all of whom were constantly levying forced contributions upon him, he became exasperated, and being on good terms with the Yaqui Indians, who were really the best citizens of the country, he placed himself at their head as captain, and inaugurated a revolution, defied the laws of Mexico, and declared themselves a free and independent people. This didn't last long: the government troops came down upon them, Wilson fled to Guaymas, was captured, imprisoned, released, re-captured, escaped to California, and finally settled in Arizona … he was … we should judge from his accent, a native of some of the German States.

Wilson had accompanied Editor John Marion on a venture up the Hassayampa in 1862. The journey began at Agua Caliente and followed the Hassayampa to Wickenburg. They then went on to Prescott. Wilson settled just below the town of Wickenburg to farm near Henry Wickenburg's place. While there, he was involved in installing the telegraph lines from Wickenburg to Phoenix.

By 1876, Wilson had located at Antelope Creek where he kept a store and station, "taking in plenty of the needful from the miners who are working the rich placer claims near his place," according to Stanton.

Possibly stemming from his days as a farmer, Wilson had a deep affection for hogs. That affection would play an important role in the events to come.

William Partridge

Coming to Arizona from Shasta, California, Partridge settled at Antelope Creek in 1863. In 1866, Partridge purchased 160 acres of land on Antelope Creek which had been designated as Auxiliary Lands for Mining purposes.

Partridge was an Irishman according to the census of 1880. A miller by trade, he became interested in the mines at Antelope Creek and was at least part owner of the Sexton mine near there.

Partridge didn't become involved with building a station at Antelope Creek until April of 1877, after the C & A Stage company had built a corral and barn near his place. He purchased some of the lumber for that construction as late as July, 1877.

John Timmerman

Little is known about John Timmerman except that he was a native of Holstein, Prussia, born about 1845. Like many men in the West, Timmerman was single.

Barney and Rosa Martin

Another Irishman, Barney Martin, came to Antelope Creek from California around 1878 with his two boys, William and John. There, on January 12, 1881 he married a widow, Rosa Sherline, who may have previously been married to the station keeper at Partridge's old station. Already living together, Rosa was listed as Rosa Martin in the 1880 census.

George Curtis had purchased Partridge's station in February 1878 from a Sheriff's sale when Partridge could not pay for the lumber used to build his station. Apparently, Curtis tried to operate it for a while but ended up selling it to Rosa Martin for $1,000 the day after her marriage to Barney. At the time of the purchase, she was said to already be an occupant of the station house.

Rosa Martin was one of the few women of the time who insisted that her property be held separately from that of her husband. Finally, she sold the station to her husband for one dollar in June of 1882. Presumably this occurred only after she felt the marriage would last!

Rosa was never bashful about complaining to the Justice of the Peace if she felt her rights were being infringed upon, even if the perpetrator happened to be her husband. Rosa brought two actions against citizens of Antelope Creek. The first was against Dennis May, in August of 1881, for discharging a firearm in her house. The second was against her husband, Barney, in March of 1884, for assault and battery. Barney's long time rival, C. P. Stanton was Justice of the Peace for both actions.

In the second case, Barney had reacted violently to her complaint that he had sent the boys out to fetch a cow before they had eaten their breakfast. Barney started out by calling her a "damn bitch" to which she called him a "cur." Barney then took a plate off the table and hurled it in her direction, presumably striking her with it. No doubt Stanton delighted in getting the opportunity to hear this family squabble, especially since Barney Martin had brought charges against Stanton in November of 1880 for assault with intent to kill. That action was the result of Stanton pointing a gun at Barney Martin.

Froilana Lucero

Froilana may have been an English merger of Fraulein and Junna as there were many German miners in the area, including Timmerman. Her story is the saddest of all as she comes across as a very lonely young lady in spite of her attractiveness.

Was there more than one Lucero family from the Weaver area with a father named Pedro, or is the family listed in the 1880 census the correct one? They seem to fit because the youngest son is also named Pedro and one child is called Sisto, but that one was a female. The best guess at present is that Sisto was a nickname, possibly that of the Patron Saint of her birthday. In the only written record of her signature, she signs as Juana. Genung says that she was a very attractive young lady, a fact which caught Stanton's eye and led to their relationship, if there was one.

Charlie Genung

Genung came to Arizona in the early 1860s, living at various times in Vulture, Wickenburg, Peeples Valley, and the Salt River Valley. While living a few miles away, in Peeples Valley, Genung played an important role in the happenings of Antelope Creek. Possibly, his greatest contribution was his chronicle of the area which was written late in his life.

Today, Genung is considered an excellent example of the basically good Arizona pioneer who solved problems with kindness or force as the situation demanded. To say he is revered would not be stretching the truth too far, and that analysis may be valid, but it will be interesting to compare his version of the area's stories with the facts as reported by many court records.

Courtesy Sharlot Hall Museum

Charlie C. Genung

A Story of Two Stations

Just before Partridge had a chance to complete the building that was to house his new store and hotel, a confrontation between he and Wilson resulted in Wilson being shot and killed. The *Miner* carried the story on August 10, 1877.

Some time yesterday forenoon, Aug. 9th, G. H. Wilson, of Antelope Station, on the Wickenburg road, went down to the next place below on the creek, belonging to William Partridge, where he lost his life at the hands of Partridge, under the following circumstances, as nearly as we can gather them from a written statement sent to the Sheriff by the hands of John Timmerman.

Wilson went to the house of Partridge where were several persons who heard Wilson and Partridge quarreling outside. One of the men stepped out and saw Wilson running towards the creek, and turning around, saw Partridge with a gun. Wilson ran into some brush and Partridge threw stones in after him. Wilson told Partridge that he was not armed, but if Partridge would put down his gun he would fight him. Partridge called him hard names and said, I have you now. In a few moments the report of a gun was heard, and in a short time the parties in the house, who appear to have been somewhat timid about approaching too near the gun, went out and heard Wilson calling for water, which they gave him. He told them he was dying, and requested them to take off his boots. This was done and after directing Timmerman to take charge of his affects he expired. The parties present saw Partridge enter the house and come out with something tied up in a handkerchief or white cloth. He gave his affairs into the hands of one of his workmen and left in a westerly direction towards the Sexton mine. ...

We, with all who knew them, deeply regret the occurrence which has cost the life of a good citizen, and made an outlaw and fugitive of another.

Within a few days, Partridge caught the stage to Prescott where he turned himself in to the Sheriff. The June term of the Grand Jury for 1877 was still in progress and Partridge was indicted for murder. The trial started around the 20th of August and closed by the 27th.

Partridge's own testimony was of particular interest.

Defendant sworn, testifies; Name, William Partridge, reside Antelope Creek, came there in 1863, engaged in mining at that place, age about 53, knew George Wilson. Knew him for several years, not personally acquainted until "70 or 71," only saw him, never had any business transactions with him. Lived about $1/_2$ mile apart.

I saw him about the 9th of this month. I saw him on the mesa about 100 to 150 yards from my new house, coming [from the] north and going south. We met that morning; after I saw him at the new house, at the North gable end. After meeting at the North gable end of the house, he hailed me and said "good morning," and I said good morning and he says "how are you getting on," I says so-so. He went around to where I was sinking a well for water, I suppose about 16 or 17 feet from where he hailed me at first. I stopped when he hailed me. He went on the point of the well and looked down the well and from there he came back to where I was standing. He said "you sent up word that I was to keep home my hogs." I said yes, I had notified you myself and also Mr. Timmerman and he says "the hogs shall run wherever they please." I says they can run wherever they please as long as you keep them off my premises. He says "they shall run wherever they please." "God damn you," he says.

At that he struck me over the head and shoulders with a stick he had in his hand, with both hands, with all his might and main at several times. I was up against the gable end of the house. He struck me several times. I was standing by the frame of my bedroom door on the gable of the far side of the house. I turned around on my right and went into my room. He struck me as I was on the threshold of the door. In a state of excitement and passion I grabbed my gun and when I came at the door, Mr. Wilson had disappeared. I ran around to the Southwest gable end of the kitchen. I saw Wilson off from the house I would suppose about 150 feet near as I can judge. I cried out to him of his making a sudden attack upon me over the head and shoulders or something to that effect. He talked a little back, very little, but what he did say I cannot distinguish.

I pursued my course toward him. As I was going toward him he went down an embankment and I went on the bank of the mesa, somewhere, might be, 25 or 30 feet above, to the north, where he went over I went down the embankment

towards the creek, sharp embankment and brush. As I went down I suppose about 70 or 75 feet I heard a noise in the brush. I whirled around on the left hand. I didn't see anything. I saw a rock rolling down the hill and I immediately shot into a bushy place about 25 feet above where I was standing. I came up the embankment and saw Mr. Wilson sitting, his back up the hill. I never spoke to him. I went to the room in my new house. Whether I saw Mayne when I was going to my room or spoke to him, I really forget. From there I went to my cabin on the west side … I then went up over the bank on the west side of the creek … I struck into the trail that leads to the Sexton mine.

Numerous other witnesses were questioned, but the only new information revealed was that Wilson had yelled out, when he was in the brush, or just before, that he was unarmed and if Partridge would put down his weapon they could fight it out with fists.

Some of the witnesses used had not watched the altercation, but had been summoned to testify to Wilson and Partridge's character. All agreed that Partridge was "quiet and peaceful" while Wilson's old neighbor from Wickenburg, Fritz Brill, avowed that Wilson used to have trouble with his neighbors.

Charles P. Stanton said that Partridge's character was exemplary. Stanton had even brought to court the wooden club, supposedly a sledge hammer handle, used by Wilson in the assault, to assist in Partridge's defense.

The verdict came in "Second degree murder," to no one's surprise. The sentence was onerous, "Life in Yuma Territorial prison." The case was pleaded up to the Territorial Supreme Court to no avail. Partridge was off to prison.

Charles Genung's name was on the list of witnesses to be summoned, but apparently did not appear at the trial. In Genung's memoirs as compiled by K. C. Calhoun in *The Smoke Signal* for Spring and Fall, 1982, he noted the event, but with quite a different twist.

When the mill [Vulture] closed down Stanton went to Antelope Creek near the Leviathan and built a small cabin in which he made his home for several years. His cabin was near the station of Yaqui Wilson and, as Wilson was pretty busy some times, he got Stanton to assist him. There was an old Englishman named Partridge living on the creek about half a mile below Wilson's. The stage company decided to build a barn of their own at Partridge's place, as he had plenty of water. After the barn was built there was no place for the stock tender to eat and as the stage passengers were in the habit of eating when the stage stopped at Wilson's, Partridge concluded he would start a station, so he put up a house with several rooms and had everything fixed up for store and station but the passengers would get off the stage at Partridge's place and walk to Wilson's and get their dinner, the stage picked them up as it came along on the way to Prescott.

Partridge was an Englishman and very veracious; wanted to get everything in the country. Stanton worked him up to kill Yaqui Wilson by telling him that Wilson had threatened to put him out of the way as he did not want him there with an opposition business. Wilson had some pigs and he would go out every day with a pole and knock the fruit off of the prickly pear which grew in abundance and the pigs followed and ate the fruit. One day he was near Partridge's house with a sledge handle, knocking off the prickly pears, when Partridge started after him with a rifle. Wilson had no gun and made a run for a short, bushy gulch and crawled into the brush and hid but Partridge ran around to the mouth of the gulch to where he could see Wilson and shot him to death. He hid out for a few days, but as it was impossible for him to get out of the country, he made his way to Prescott and surrendered; was tried and sent to the pen for life. Stanton had thought if he could get rid of Wilson that he would have no trouble in getting the station, but Wilson had a partner who had put up a part of the money to start the business. At the time Wilson was murdered Timmerman, that was the partner's name, was cooking at Smith's mill on the Hassayampa. He at once quit his job and went and took charge of the station.

Genung was entitled to his own view of the matter. Nevertheless, the obvious differences between his recollection, at an advanced age, and the evidence presented in sworn testimony make his writings on this subject somewhat suspect.

Getting back to the real story, Timmerman produced what must have been a contested will for Wilson which named himself as administrator but not beneficiary. The court put Timmerman through a lot of work before naming him Special Administrator to the estate. After finally receiving the appointment, Timmerman went about using Wilson's assets to pay off his creditors.

To accomplish the sale of those assets most effectively, Timmerman was allowed to run the store and station for the interim, selling off merchandise while keeping the station open for travelers. This was essentially just doing what he had been doing previous to Wilson's, death while in Wilson's employ.

Within a couple of months it became apparent that the real estate would also need to be sold to satisfy Wilson's many creditors. On December 4, 1878, James Bright successfully bid for and supposedly purchased Wilsons real property which consisted of a twenty acre placer claim with buildings thereon located on Antelope Creek. Also thrown into the sale were claims on the Western Extension of the Sexton mine as well as a portion of the Vulture mine by Wickenburg. The sale price was around $950 but there was one minor problem, Bright never paid the amount to the estate. Nevertheless, Bright and Timmerman ran the stage station just as if they owned it!

By mid-January, 1879, Timmerman had completed the administration of Wilson's estate, except for the distribution of about $1,500 to the remaining creditors (an amount he didn't really have since he had not collected anything from Bright).

Then a strange thing happened. Timmerman was murdered. The Coroners Inquest describes what took place on that day in January, 1879.

John Timmerman Inquest

Proceedings of the Coroner's Jury which was summoned by order of A. H. Peeples, Justice of the Peace, of Wickenburg precinct, Maricopa County to examine into the death of John Timmerman of Antelope Creek Station whose body was found lying dead on the road about halfway between Antelope Station and Wickenburg on the 26th day of January, 1879.

The jury assembled on the 27th day of January, 1879 at Antelope Station.
Jurors names:
George E. Treadwell
James N. Bright
Charles P. Stanton
Thomas Napper
John Aldenburg
Hans Paulson
Samuel Smeeton

James Bright
—sworn and examined, testifies that from information received from a Mr. Brown that he saw a dead body lying on the main road about 7 $1/2$ miles from Antelope Station on the Wickenburg Road—I went in company with John Oldenham and Hans Paulson to the spot indicated and there found the dead body of the late John Timmerman. We took charge of the body and brought it to the Station. On searching the body, I found thereon three dollars and seventy five cents in silver coin. I found his pistol lying within 6 or 7 feet of the body in the road. There was one charge discharged out of the pistol, as I found one chamber empty. To the best of my knowledge, the pistol was fully charged when he left the house. On examining the ground the next morning where the body was found, I saw the tracks of a man on foot where he had jumped from the rocks into the Wagon Road. I followed the same tracks down the road towards Wickenburg two miles or more till I met a buggy containing Mr. Peeples and Treadwell. I found the horse that the deceased was riding with saddle and saddlebags on and the bridle reins trailing on the ground. All the saddle bags contained was one small package of smoking tobacco. His clothing on the left side was burned and his body scorched under the arm pit near the wound. The space burned was about 8 by 10 inches. The clothing there burned was all woolen.

I do not know what money the deceased took with him, but I do know that he had some considerable in the house which money I cannot now find on examining the whole house in search of the same. He wished to see Mr. Peralta at Wickenburg to negotiate for having some flour sent up from the Salt-River. He owed Mr. Peralta some money and Mr. Peralta was then at Wickenburg.

Samuel Smeeting
—sworn and examined testifies, that the late John Timmerman left his house to go to the town of Wickenburg about 2 o'clock on the afternoon of the 26th day of January 1879 and left me to attend to his business. On the point of leaving he said to me "I require some change," at the same time taking some greenbacks out of the desk, one of which was a ten dollar note and some other small bills leaving at the same time, in the drawer, change in small bills and silver to the amount of ten or twelve dollars.

Ten days ago he informed me that he had gold dust in the house amounting to three or four hundred dollars which he requested me to run into gold bars for him as soon as we got some charcoal. This gold cannot be found in the house at present.

I also saw him put two or three dollars in silver into his pocket as he left the house. I have been here sick two or three months. On leaving the house he [Timmerman] requested me not to give credit to some Mexicans whose names he mentioned but which I now forgot.

Thomas Napper
—sworn, testifies that on the 26th instant at the time the late John Timmerman left for Wickenburg, I accompanied him as far as the new house [Partridge's place] and he said to me that he would see Mr. Peeples and find out what he paid for sending gold in that Grant charged him too much the last time, that he would ascertain what Peeples paid and would not pay anymore than what he [Peeples] paid. I know that he had money with him for he told me that he ought to have taken it down the day before. On the question being asked if any person knew that he had a large amount of money in the house, or knew of his going to Wickenburg, no person but a Frenchman, named Peter Verdier who was here on the morning of his leaving. He [Verdier] knew that he was going to Wickenburg for I heard him [Timmerman] tell him so. I do not think that he had any money. [Verdier later was murdered at Walnut Grove.]

I do not know whether the Frenchman knew he was about to take away money with him or not. The Frenchman lives in the town of Weaver.

The new house is about half a mile distance.

I have been here sometime employed at Antelope Station with Timmerman and Bright.

John Oldenburg
—sworn and testifies that he saw the body as described by Mr. Bright.

Hans Paulson
—sworn and testifies that he left Bright and Oldenburg to go to Wickenburg to inform Mr. Peeples of the circumstance. Also, he saw the tracks leading to Wickenburg as reported by Bright.

George E. Treadwell
—sworn and testifies he saw the tracks as described by Bright and also noted that no tracks could be found leading north to Antelope Station or Weaver.

We the jury summoned to examine into the death of John Timmerman find that he came to his death by a rifle or pistol shot which entered his left breast in the neighborhood of his heart and passed diagonally through the body passing out under the right shoulder ranging a little down and inflicted by some party unknown to the jurors.

We also find that a portion of his clothing and body was burned as described by the witnesses. The deceased was from 33 to 35 years old and a native of Holstine, Prussia.

Genung had his version of this story too and, as might be expected, it included more deviltry on the part of Stanton.

Timmerman went and took charge of the station. That blocked Stanton's game for a time but he had some old pals in the country and put up a job to get rid of Timmerman the first opportunity. So Timmerman, having taken in quite a bunch of gold dust, started one day to go to Wickenburg to send $700.00 by Well's Fargo & Co. to Schrofe & McCrum, wholesale liquor dealers of San Francisco. Stanton was still attending to the P.O. and making himself generally useful around the place and when Timmerman started for Wickenburg on his mule he passed a Mexican in a canyon about half way between Antelope and Wickenburg. After he passed by, the Mexican shot him through the heart with his six shooter, being close enough to set Timmerman's clothes on fire. Stanton had followed Timmerman and was in sight when he was killed. The Mexican divided the gold with Stanton and they separated, Stanton going back to the station. In a very short time, one Douglas Brown, of Brown Bros., of Prescott, came along, with his sister-in-law, Mrs. Wm. Brown, who had just come from Scotland, and found Timmerman's body lying in the road and his clothes still burning. That was rather a strange introduction to the country to which Mrs. Brown had traveled so far to make a new home.

How does Stanton fit into this picture? There were no tracks leading back to Antelope Creek. The only ones led to Wickenburg. Then, too, Timmerman was riding a horse, not a mule. The man with the opportunity and motive to murder Timmerman was, of course, James Bright. Later on we will learn how Genung went about getting information from Mexicans.

Stanton also had a version of the Timmerman affair which appeared in the *Miner* dated June 20, 1879. In that, Stanton claims that while in jail for a trumped up offense of stealing a gold specimen, he had a long talk with another prisoner by the name of Nicanora Rodriquez.

Rodriquez advised Stanton that, "there was a terrible conspiracy formed against him which he didn't seem to see yet." At the heart of that conspiracy was C. P. Raines. It seems that Raines and a Wells Fargo detective by the name of Thacker were interested in proving that Stanton had killed Timmerman and were trying to get Rodriquez to lie in court about it. The motivation was their desire to own Stanton's Great Sexton, later known as the Leviathan mine.

When Stanton questioned Rodriquez, asserting that he (Stanton) and Raines were friends, Rodriquez replied that in spite of Raines negotiating with Stanton to get him to sell the mine, the real plan was to have Stanton hung for the murder of Timmerman so that Raines could jump the mine , along with some friends from Prescott. Rodriquez further asserted that it was well known that Stanton and Timmerman were not on friendly terms. By hiring men to slander Stanton to his friends, it was hoped that public opinion could be turned against him.

Furthermore, Rodriquez told him that the man who had sworn out the warrant against Stanton and the Justice of the Peace, C. F. Cate, who had heard the case on the theft of the gold specimen, were planning to have Stanton's ranch to run cattle upon.

What can be verified from Stanton's letter to the editor of the *Miner*, that which appears in the case against Stanton, and the case against Rodriquez, checks out perfectly. After talking to Stanton, Rodriquez was whisked out of jail with his bail reduced from $2,000 to $1,000. James Bright and Fred Williams provided the bail and, of course, Rodriquez was never seen again.

After Rodriquez was released, another prisoner, Juan Rubal, who was being held for the stage robbery near Date Creek, told Stanton that he and Rodriquez had killed Timmerman for his money. Rubal turned state's witness to save his life after Bright swore out a warrant charging Rodriquez and Rubal with killing Timmerman.

James Bright was then, according to Stanton, coerced to swear that Stanton had stolen a gun from one Mr. Bennett. That gun was, as indicated in the court records, found in a search of Stanton's home along with the gold specimen. Bright's involvement in this matter is of interest when considering what he had to gain.

When it was determined that Mr. Bennett had not lost a gun, the charges were changed to state that it must have been stolen from someone else. That was dismissed by the Justice since no one would take the stand to testify to anything.

When W. J. Tompkins, the man who swore out the original charge that Stanton had stolen the gold specimen, took the stand, he admitted he knew nothing about it. Johnson, from whom the specimen had allegedly been stolen, was the only witness against Stanton. To neutralize his testimony, thirteen prominent citizens of Prescott swore that Stanton had been in Prescott, up until the day before the supposed theft, with the specimen in his possession! Stanton had sworn to the fact that the gold specimen was his property.

Unfortunately, none of that testimony exists today. The Commissioner of the Court found that the 250 page testimony was not properly recorded or signed, and threw it out. The whole case, as Stanton suggested, certainly smacks of a trumped up charge intended to put Stanton away for the murder of Timmerman.

Genung had more to say about this matter as well.

> Reval [Rubal] also told of being one of a party who robbed the Prescott and Ehrenburg stage and got away with three bars of Peck bullion. Stanton engineered the job and C. P. Raines and some of Stanton's band did the work. They drove a band of horses over the road to obliterate the tracks as the stage was held up on the edge of the great stretch of open country lying between Date Creek on the north and Cullings Valley on the south, known as Cactus Plain. The Mexicans got one bar of bullion and carried it to Rawhide on Bill Williams fork where they melted it down in an old Mexican smelter and in that way destroyed the chance to identify it. C. P. Raines carried his bar to Prescott and sold it to a citizen of the place for $700.00. It was later recovered by a W. F. [Wells Fargo] & Co.'s detective, a man named Hume. Hume also arrested Stanton but never could locate the bar of bullion but in searching for it found a Winchester rifle that had been stolen from a man at Minnehaha flat a short time before. Stanton was suspected of the theft at the time. The gun was identified by men who knew it, but the owner who was working for Barnett & Block in their store at Maricopa would not leave his work to come to Prescott to prosecute. The gun was found under the floor of his [Stanton's] cabin near the Wilson station. There are people who still hunt for that bar of Peck silver as people who live near the old Wilson station often find where parties have dug new holes in the ground in the vicinity. Supposedly this was done by some of Stanton's confederates who knew that he had the bullion and much other valuable plunder. Just a short time before he was killed he showed a man named Waterman, who was boarding with him, several good gold watches and tried to sell him one. Those watches had probably been plunder from some train or stage robbery in Colorado or New Mexico, as the band did business from

Colorado to Lower California, stealing horses and driving them from one part of the country to another. They, stole two bands of good mares each of which had a fine stallion with them and ran them off to Lower California. The last raid they made they took a very fine band of mares and a stallion that cost Frink $500 in California. Frink belonged to the Stock Men's Association of Yavapai County and went to some of the members to get help to follow the thieves. The last man he went to was Fred Gaines, of Kirkland Valley but he got no assistance. Then he came to me although I was not a member of the association. An old timer, named Sam Dennis, was staying with me at the time and he volunteered to go. They followed the trail of horses to and across the Colorado River and recovered the stallion and some of the mares on the California side, not far from Yuma but never got a greaser. One of the band is now living near Wendendale in Yuma County and his name is Trinidad Gonzales.

Stanton agreed that Raines was involved in the stage robbery and that he had sold a bar of Peck bullion at Wickenburg. According to the court records, Stanton was not arrested by a Wells Fargo detective, and his home was searched by the Under Sheriff, not the detective.

Wilson's Station Sold Again

James Bright was required to deed the Wilson place to Timmerman's Estate for one dollar. Although not the original owner, Timmerman had been the administrator of Wilson's Estate and had died before completing his work.

Therefore, Timmerman's estate became responsible for the resale, this time for real money, of all of Wilson's real estate. By late 1879, Timmerman's administrator, W. J. Tompkins, the same man who had put the finger on Stanton concerning the gold specimen, declared the Antelope Creek Station (Wilson's) to be vacant and practically worthless. Previously it had been appraised at $350.

In July 1881, Tompkins completed the administration of the Timmerman Estate and on the tax roles for that year we find Stanton being assessed for the George "Yaqui" Wilson Station. Stanton may have just moved the boundaries on his 160 acre ranch to include the Wilson place, or he may have purchased it at the "private sale" Tompkins proposed to get rid of the balance of Timmerman's real estate holdings. The Yavapai County deed book does not report the transaction.

Within a few months of his acquiring the "Antelope Creek Station," formerly belonging to George Wilson, Stanton had a run in with a man by the name of John McCue. Apparently, Stanton had fired a rifle in McCue's direction and ended up in court for it. Such were the hazards of being a station keeper.

This time Stanton lost and was sentenced to a $250 fine or 250 days in jail. The original crime charged had been, "assault with attempt to commit murder." The conviction was for, "assault with a deadly weapon," but the fine was interesting; only $250 for attempting to take a mans life.

Partridge's Station is Sold

Meanwhile, William Partridge's property had been sold off to satisfy a judgement in favor of L. Bashford and Company of Prescott. Partridge's place, at the Sheriff's sale, brought just over $600, and the new owner was George W. Curtis, pioneer lumberman of Yavapai County. Barney Martin acquired the station and land in 1882, from his wife Rosa who had purchased it from Curtis in 1881.

Once again, there were two competing stations at Antelope Creek. The new owners were no more fond of each other than the previous ones had been.

In addition to the incident of 1880, when Stanton had pointed a rifle at Martin and Martin had filed a complaint with John Pierson, but lost the case, another situation arose in 1884 involving Stanton. This time Stanton was the alleged victim and Cisto Lucero was the supposed perpetrator. Lucero was indicted for the act of having shot off a pistol in the direction of C. P. Stanton. Although the indictment was not filed until November of 1884, the alluded act had taken place in December of 1882. The lack of court records for this case may indicate that Lucero was ever found to be brought to trial.

Barney Martin had trouble with a man named Lucero as well. On May 15, 1884, Martin ran across three Mexicans who had in their possession two horses which Martin recognized as belonging to men from Weaver. Eventually the three, Manuel Mirando, Hercutano Sanches, and Simon Lucero were brought to court on the charge of stealing horses. In his testimony, Martin refuted the allegations that the Mexicans knew nothing about the horses. Martin related that when he closely examined the horses, he realized that they belonged to William Church of Weaver, but he thought the Mexicans would not take them back to their owner.

Charles P. Stanton was Justice of the Peace at the time, and as might be predicted, let the three go on insufficient evidence. Stanton frequently championed the cause of local Mexicans, much to the disgust of his white American neighbors. Simon Lucero may not have been related to Cisto Lucero, but within a couple of years, Simon would meet Barney Martin one last time.

By the Spring of 1886, the Martin family must have had their fill of back stabbing, as they sold out to the Piedmont Cattle Company of Kentucky for $2,500. Apparently, the Cattle Company was most interested in the mill site and water rights that had been originally obtained by Partridge and passed on along with the station to the Martins. Of course, the transaction also included the station and land upon which it stood. The cattle, belonging to the Martins, were to be purchased later that year by the same company.

By mid-July, the Martin family was off to Maricopa Wells so that Rosa and the children could catch the train there to, presumably, go home to visit her parents in Pennsylvania. Barney was intending to return to Antelope

Creek to make some repairs on the station and continue to run it for at least a while.

Unfortunately, they never got to their destination according to the *Phoenix Herald*, August 9, 1886.

The Martin Family Murders

The Missing Family

There are some very ugly features about the disappearance of Mr. Barney Martin and family. Mr. Martin sold his stock and ranges north of Wickenburg, paid his debts there and left with his family with about $5,000 [sic] in their possession on the way we believe to the east coming by way of Phoenix. They have never reached Phoenix. Two weeks ago last Thursday at about 2 o'clock p.m. they were at Seymour passing Dan Congers at that time and intending to camp at the forks of the road some distance this side of the Hassayampa. Since the time stated they have not been seen or heard from. Telegrams have been sent west as far as Gila Bend on the railroad and east to Casa Grande but it seems that they have not reached the railroad which they were making for intending to travel by cars to their destination. The family was composed of Mr. Martin, his wife and three [sic] little children. Since their disappearance events have transpired which together with the fact that they have disappeared and were known to have considerable money, excite the strongest suspicion that they have been foully murdered and robbed while on their way to this place and somewhere between here and Seymour.

The supervisors of this county should offer a reward for the finding and arrest of the murderers. The sheriff's office of this county has done about all it can afford to do in the matter and the time and the severe labor of the search by the officers should be rewarded. Yavapai county is interested in this matter also and should assist in the hunt and punishment of the murderers.

A few days before the above article was printed, the scant remains of Martin and his family were found, with a few charred wagon parts, north of Negro Wells. A coroners jury was hastily impaneled to examine the evidence in this the most brutal of murders.

Barney Martin Family Inquest

Wickenburg Precinct, Maricopa County, A.T. (On the plains ten miles east of Seymour and four miles north of Negro Wells.)

The following men were sworn in as Coroner's Jurors this day, August 9, 1886: F. L. Brill, Justice of the Peace, acting coroner, Henry Wickenburg, John Kenton, Charles J. Taylor, Ramon Mesias, Ignacio Valles, and Pedro Valdenegro.

Henry Wickenburg chosen foreman of jury to hold inquest over the burned remains of human beings.

First witness sworn and examined; Adam Bender; age 26; occupation farmer.

Q. What day did you start from Phoenix?
A. Wednesday evening, July 21. Started from Agua Fria 3 p.m., Thursday; about two miles past the forks of the road, I saw a large fire in a northwestern direction about four miles from the road. I traveled till two o'clock at night and still saw the fire. It struck me at the time it was an unusually large fire.

Second witness sworn, F. L. Brill

I left Phoenix July 22, at 4 p.m.; stopped at Agua Fria overnight, starting early, traveled until I arrived on the telegraph line on my way to Wickenburg. Pursued the trail along the telegraph line, traveling horseback. About three miles west of the forks of the road I observed a new wagon track crossing my trail and heading north. This circumstance I thought very strange at the time. On reaching home and hearing. In the course of two weeks afterwards, that Barney Martin and family had disappeared on the desert and been last seen between Seymour and Agua Fria, I remembered this circumstance, and requested George Daniels to examine into the matter.

Third witness sworn, George Daniels;

I went to Negro Well Canyon, and there struck the wagon track of a team leaving the road, and going east and afterwards north. I followed the track back to the road and found where a team had been camped on the bank of the road, east side of Negro Wells, but I could see no sign of struggle or bloodshed, the rain in the meantime having erased all signs of the kind. I

again followed the track north for four miles and there I found the remains of a wagon and bones of human beings of different sizes, the remains of a churn with a bullet hole through it, and a trunk containing utensils, etc., all burned more or less. There were no traces of any murder left, except five horse tracks starting north from the fire. In following them about three miles I found a sorrel, bald-faced horse, with its throat cut; the same I knew belonging to Barney Martin. I again followed the trail a mile further north, and the tracks turned southwest about five miles—two men having four horses, each man leading one, apparently, to judge by the tracks. The tracks turned due north again. I followed six or seven miles further and lost the tracks in the foothills. On the 22d day of July, in the morning, I saw Barney Martin camped at Seymour. He had a wagon and three horses, his family consisting of a wife and three [sic] boys.

We the jury empaneled to inquire into and about some human remains lying on the desert between the Hassayampa and Agua Fria rivers, about midway, and about four miles north of the road leading from Seymour and Smith's Mill, on the Hassayampa, toward Phoenix. The persons of said human remains have apparently been murdered on above mentioned road, then hauled on their own wagon and team to the above mentioned place, then together with the wagon and some wood added, burned so that nothing remains of said bodies except some fragments of bones as jaw and skull bones, besides one human foot, recognizable to be human bones. Said remains we believe to be those of Barney Martin and family—the perpetrators of this crime unknown to us.

(Signed) Henry Wickenburg, etc.

Another Charlie Genung version, from the same *Smoke Signal* publication, covered this story as well.

On July 18th, 1886, before the Martin family was murdered I was at Prescott, and the news was wired to there that one Lucero boy had fired a shot at Stanton from long range; that gave Stanton an excuse, and he, as soon as he returned from the scene of the murder made out a warrant for the parent, Pedro Lucero, father of the boy who he claimed had shot at him. He also made out subpoenas for all of the citizens of Weaver, but two, whom he forgot. I suppose, his object was to get all of the people out of the way and get Rodgers saloon and store closed until the gang that had done the killing should get back and scatter out of the neighborhood, as they might get to Weaver and get drunk and talk too much. Mick Hickey who was deputy sheriff made the arrest and served the subpoenas, Stanton issued the papers out of his own court, he being a justice of the peace. While en route to Prescott, Hickey claimed that Lucero tried to escape and had his head badly beaten with a six shooter. The boy that Stanton claimed shot at him on July 18, had shot Stanton through the ear some time before for insulting his mother and sister and Stanton offered $5000.00 reward for him dead or alive, which had caused the boy to leave the country for a time and stay in hiding. I learned that at the time that Stanton claimed he was shot at and had Lucero arrested as an accessory, Lucero was at the Vulture mine on a visit to a married daughter and knew absolutely nothing of the matter. I went from Phoenix to Prescott and succeeded in getting Lucero out of jail where he was held under $3000 bond, Dr. O. Lincoln going on the bond with me. I took him to my ranch in Peeples Valley, armed him and sent him home through the hills. He told me he thought his boy was in hiding near Weaver. I told him I would like to see him, the boy, and talk to him and set a date to meet him at a certain place.

The boy, Sesto [Sisto], was at the rendezvous on time and I had a long talk with him. He told me that he did not shoot at Stanton on the 18th but that Stanton had caused the shot to be fired by an Indian who was staying with Vega's family in his absence and that he thought it was part of the plot to give Stanton an excuse to get the people out of Weaver. He gave me a lot of information that was of much help to me during my struggle with Stanton and his gang. Told me who I could depend on among the Mexicans if I needed help, and who to look out for. Told me that his little brother, Becente, had been told by Elano Ernandes, the man who used the knife on the Martin family, that the Martins were all dead: (Becente is now serving a life sentence in the Territorial prison for a crime of which he is innocent). He told me also that an old man named Marco knew which way Ernandes went when he left Weaver and I got Marco to go with Sheriff Mulvenon and his deputy and put them on the trail of the mule that Ernandes rode and they arrested the man and put him in jail at Phoenix.

As soon as Stanton heard that I was on the trail, he went to Prescott leaving a man named McGowan in his place. While he was gone McGowan kept Stanton posted as to what was going on at the station by sending a courier two or three times a week to Prescott. Stanton hung around the Sheriff's office most of the time while in Prescott. While Stanton was in Prescott, Vega and several others of the band were in hiding at an old deserted miner's cabin about two miles up the canyon from Stanton's place. The night after he returned Vega and the others of the party that were with him moved to an old tunnel on one of Stanton's claims. I had two Weaver Mexicans watching every move, and before day one of them came and told me that Vega had moved and that Stanton had sent the Indians that were staying with Vega's family, out to them with a lot of provisions. These two Mexicans had lain out all night in a heavy rain to watch the movements of the gang. Sheriff Mulvenon had promised me to come to me on the day before Vega moved and had he kept his promise we would more than likely have captured or killed several of the gang but he did not come until the afternoon of the next day. In the morning after the murderers had changed camp I took their trail and followed them to where I found the ashes still warm in the fire that they had built in the tunnel. I tracked them to near the Martinez Ranch where they had separated. I then returned to Antelope Creek where Mulvernon had promised to meet me. Late in the afternoon he came bringing with him a man named R. C. Talcott: came in a buck board. Had they come the day before we could have done something, for Talcott was a good and fearless deputy. As it was, there was little use to follow the murderers, who had forty hours start and were not following wagon roads much to speak of. A buckboard was always a poor tool to hunt outlaws with in Arizona. They were headed for their stamping ground on the Colorado River where it would have been folly to try to find them.

I then arrested the Indian [Mexican?] that was living with the Vega family and took him to Phoenix and locked him up. I got some information from him which would have been of much help if Stanton had been brought to trial. I then returned with a deputy from the Sheriff's office in Phoenix and had Stanton arrested and taken to Phoenix where he was held as long as the law would hold him without a trial. Jack McGowan went as far as the Vulture mine with Stanton riding one of Barney Martin's horses. The last word that McGowan said to Stanton when they separated at the Vulture was, "I'll stay with you," and rode back toward Antelope Creek.

Indeed, Stanton and a Mexican were brought to Phoenix by Deputy Blankenship and, probably, Genung. In fact, it caused an international incident when Blankenship held the Mexican for sixteen days without a hearing, and a mob, led by Genung, tortured him nearly to death. The Mexican government was outraged to think that a citizen from that country would be so treated in the United States.

A letter from M. Romero, at the Legation of Mexico in Washington, to the Secretary of State, written on January 13, 1887, detailed the events of August 1886.

Mr. Secretary:
Referring to the notes addressed by me to you under date of Sept. 25th and Oct. 26, 1886, relative to outrages committed at Phoenix, Maricopa County, Arizona Territory, upon a Mexican citizen named Manuel Mejia, I have the honor to inform you that I have received instructions from Mr. Marical, Secretary of Foreign Relations of the United States of Mexico, dated City of Mexico, January 7, 1887, directing me to present a formal complaint to the United States Government on account of the failure of the Arizona authorities to punish the parties who were guilty of those outrages, to present a reclamation based upon the evident lack of the proper administration of justice which, in the opinion of my government, there has been in this case, and to ask for the punishment of the delinquents and of the authorities that have been derelict in the performance of their duties.

From the information furnished by several persons who were cognizant of the facts, at least one of whom was a citizen of the United States [Stanton], and was the victim of an assassination at Antelope, A. T., November 15, 1886, who wrote me two letters relative to this matter, dated, respectively, September 13 and November 6, 1886, of the former of which I sent you a copy with my note of 30th of September last, and send you one of the later now, together with the sworn statement of Manuel Mejia, a copy of which I also enclose, it appears that Mejia was arrested at Wickenburg, A. T., on the 17th of August, 1886, by J. W. Blankenship, Deputy Sheriff of Maricopa County and that he was handcuffed and taken to Phoenix, sixty-five miles distant, where he was confined in the jail of that town, that the Deputy Sheriff made the arrest without having been ordered to do so, and without any complaint (as it appears) having been made against Mejia; that he later was kept in the Phoenix jail from August 17th until September 3d, during which time he was not informed of the reason of his arrest.

From the information obtained since the notes on this subject were sent by the Legation to your Department, it appears that Deputy Sheriff Blankenship, who arrested Mejia, says in his statement, a copy of which I herewith enclose, that he arrested him because he found in his possession a horse that was said to have belonged to Barney Martin, who had recently been murdered; but from a statement made by Frank Cox, the District Attorney of Maricopa County, dated November 22, 1886, a copy of which I enclose, it appears that Mejia was first charged with complicity in the murder of Barney Martin, and that, it having been found impossible to sustain this charge, he was afterwards accused of having been found with a horse that had belonged to Barney Martin, in his possession. From another statement, made by Charles P. Stanton and dated, Oct. 26, 1886, a copy of which I likewise enclose, it seems that Mejia took the aforesaid horse, in obedience to an order of Deputy Sheriff Blankenship, in order to accompany him for the purpose of making an arrest. From the statement made by Mr. Cox, the District Attorney, it appears that, even if Mejia had stolen the horse, the theft, would not have been committed in Maricopa, but in another county, and that he consequently could not have been tried in Maricopa County for that crime, which circumstances induced the District Attorney repeatedly to order the Deputy Sheriff to release Mejia, which Blankenship delayed doing for several days.

As I have already stated, Mejia was released during the evening of September 3, 1886, and at half past nine o'clock that same night, he was set upon in the streets of Phoenix by nine men, led by Charles B. Genung and Thomas Bryan; his assailants beat him brutally, gagged him in order to prevent him from calling for assistance, after which they put a rope around his neck, and dragged him with great violence for nearly half a mile, to a secluded spot, where they tied his hands and feet, and hung him to a tree, probably for the purpose of intimidating him, since they soon asked him where the $4,000 were that were said to have belonged to Barney Martin. Mejia replied that he knew nothing of the matter about which they asked him. The blood was now flowing from his mouth and nose. He was hung up a second time and let down again, after which the same question was put to him, and when he again replied that he knew nothing about the money, he was kicked by Genung in the back and face. He was hung up for a third time and let down again, and asked whether the money was in Mr. Stanton's house. Mejia repeated his previous answer. Finally, they hung him up for the fourth time, intending to kill him, having tied a knot in the rope, which Thomas Bryant put under his ear. Mejia then succeeded in freeing his hands, and in pulling out a knife which he carried in his pocket, with which he cut the rope, whereupon he fell upon a barbed wire fence, which lacerated him terribly, he then rolled to the bottom of a ditch, whereby he was still further injured; when he reached the bottom of the ditch, he cut the rope which fastened his feet. His tormentors, who desired his death, when they saw him fall were unable to get at him, being prevented from doing so by the wire fence, fired five shots at him, none of which hit him, owing to the night being very dark.

In consequence of these outrages, Mejia is maimed for life, having lost the sight of his right eye and the use of his left arm, and having received internal injuries which render it impossible for him to do any work.

The statement of Dr. Louis Stern, taken at Phoenix on September 11, 1886, a copy of which I enclose, shows what was Mejia's condition on the 4th of that month. Charles Genung and Thomas Bryan were the only ones of his assailants whom Mejia recognized, and he made a complaint against them before the competent magistrate. After an investigation which lasted eight days, they were set at liberty by the judge, having pleaded an <u>alibi</u>, and are now walking unmolested about the streets of Phoenix. A letter that was addressed by the District Attorney of Maricopa County to the Vice Consul of Mexico at Tucson, a copy of which I also enclose, shows that the District Attorney doubted whether the evidence presented by the accused to sustain the plea of an alibi was sufficient. In the opinion of Mr. Marical, it appears from the aforementioned antecedents of this case, that the judicial authorities did not act with proper energy in administering justice in this case; it further appears that Deputy Sheriff Blankenship not only arrested Mejia without any reason for doing so, but that he failed to obey the order to release him which he several times received from the District Attorney. All this furnishes grounds for the belief that justice has not been properly administered in this case.

I have therefore received instructions from my government to present the reclamation contained in this note, and to ask, at the same time, that both the delinquents and the authorities that have failed to perform their duty may be punished.

M. Romero

Seemingly, Mejia's only crime was being a friend of Stanton. Certainly, he would have talked, under such duress, if he knew the whereabouts of the money. And, why were Genung and Bryant so interested in the money? If their real concern was for the Martin Family, you would think they would have wanted to know who committed the crime.

Apparently, the assumption was that Stanton was the culprit, and forcing Mejia to talk would prove it. Certainly, something foul had happened to Mejia, according to Dr. Stern. Genung and Bryant's action proved that they could be nearly as vicious as the murderers of the Martins.

Governor Zulick took his time in responding to the Secretary of State, if indeed he ever responded. A full year after the State Department requested information from Zulick, a subsequent letter asking for the same report was sent out. Zulick's outgoing correspondence was never found.

On October 20, 1886, Dan Conger, M. M. Elders, C. B. Genung, Pedro Ledisma, Pedro Rodriquez, Antonio Rodriquez, Lou Banbry, Geo. A Wallace, Rufino Repetta, Marcus Avala, Francisco Ganiez, Dollores Sortellon, J. W. Bramlett, Adam Binder, Elano Fernandes, Manuel Mejia, C. P. Stanton, J. W. McGowan, and F. L. Brill appeared as witnesses before the Grand Jury in Phoenix. That body brought an indictment against Francisco Vega, Jose Vega, and Simon Lucero for the murder of Barney Martin, and a warrant was issued.

Within days, a key defendant was himself murdered, possibly by the gang that got the Martins, but more likely by a trio of Mexicans encouraged by Charlie Genung, as Genung later suggests. Charles P. Stanton was murdered at his home on Antelope Creek on November 15, 1886.

Inquest on an Unknown Mexican

Following the murder of Stanton and the coincident death of one of his attackers, an inquest was held at Stanton Precinct, but strangely was titled, "Inquest on an Unknown Mexican." Fortunately, both deaths were addressed.

The first witness was E. A. Kelley, Stanton's so called bodyguard.

E. A. Kelley, age 38, native of Ohio.

Q. State what you know about the case.

A. On Saturday night, a few minutes I think past six o'clock, three Mexicans came up on foot asking for a place to camp where they could find water. They said their burros would be along in a few minutes.

One of them asked me if I would sell him some tobacco. I opened the door and asked them in. As soon as he got not quite into the door, he commenced shooting at Stanton as he was reading at the table. I then threw the top of a barrel at them. Their shots put out the light on the table where he was and the force of the wind from the top of the barrel put out the candle on the counter.

I then went to get into the back room where the gun was and when I got there there was a man shooting in the window, and he is the man I shot through the window, the only one I saw after leaving the front room.

Q. You did not see but one man when you shot?

A. The one man was all I saw.

Q. You did not chase the other man away?

A. No, I heard a shot from the fence.

Q. When the man came in did he make any remarks?

A. I did not hear any.

Q. How many shots did he fire?

A. I cannot tell. I think the three men shot ...

Q. You think that one man shot at Stanton?

A. I think there was but one.

(Several unreadable lines)
Q. Did Stanton make any remark?

A. "My God, I am shot."

Q. How long was it after Stanton was shot did you feel Stanton's pulse?

A. About ten minutes I think.

Q. You say there were three Mexicans? How did you know?

A. Because they spoke Mexican.

Q. What were you doing when the Mexicans fired at you?

A. I was getting them tobacco and had my side to them.

Q. Was anything found with the Mexican?

A. I did not find anything.

Q. Who came after the shooting?

A. Briget, Vandeburg, Partridge and Henning.

Iscinto Kroter, native of Italy, was sworn in as interpreter.

Pelar Bajorca, native of Mexico.

He has never seen the dead Mexican. I live in Weaver but I have seen no suspicious Mexicans in Weaver. I can sign my name badly. **I have never heard of Mexicans threatening Mr. Stanton for they all like him**. I got some whiskey from Vandeburg on Saturday. Nobody got me up at 12 o'clock last night.

I do not know the cartridge belt or these two knifes. I do not know where Sisto Lucero is now. I saw him last at Weaver, coming out of the store with a sack of tobacco in his hand, about two months ago.

This man is new to the place for I have not seen him before. I did not sell any whiskey to any strange Mexicans on Saturday.

The next witness was fascinating as she is probably the Froilana mentioned in so many "hand me down" stories about C. P. Stanton.

Juana Lucero

I can write a little, but have no lover. I do not know the writing of this letter and do not know of any other people that can write in Weaver. I do not know the corpse and have never seen him before. I do not know of anybody having the initials of the letter.

Apparently she was shown a love letter but denied having been the author. If she was lying, it would disprove the old theory that she had been somehow forced into an affair with Stanton. If she were truthful, then it must have been some other woman, and the old theories still would not stand up.

In either case, was that really her brother, Sisto, lying dead on the ground? Several other Mexicans were questioned at the Inquest but none of them admitted to recognizing the dead Mexican. Most of them knew Sisto but had not seen him for months or years. One man said that the only Lucero currently living at Vulture was a daughter. We will probably never know, but this is the last time Sisto's name is mentioned.

Most of the witnesses testified that they had not seen any unknown Mexicans around the place recently, but one man sold a drink to a Mexican the night before, and another man had seen a wagon with three men in it on the road from Wickenburg to Weaver.

Genung came close in his version of this story in the *Smoke Signal*, but in the end he alludes to the idea that he engineered the murder of Stanton.

A few months later, Stanton had a man staying with him named Charles Kelley. One evening Kelley was attracted to the front door by hearing men talking. The men proved to be three Mexicans. When Kelley appeared at the door one of the Mexicans asked him where they could find a place to camp as they had a pack train coming behind. Kelley told them of a good place near the house. Then one of the men asked in Spanish if he, Kelley, had any tobacco for sale. Stanton, who was sitting inside the room, answered in Spanish and invited them in. Two of the Mexicans stepped into the room and fired on Stanton, killing him on the spot. Kelley started to run behind the bar but when he saw the rifles pointed at him he grabbed a barrel cover and knocked the light out. Then he rushed to a room on the side of the building where there were several guns. The third Mexican, the one who remained outside, was at the only window in the room where the guns were and shooting through the window which was in range of the corner where the guns stood. The two men who were inside came out and saw their companion, mistook him in the dark for Kelley and shot him dead. Kelley said that he had fired the shots that made the holes in the window glass, but it was imagination on his part, for every shot had passed through from the outside. When an official of Yavapai County went to Governor Zulic [Zulick] and asked him if he was not going to offer a reward for the capture of the murderers of Stanton, the Governor told him that the reward fund was entirely exhausted. A short time after the killing I met Governor Zulic [sic] and Secretary Tom Ferish [Farish] in Prescott, the Governor shook hands and remarked: "Well, Charley, you got rid of that _____ down there, didn't you?"

Together in Death

After thoroughly annoying each other for over six years while both were residents at Antelope Creek, one would think that Stanton and Martin would have preferred to be separated for the rest of eternity. That, unfortunately, was not in the cards as Patrick Ford, Yavapai County Coroner and Public Administrator, took over the probates for both Stanton and Martin.

Now, Ford, yet another Irishman, would decide how the estates of these two men, each detested by the other, would be divided between their creditors. Of course, Martin's estate had for the most part been sold off to the Piedmont Cattle Company. Stanton's, on the other hand, consisted of real as well as personal property.

Nothing went smoothly in either case. Martin's estate was thought to have been raided by the man whom Martin left in charge of the station when he started with his family to the train at Maricopa Wells. Eventually, that man, George Wallace, was exonerated when each item of the estate which had been found to be short was explained. The only unexplained shortage was from the whiskey barrel which it was determined had been depleted by the posses from Maricopa and Yavapai Counties.

The problem with Stanton's Estate was that his friend Kelley produced a will allegedly written between Martin's and Stanton's deaths. Was this a premonition on Stanton's part that something would happen to him after the Grand Jury indictment of the Vega Brothers and Simon Lucero? Or, was this a forgery, considering that Kelly was to receive the station and most of Stanton's personal property while Dennis May and J. W. McGowan were to inherit the Leviathan mine? Although the Will was not recognized as authentic by Patrick Ford, the Maricopa County Clerk was more than happy to send a copy to McGowan, for a small fee!

Ultimately, Ford was replaced in his position as County Administrator before he had a chance to complete either probate. Because the accounts had not been completely settled in either case, Ford was admonished by none other than Probate Judge, "Bucky" O'Neil, for failure to complete the job. At last, both estates were settled by the new administrator, Charles Randall. Martin's goods were sold for a pitiful sum and Stanton's Station went for only $65 to Coles A. Bashford and F. G. Parker.

Courtesy Sharlot Hall Museum

A Building at Stanton After Stanton's Death in1886

William Partridge Returns

Ironically, the man who drew first blood returned to Antelope Creek, by then known as Stanton, peacefully living out the rest of his life there. Having been sent to the Territorial prison at Yuma in late 1877, Partridge was pardoned by Governor J. C. Fremont on January 16, 1880, just in time to be back home at Antelope Creek for the census of 1880. Partridge was granted Executive Clemency in compliance with the wishes of the community and at the recommendation of the judge before whom he was tried.

On July 7, 1881, Stanton sold to Partridge the Second Eastern Extension of the Great Sexton Mine for one dollar. It was not until the 23rd of August, 1899 that Partridge finally resold that claim, but this time the price was $1,800.

Three weeks later, Partridge died in the county hospital at Prescott having outlived every other person involved in the story of "Two Stations" except one, Froilana Lucero. Her death came by suicide on January 1, 1900 at Weaver.

Froilana apparently ceased wanting to live when her two brothers, Pedro and Vincente, also called Becente Lucero, were convicted of being involved in the murder of another store owner, William Segna, from Stanton. Vincente was convicted of the crime and sent to the Territorial prison for life.

Ten souls perished violently, including the man that Charles Genung would have us believe was at the root of the trouble. Certainly this story rivals, in number of victims, the Pleasant Valley feud. In pure meanness, it stands head and shoulders above that conflict.

Most notable is the fact that both altercations took place in Yavapai County and a lot of it happened while Sheriff William Mulvenon was in office. Maybe it was just the time, or possibly this was a last gasp for lawlessness on the Arizona frontier. Either way, the stories of both places will long be remembered.

An Old Dry Placer Miner Near Antelope Creek

Photo L. J. Hanchett Jr.

Possible Site of Nigger Wells

Photo L. J. Hanchett Jr.

Barney Martin Family Grave

Whereas, I am informed that Cyrus Gribble, superintendent of the Vulture mine, and his guards, John Johnson and Charles Doolittle were brutally murdered by some unknown person or persons, about eighteen miles from Vulture, and near Nigger Wells, Maricopa County, on the night of the 19th inst, while en route to Phoenix.

Prelude to Governors Proclamation, *Phoenix Daily Herald*, March 27, 1888

Chapter Seven
Nigger Wells

The article goes on to say:

Now, therefore, I, C. Meyer Zulick, Governor of the Territory of Arizona, by virtue of the authority in me vested, do hereby offer and proclaim a award of five hundred dollars ($500) for the arrest and conviction of the person or persons committing said murder.

In witness whereof I have set my hand, and caused the Great Seal of the Territory to be affixed hereto.

Done at Prescott, the Capital; the 21st day of March, A. D. 1888.
C. Meyer Zulick

Murder at Nigger Wells. Where in the world was that and why would it carry such a hateful name? Part of the answer lies in an article from the *Miner* dated October 22, 1870.

Death of a Negro

Parties recently from Salt River and the Gila, inform us that a Negro named "Joe" who formerly resided in this town, lost his life in the following manner: About two weeks ago—perhaps three—Joe and two other men—a Mexican and an Italian—were engaged in sinking a well on the plain between the Hassayampa and Agua Frio [sic] rivers, in this county, and had got down about 100 feet, when, the earth being saturated with water, the walls commenced to cave in. Wishing to prevent this,

a bundle of poles and willows were procured and fastened to the rope, above the bucket. Joe stepped into the bucket, and while descending, the bundle of poles became unfastened, and falling upon Joe, threw him to the bottom of the well, where we are told, his lifeless body was allowed to remain until the smell arising from it deterred all who passed that way from attempting to bring it to the surface. The two men who were at work with the deceased, say it was impossible for them to get the body out alone, so they left and went to Wickenburg.

The *Miner* of July 4, 1868 may have been referring to the same man when it reported that a Portuguese Negro and two Mexicans had been fighting at Wickenburg. The result of that affray was one man dead, one nearly killed, and the third badly injured. From 1870 on, the papers regularly carried references to Negro or Nigger Wells.

Gus Swain, who was killed soon after by Apaches on the Hassayampa, was the next man reported to be trying to reach water at, "Nigger Wells, situated half way between Wickenburg and Agua Fria on the road to Phoenix." Even Darrel Duppa, according to the *Miner* of February 1, 1873, got into the act.

D. Duppa, from Agua Fria, is in town to employ men for the purpose of sinking a well between his place and Wickenburg, at or near

Nigger Wells. He says, although the former attempt to get water in that locality was a failure, he is determined to dig at least 200 feet before throwing up the sponge.

William Gillespie was next. In May of 1873 some travelers found him alone, waiting help to dig his well even deeper than the 100 feet already achieved. The traveler titled his article "Nigger Well." Gillespie felt sure that water was near the bottom of his shaft. A few weeks later, on June 14, 1873, the *Miner* noted:

> While the workmen were digging in Gillespie's well they discovered ants at work 90 feet below the surface of the ground, and 110 feet down they found an animal about nine inches long imbedded in the cement, alive and active which resembled a lizard in all respects save that it had a short tail.

Why would so much effort be spent to provide a source of water in the middle of nowhere? The answer is simple, there was no other source of water in the eighteen miles of road from Lambey's station on the Hassayampa to Duppa's Agua Fria station. In the heat of the Arizona summer, eighteen miles was a long way to go without water, especially for the animals pulling the stage or freight wagon. Establishment of a reliable source for water, coupled with a resting place for the weary traveler could be of definite economic gain to the person determined enough to succeed in finding water. Nigger Wells would have been half way between the existing stops.

As far as we know today, water was never found at that location, so Nigger Wells would have to win fame by some other means. Mysterious killings took the place of life giving water at the station that never was.

The Death of Negro Joe

Even the death of the first man to try for water at that location is shrouded in mystery. There were of course other versions of Joe's death that circulated in the area for many years.

A different version has Joe as a Portugese Negro who ran a bakery in Wickenburg. Joe decided to spend his hard earned savings on a well between Wickenburg and Agua Fria, so he and another man went to work digging there. Passersby later noticed a caved in area and a camp that had been looted. No one ever bothered to clean out the well site thinking that both men had met their fate there.

Another account was given by Thomas D. Malloy of Yuma in an article carried by the *Arizona Republican* dated April 13, 1921.

> Nigger Well is so called because tradition says that in the digging of the well one of the owners of the venture, a colored man, was murdered down in the well about one hundred feet or thereabouts by his partner piling rocks on top of him …

Gus Swain and the Apaches

About six miles east of Smith's Mill on the Hassayampa, Gus Swain and a partner were digging a well with the idea of establishing a station for travelers on the Phoenix–Wickenburg road. Twice each week Gus had to travel from the Nigger Wells area to Lambeys ranch to procure water for his camp. On a fateful day in 1873, Gus had just turned onto the road as it passed through the Hassayampa Canyon when he was ambushed by a large band of Apaches returning to the Central Arizona mountains from a trading trip to the Colorado River. Gus barely escaped Apache torture on that day as he died instantly from the first bullet to enter his breast. His friends, who found him a day later, felt thankful the end had come so quickly.

Barney Martin Family Murders

When the Barney Martin family was murdered on July 22, 1886, the actual killing took place at Nigger Wells. From the Coroner's Inquest we learn that George Daniels, P. L. Brill's employee, had followed the tracks of Martin's wagon finding that they had been camped on the bank of the road on the East side of Negro Wells. This was apparently located close to Negro Canyon, but where was that?

Charlie Genung sheds some light on its location in his memoirs.

> From the Agua Fria to the Hassayampa it is about eighteen miles and Blankenship rode on one side of the road and I on the other, watching for any wagon tracks that might lead off from the road … That night we camped at a point about half way from the Agua Fria to the Hassayampa … About six miles from where we camped we crossed a gulch, about the only one from the Agua Fria to the Hassayampa. Blankenship who was cutting tracks on the north, came back to the road just a short distance before he got to the gulch. I noticed this and fired a shot to stop the wagon [which was accompanying them], the driver having been instructed to keep in sight of us and stop the wagon if either of us fired. We rested here a short time and walked back to the gulch, but did not cross it. If I had I would have found the tracks of Martin's wagon, for it was in this gulch they were held up and as soon as the wagon was on the east bank it was turned off the road and driven along the bank for some distance. [In fact, nearly four miles according to the Coroners report.]

At that point the wagon was piled high with mesquite branches and set afire, no doubt to destroy any evidence of the slaughter. Now Nigger Wells had touched the lives of at least six different people in a most horrible way.

The Gribble Murder

Not quite two years later, Cyrus Gribble, Thomas Johnson, and Charley Doolittle met a similar fate while crossing Negro Canyon at a point that was actually some three miles below Nigger Wells, on the road to Phoenix. The first report to reach Phoenix was carried in the *Daily Phoenix Herald* dated March 20, 1888. Admittedly, the information was sketchy, but the paper did its best to fill in the details.

Shocking Murder

Of Supt. Gribble and Tom Johnson

The Murderers Escape With $7000 in Bullion

Two Posses on the Trail—The Particulars

At mid-night last night Sheriff Halbert was aroused from his bed by Assistant Supt. Turnbull, who had just arrived from the Vulture mine with the shocking news of the murder of Capt. Cyrus Gribble and Thomas Johnson, his driver. The bodies had been found lying on the stage road some twenty miles this side of the mine, and the Sheriff immediately dispatched Deputy Murphy with a posse to the scene of the murder, with directions to take the trail as soon as possible, and to leave signs which could be followed quickly by an additional posse which would follow this morning.

As the spot where the crime was committed is forty miles from this city no full particulars can be attained until the return of the coroner, Judge Richards, who hastened thither early this morning.

At 10 o'clock a.m., a posse composed of Frank Cox, Tom Davenport and George Wilder also started out. The ground is so soft owing to the recent rains that there should be no difficulty in following the trail of the murderer or the murderers, if there are more than one.

The Discovery of the Crime.

At 10 o'clock yesterday morning, Ramon Olea, who was on his way from the Vulture pump to Phoenix, was met by a Mexican man and woman in great excitement and alarm who told him they had seen two corpses on the road, a few miles back. From the description given him he suspected that the corpses were those of Gribble and Johnson, who had passed the pump that morning before daylight, and without going to see, he hurried back to the Vulture and gave the alarm.

Ramon Olea is in the employ of the Vulture Company, and the man and woman who informed him are two old people who drive a little rickety peddling wagon between Phoenix and the various mining camps.

Assistant Superintendent Luke Turnbull, making all haste to the spot indicated by the informers, which is about three miles beyond "Nigger Well"—the scene of the Barney Martin murder— found both bodies piled together with the body of one of the horses and the smashed up wagon. Had it not been for the bullet marks on the bodies the scene might have been taken for the result of a runaway smashup.

The horses had evidently started and ran some distance off the road, and the shooting did not take place until the team returned to the road. Gribble was shot in the back of the head and also in the arms and lower part of the back, but no wounds were seen on Johnson. The horse had also been shot, but in the hurry to inform the authorities as soon as possible, no very particular examination was made, nor were any tracks searched for.

The bar of bullion which Mr. Gribble was transporting to Phoenix was missing and no doubt was the incentive to the crime. Its exact value is not divulged but it is known to have been between $7,000 and $10,000.

Mulvenon on the Alert

Sheriff Halbert received this morning the following telegram from Mulvenon, Sheriff of Yavapai county:

"Prescott, March 20—How far from Vulture were they killed? Which way did trail lead? Answer quick."

Theories of the Crime

As the buggy is smashed up and the bodies have every appearance of being roughly tumbled out, it is thought that the horses took fright, probably at the first shot which killed Gribble, and the murderer then shot the horse in order to stop the team. Then the sudden stoppage pitched out Johnson who falling on his head broke his neck.

————————

Some say that the deceased Superintendent was hated and feared by many of the men working under him, and had frequent trouble with them, from this fact they deduce a theory that the murder was partly of revenge. On consideration however, this supposition does not seem plausible. Miners as a class do not furnish many murders to swell the calendars of crime, and any who had been having a personal quarrel with their superintendent would scarcely resort to a crime of which they would be the first to be suspected.

Another theory, and a much more natural one, is that the murder was committed by the same gang who were guilty of the Barney Martin massacre nearly two years ago, and of the Stanton murder which followed it. This gang has never been brought to justice, though there are several parties who claim to know them, and say that they could bring them in at any time if the county would only put up a little.

On the following day the *Herald* had more first hand information. The County Coroner, Judge Richards, had by then returned with the bodies of the three murdered men. There were three because Charley Doolittle had been found nearly two hundred yards north of the road, and was just as dead as the rest.

Doolittle had been a machinist at the Vulture mine and had agreed to accompany Gribble as a guard for the bullion shipment. For the trip he had borrowed a large horse from James Hammond. Even the horse played a major role in the case.

The coroner had noted that five sets of horse tracks left the scene of the crime. Fortunately, for the posse, it had rained just days before and the tracks were easily seen. The conclusion was that just three men were involved in the shootings, the other two horses being those belonging to Hammond and a horse that was following the buggy.

Gribble's shotgun had one chamber discharged which led the coroner to believe that he had fired it spontaneously when he had been shot, wounding one of the buggy team mares. That mare charged on about one-hundred yards and then died bringing the buggy to a crashing halt.

Examination of the bodies brought the conclusion that although each man had been seriously wounded by the first volley, they were in turn shot many more times as they lay rolling on the ground. The citizens of Phoenix were outraged, demanding immediate response from the Territory and County in way of offering a reward for the capture of the assassins.

Thomas Malloy, in his 1921 article on the Gribble and Martin murders, describes the point at which Gribble and his party were attacked. His description makes sense because one can still clearly see the place today, especially when armed with a copy of the photo of the exact spot, taken a day or so later by the noted photographer George Rothrock.

Judging from the map, it is a few miles west of the station at Nada [Wittman] on the Phoenix and Prescott railroad. It is the first material depression on the old freight road from the Agua Fria to the Hassayampa and it is some six or eight miles from the Desert Well and about ten miles to Smith's Mill. This depression was at one time an old water course carrying water from the Castle Creek into the Hassayampa, but in those early days there was no indication of its having carried any large quantities of water in recent times. I would say that this depression is about seven feet below the general level of the desert, and is perhaps 100 yards in width. Immediately at the foot of the steep declivity on the south and Phoenix side of this depression there was in those days a very small water course, or gutter, about one foot deep, and an average of 14 inches in width, and, as is common where greasewood grows, the north bank of this little water course had on it a slightly thicker growth of greasewood. On the morning of March 19, 1888, someone had cut some other greasewood, and had, on each side of the road, inserted some of the cut greasewood among the branches of the greasewood there growing, and thereby making a thicker screen for anyone who might chose to lie down in this little gutter and hide himself. At least two men did lie down and hide themselves behind this greasewood screen, and at least one other laid down in a little rifle pit on the west side of the road and about 200 yards southeasterly from the top of the little declivity. The out rider passed in safety the ambuscade at the foot of the declivity, without noticing anyone secreted there, and passed on up and out onto the desert, where he was shot by the man lying in the rifle pit; and Gribble and Johnson came along in the buggy, and were not assailed until they were practically at the foot of the little hill, when they were both riddled with bullets and the only effect that Mr. Gribble's shotgun had was that when he was shot he pulled down the shotgun to shoot in the general direction of his assailant and the off mare was fatally shot in the rear, and both mares stampeded and ran up the little hill and about 20 yards from the top of the hill the off mare fell dead and the living mare, endeavoring to keep going, upset the buggy and threw out the bodies of Gribble and Johnson. Doolittle had borrowed Jim Hamond's big horse and was riding him at the time of the tragedy. The bullion and the horse were both taken.

Courtesy Arizona Historical Society/Tucson

Rothrock Photo—Phoenix Stage Approaching the Gribble Murder Scene

Of course, this was only speculation on Malloy's part, but he had been a wagon driver on this very same road during the 1880s and had passed that place many times. A trip to the spot where it all occurred, coupled with the photograph taken by George Rothrock, only adds to the opinion that Malloy had the story pretty close. The little water course on the east side of Trilby Wash is still in place today.

The Rewards are in Place

On March 22, 1888, the *Daily Phoenix Herald* broke down the rewards offered by various government entities as well as the public offering:

Territory $3,000
Gov. Tabor (Mine Owner) 2,000
Maricopa County 1,500
Private rewards 500
                                     _____
Total $7,000

"With a bounty of $7,000 hanging over their heads the chances for the final escape of these wretched criminals is diminishing by a very rapid rate."

A telegraph from C. Meyer Zulick, Governor, added that "their" posse had also gone to the scene. That posse could only have been men from Yavapai County, including Sheriff Mulvenon.

Why were rewards so important if there were men on the trail whose job it was to bring in the culprits? On the other hand, what amount of money would convince a man under threat of death to reveal the name of the evil doer?

Yet another posse was dispatched from Phoenix at 10 p.m. on the evening of March 21, 1888. This one was called the citizens' posse and consisted of: Will Smith, Captain; Wm. Breckenridge, Lieutenant; W. W. Pomeroy; Geo. Craighead; Ed Eads; Lee; Henly; Smith and two Maricopa Indian trailers. They were equipped for a long trip and had three pack animals.

The murderers had a two day head start, but the posse was optimistic due to the Salt and Gila Rivers being so high as to be impassable. To get across the Colorado the murderers would need to use one of the ferries but would still be on American soil. The greatest fear, of course, was that they would escape to Sonora, Mexico and be swallowed up in the population there. By treaty with the Mexican government, extradition across the border was not permitted.

News of the first two posses was printed in the *Daily Herald* of March 24.

> Tom Malloy, a teamster who arrived today from Vulture, brought the following news:

> Frank Cox, Davenport and Wilder trailed as far as the Hassayampa the first day, and proceeded to the Pump on the top of the Vulture divide to obtain feed for their horses. Here the Mexicans would sell them no feed for love nor money, and they were compelled to return to Seymour on the Hassayampa where they spent the night. Following the trail all the second day it led them to a point about five miles south of the Vulture mine, and was leading westward when they left it and came into Vulture to rest and refresh their horses. The next morning they started south to recover the trail taking a Mexican with them to some water tanks near the Osborn mines.

> Malloy also states that the trailers say there were five of the murderers and that on reaching the Hassayampa, three of them took a westerly course, and were followed by McGinnis and Elders, while two turned up at the Hassayampa and were followed by Deputy Murphy and Pedro. From the start, the fleeing party had done their utmost to conceal their trail in every possible way and to otherwise confuse possible pursuers ... Mulvenon with a posse is said to be somewhere in the vicinity, but it is not known where.

This was no doubt the same Tom Malloy who authored the article in 1921. Certainly he knew the subject matter well.

Two days later, March 26, the reading public was further excited by news that the Sheriffs of Yuma and Mohave Counties, along with the Sheriff of San Bernardino County, California, were watching those avenues of escape. The search area was defined as a vast desert, about one hundred miles square, bordered on the west by the Colorado River, the east by the Hassayampa River, the south by the Gila River, and the north by the A and P Railroad. There simply was no way to get out unnoticed.

On that same date the posse reported in once more. This time the word came from Smith and Breckenridge to the effect that they were on the trail of the robbers who were heading due west for the Colorado River. Murphy was said to be two days ahead, but why did he leave the trail of the two who had headed north? McGinnis must have abandoned the search altogether as he was the one to bring the news back to Phoenix. Cox and Mulvenon were reported to be at Vulture.

A telegram brought more items of interest.

Sunday evening Sheriff Halbert received a telegram from Robert Stein, Sheriff of Mohave County at Kingman, stating that Francisco Vega, the supposed Barney Martin murderer, and three suspicious looking men, had just reached there from the direction of Vulture, and were under surveillance. Sheriff Halbert wired him to arrest them immediately.

This is very important as there are many reasons to believe that these are the very men wanted. The distance between the scene of the murder and Kingman is not more than 150 miles, and the men had six days in which to traverse it.

The same issue of the *Herald* reported that the two horses which had proceeded north from the scene of the crime had been located at some unknown point. One was shod while the other was barefoot, but neither were recognized as belonging to that part of the country. Somehow, this led the editor to presume that there were only three murderers involved in the crime.

The next piece of news was what the whole county had been waiting to hear. According to the *Phoenix Daily Herald* for March 27:

The following telegram was received by Sheriff Halbert this morning:

GILA BEND, March 27, 1888—We overtook one of the party, who was shot and killed resisting arrest. Found jewelry belonging to Gribble on his person and recovered the bullion. Tell Y. T. Smith to send a photographer to Vulture at once. It is important. We will take the body to Vulture.

Murphy and Smith

The next day, details of the chase were published in the *Herald*.

The Man Hunt

———

One man Killed and the Bullion Recovered

———

The Posses Return—
Full Particulars of the Pursuit and Capture

———

The Story of the Trail

Frank Cox, who went out with the second sheriff's posse, consisting of Geo. Wilder and Tom Davenport, arrived in town last evening pretty well tired and toughened by a hard week in the saddle, over some of the roughest country to be found in Arizona. He describes the chase as follows:

Starting at the scene of the murder, the footmarks of horses indicated that after going a short distance north from the body of Doolittle, a transfer was made, and two horses were turned loose to the north, while the murderers proceeded directly west some 18 miles, and crossed the Hassayampa. There they separated, each of the three men riding a quarter of a mile from the other, but all keeping exactly parallel routes and heading due west, as Frank and his two companions found out by each taking a trail. This led them to the black butte some 24 miles west of Vulture …

Thence the trail turned down the Harquahala mountain range, always choosing the most difficult places in a range where the easiest places are almost impassable, and finally led toward the Eagle Tail range further south. Up to this time—Friday noon—our brave scouts had been alone, here in a rough canyon they suddenly came upon Murphy and Prether, both parties being startled at the meeting, as each at the first moment took the other party for the party both had been in search of. At this point Murphy and Prether had been nearly four days without food, and Cox and party had been keeping Lent for nearly two days. Murphy, it seems, had followed the trail forty-five miles further west towards the Colorado, and here the fugitives must have changed their minds, for they turned back on their tracks, thus making an extra ninety miles of traveling, and fortunately bringing the two parties together: for if they had not thus joined forces it might have gone hard with Murphy and his companion, as the sequel will show.

The party now journey on towards the Eagle Tail mountains, Prether following the track as easily as a tramp follows the railroad track. Their horses were fagged, and suffering from thirst, and they themselves were hungry and worn and weary, but their spirits were firm, and their hopes were high, for the trail looked fresher and the end seemed near.

At ten o'clock the next morning (last Saturday) the trail led them around the craggy summit of an isolated hill, and looking beyond and below they described the murderers laboring slowly down a rocky ledge, less than a quarter mile distant.

The pursued had apparently not noticed them, and the pursuers changed their course in such a manner as to flank them when they reached the bottom of the ridge. The Mexicans—for Mexicans they were—discovered them in time, and dashed down the side of the ridge into the canyon, where they halted but were only partly visible.

It being impossible to dislodge them, and there being but two rifles in the party, Frank Cox cut across the country to Vulture, some sixteen miles for reinforcements. After his departure the Mexicans broke cover and the chase commenced once more.

It was now headed for Wickenburg leaving Vulture a few miles to the east. So, Frank returning with six men from Vulture, met and joined his party in an hour and fifteen minutes after leaving them. Now the trail was warm and easily followed. Within four miles of Wickenburg they came upon two horses which the Mexicans had just abandoned, but the third and largest horse still kept on, and the trail turned back

through the mountains to within a quarter of a mile from Vulture where the rider had tied his horse and gone into Vulture, returned and started off in a direct line for the mountains at which the Mexicans were first jumped at ten o'clock the same morning. From here the trail turned southward towards the Gila, and here Frank Cox, whose horse was jaded, left the party which by this time had swelled to nineteen men. This is the story of the trail as long as Frank Cox was on it.

The two fugitives who abandoned their horses near Wickenburg, were supposed by the Murphy party to have mounted the large horse behind their compadre, thus vanishing entirely from the trail. Perhaps, indeed they did so, and leaving him at Vulture safely mixed with the motley crowd of their countrymen which is always to be found there. Frank Cox on his return from the trail informed Supt. Turnbull that the two had taken to the brush and a party had been put upon their trail.

The sequel may be told in fewer words. There is one innocent victim of the exciting tragedy which has just closed, deserving of kindly notice. The noble horse which its inhuman rider sacrificed when so vainly fleeing from his doom. On the third day he carried his rider over 100 miles without a drop of water to drink, and no doubt would have brought him safely across the line had it not been for the treacherous quicksands.

The Smith and Breckenridge party followed the same trail through all its windings, until they reached the place of the meeting between Cox and Murphy, and here they saved the extra ninety miles traveled by Murphy and took over the same course as the others after the joining of forces. The trail being by this time well worn they followed easily, part of the time at a gallop. They reached the Gila River just below the mouth of the Hassayampa Monday afternoon at two o'clock, just one hour behind Murphy's party. The combined party then continued on the trail, and found the horse of the fugitive stuck in the quicksand of the Gila abandoned by his rider. The horse could not be extricated and as he had broken his leg in the struggle he was shot. From this place a small heel track was followed down the river some ten miles to the house of Gov. Powers, about eight or ten of the party in the lead, and others strung out along the road for miles—for the horses were fast giving out. It was now just sundown, and riding up to the house, Smith inquired if there were any strange Mexicans there. Powers pointed to a Mexican who was sitting on the wood pile, who as soon as he saw he was attracting particular notice, started to run. He was ordered to halt but refusing, and being at that time nearly one hundred yards distant the shooting commenced. He was over two hundred yards distant when he received the fatal shot. He had the bullion rolled in his blankets and the watch of Capt. Gribble on his person. He had come to Power's ranch but a short time before and asked to be put across the river, and was persuaded to wait until morning when others were going to cross.

Two days later the *Phoenix Daily Herald* carried its last full column article on the subject.

The Man Hunt

—————

Two Suspects Gathered in by the Posse
—Arrival of the Bullion

—————

Late last night, Wm Blankenship, Tom Davenport, George Wilder and W. E. Eads arrived from Vulture, with two Mexicans, suspected of collusion with the murderers and the bar of bullion which instigated the crime. The prisoners were quietly turned over to Sheriff Halbert who introduced them to their cells, and also took charge of the bullion.

The Mexicans, Ignacio Valles, who confesses to have furnished the bandits horses and provisions, and Juan Vaquez, who is expected of hiding them in their escape, were visited by the reporter this morning and do not appear to be very talkative. They look frightened and anxious, as if uncertain of the fate in store for them, though expecting the worst. Aside from the fright depicted on their faces, the countenances are by no means prepossessing, though if men were to be hung for bad looks, few of us would survive.

Will Smith, Murphy and two Indian trailers are still on the track of Valenzuela's companions, who were two days ahead of the pursuers and heading south. There is no doubt of their final capture.

Rothrock succeeded in taking a very good picture of Valenzuela, the defunct bandit, and also a view of the crime. The man is rather good looking than otherwise, and appears about thirty years of age........

The Mexican, Juan Vaquez, who was brought in this morning was arrested by Blankenship on several serious grounds of suspicion, one of which may be mentioned. Vaquez disappeared from Vulture on Sunday, the day before the murder, and nothing was seen of him again for several days. Also one of the foot trails which led from the scene of the murder was made by a man who chewed tobacco, as here and there along the trail a stick or a stone was covered by tobacco juice. Mexicans do not take kindly to tobacco chewing, in fact it is a proverb among them that a Mexican who chews tobacco is generally a bad man. Vaquez is said to be the only Mexican in Vulture who indulges in the habit.

Inocente Valenzuela was so extensively known among the Mexican population that among the crowds of his countrymen who viewed his picture today, one out of every ten recognized him.

The article went on to describe the "fatal bar" which contained a cut in it that was one-eighth inch wide and one-quarter inch deep. Apparently the murderers had attempted to cut the thirty-six pound bar in half with an ax in order to make it easier to carry. The writer of the article was amazed that someone could have carried the bar on horse back and on his person for over 500 miles through some of the roughest country Arizona has to offer.

On Valenzuela's body the following articles were found: a silver watch, a gold chain, two gold rings, a pair of buckskin gloves, an old buck handled pocket knife, a pocket comb, and a diamond collar button. All of these had belonged to Gribble.

The balance of the posse's collection consisted of only a pistol that had been left behind when the murderers dropped off their horses near Wickenburg. It was a new model Colt 45 caliber revolver, serial number 3995. It had three chambers discharged.

By March 31st, Mr. E. H. Hiller of the Hartford Banking Company received a letter from the mine owner, Gov. Tabor, requesting him to thank the people of Phoenix for their, "kind, enthusiastic and prompt action concerning the murder of Capt. Gribble and his

Grave of Inocente Valenzuela at Vulture

associates." Additionally, he authorized payment of the $1,000 reward.

To one looking back from the twentieth century, it would seem that recovery of the bullion and payment of the reward was what this was all about. Two other murderers were still at large, but concern by the authorities died as quickly as the three men in the desert.

Around mid-September the Sheriff of Cochise County did arrest two men, Nabor Escalante and Angel Demarra, at Fairbank. The most significant evidence against the defendants was that one of them possessed the watch thought to have been in the possession of Johnson on the day of the robbery. Supposedly, the watch had belonged to Harvey Howe and had been loaned to Johnson for the trip.

Once the Grand Jury had bound the two over for trial, two further witnesses, according to the 1921 article by Malloy, appeared who had seen the two at Vulture a day before and at

Smith's Mill the morning of the crime. Chris Rodriquez had seen them at Vulture and Bill Gahan noticed them at Smith's Mill. Howe knew the watch for certain because, as he testified, it had suffered a broken crystal and subsequently had been repaired in San Antonio, Texas.

In spite of the able job done by the County Attorney, Frank Cox, skilled defense attorney, Ben Goodrich, got both men off by finding a witness who swore that both men were in his employ at the time and two jewelers who testified the watch had never been repaired. Arizona was satisfied and no one else was ever brought to justice for the crime. Apparently, one out of three, or one out of five, was good enough in those days, at least after the gold was recovered.

Four years later, the *Arizona Weekly Republican* carried an article that could keep the name Nigger Wells in the minds of the public for a long time to come. Tuesday, July 28, 1892:

A White Shadow

**A Ghostly Presence Recalling
Bloody Deeds**

The four drivers who pass on the Wickenburg route between Phoenix and Prescott tell an interesting story of what may be seen almost any night near Nigger Wells about midway between the Agua Fria and the Hassayampa.

The spot itself is ghostly and rendered still more so by the bloody memories which hang around it. But first it is better to tell what these stage drivers have seen. It may also add force to the story to mention that their vision is supported by the evidence of several passengers.

The stage passes near Nigger Wells late at night. Nearly a month ago a driver was startled by a shadowy presence which appeared at the side of the coach and seemed to touch it and travel alongside it for a considerable distance and finally vanish by degrees.

The driver at first believed this was an hallucination but it occurred so frequently that he finally spoke to another driver about it. The second driver had also seen the presence.

A further comparison of notes showed that all had seen it. After this the shadow seemed to become more distinctive and to take the form of a man still white and shadowy, he nightly approached the passing coach at that point and was plainly seen to lay his hand upon the vehicle. It always vanished at the same spot. One of the drivers swore that he would take his shotgun along and on the next visitation and would shoot into the fearful white shadow.

The opportunity was given that night but the driver had not the strength to raise the gun. These drivers have all related their strange vision here; they are men of undoubted veracity and courage, so considerable talk and excitement has been aroused …

Was the white shadow seen by the four stage drivers that of the Englishman Gribble, Barney Martin, or the unknown Portugese?

But where was Nigger Wells, the site of all these atrocities? The best guess today is that it was located in the southeast corner of section nine of Township 5 N, Range 3W, a couple of miles west of Whittman. This point is right on the old stage road and a few hundred yards west of Trilby Wash which was known for many years as Niger Wash.

There you can see two or three significant depressions in the ground, where deep holes may have been dug in the past. Significantly, it is also just three miles above the point, also on Trilby Wash, where Gribble and associates were ambushed.

Try to find it sometime, but do it in the brightest of daylight or you may not be alone in your search!

Catch the Stage to Phoenix

Book Two

The Black Canyon Road

Preface to Book Two

In the late 1860s, when stage transportation started on the Wickenburg Road, travel south and west from Prescott rarely included a trip to Phoenix. In those days people wanted to get to California or Maricopa Wells on the trans-Territory route for travel on to Tucson, Texas, or San Diego. The Black Canyon Road was certainly a horse of a different color.

Only after Phoenix began to supply significant amounts of groceries for Camp Verde and Prescott, was a route through the treacherous Black Canyon seriously considered. Even then, it took the opening of the Tip Top mine, and its associated mill at Gillett, to give the impetus for serious road building and eventual stage coaching along the Black Canyon Road.

Of course, once the stages started rolling, it took very little time for the "Knights of the Road" to pick their best spots to rob the passengers, express, and mail. Territorial officials were quick to respond with rewards for capture or death that in some cases far exceeded the crimes being committed.

Eventually these rewards would drive men "sworn to uphold the law" to such a frenzy that any suspect in hand would suffice. It mattered little to them who the real perpetrator might be. Jack Swilling, founder of Phoenix, was a victim of such a lust for rewards.

After amassing an enviable record for pioneering and developing communities in the then sparsely settled Territory, Swilling was falsely imprisoned and ultimately died in captivity. Only after his death were the true robbers sought out, captured, tried, and convicted of the crime he had already paid for.

Swilling, along with many others of his rugged kind had established sanctuaries of safety and rest for the traveling public. Sometimes, maintaining these havens of security along the way proved dangerous if not fatal to the keeper. The stage stations at Black Canyon and New River were both attacked by "Border Bandits," resulting in death and family tragedy.

Alcohol all too frequently provided the catalyst that led to the unnecessary loss of life in frontier towns and at stage stops. Excessive drinking cost the lives of many men in Gillett and the keeper of the station at Antelope. Saloons outnumbered all other commercial establishments.

Ultimately, the stagecoach gave way to more modern and humane ways of transportation, but for pure excitement and nostalgia, you couldn't beat a hundred mile trip by stage.

Photo L. J. Hanchett Jr.

Bumble Bee Flat

Photo L. J. Hanchett Jr.

New River, Arizona

The last express came by the Agua Fria and Woolsey's ranch. The route is shorter but not so well liked by the soldiers as that by Antelope.

Earliest reference to the Black Canyon Highway found in the *Miner*, May 15, 1864.

Chapter Eight
The Black Canyon Stage Lines

Getting a Road Through the Black Canyon

By April 25, 1866 another military verdict had been passed on that route and noted in the *Miner*:

> Captain John H. Coster of General McDowell's staff, who came here with the General, has been staying at Fort McDowell, and last week arrived in Prescott via Agua Frio [sic] and Woolsey's ranch, by which route he came to see if a direct wagon road could be had from McDowell to Prescott. He thinks the country impracticable, although a direct and good road may be had to Wickenburg.

The Autumn of 1870 saw Colonel Stoneman, Commander of the newly created District of Arizona, traveling in the company of John Marion, editor of the *Miner*, and others on a grand tour of the forts of Arizona. Fortunately, Marion made copious notes which he later collected into a work entitled *Notes of Travel Through the Territory of Arizona*.

Courtesy Sharlot Hall Museum

John Marion—Editor of the *Miner* Newspaper

One of the more interesting accounts is their passage from Fort McDowell toward Prescott through the Black Canyon.

Saturday, October 1st. Since crossing the Upper Gila, we had traveled upon old and good roads, but now, we were about to take a new "road," over portions of which a vehicle of any sort had never passed. Therefore, we called upon Colonel Stoneman quite early, to learn the news. It was not very encouraging. He read us a letter from Colonel Frank Wheaton, who had reconnoitered the route, and gave, in the letter, his opinion, that Colonel Stoneman would find it impossible to take his ambulances over the route. This fell on us like a "wet blanket." But, Stoneman said he would see whether or not he could make it. This suited us, as we were exceedingly anxious to get a breath of mountain air, and to see pine trees again. Our old and reliable escorts, teamsters, wagons and teams, were ordered to turn back to Salt River and take the road via Phoenix and Wickenburg to Whipple, which they did. About 4 o'clock in the afternoon, the two ambulances were in readiness, we jumped in and followed a small escort, we made about ten miles that afternoon through a poor looking country, and camped for the night.

Sunday, October 2nd. Made an early start; were, soon after starting, joined by Captain Sanford, Mr. Grubb, and some cavalrymen. Reached Cave Creek in about ten miles travel; found plenty of wood, water and grass; rested a few hours, and put out again for the next camp—New River—distant about ten miles, where we arrived late at night, very much fatigued, for the road had been very rough and hilly. We found plenty of water in the stream and refreshed ourselves.

Monday, October 3rd. Made about ten miles today, over a rather rough road, and encamped on the east bank of the Agua Frio [sic], within plain view of the mouths of Black Canyon or Turkey Creek, and the big, black canyon of the Agua Frio. After dinner, Capt. Sanford, Mr. Grubb and a few cavalrymen, started up the mountain to search for the men of Company F, 12th infantry, who, we knew, were close by, building a road. The Captain missed the men and their camp in going up the mountain, and kept on until he reached the Agua Frio, where he got directions regarding their whereabouts. He then returned, found them, and arrived in camp early next morning, with the news, which was, if anything, more discouraging than that contained in the letter of Colonel Wheaton. But Stoneman had reconnoitered the mountains the previous evening, and knowing not the word fail, he gave orders for the wagon to return to Camp McDowell; also to lighten up the ambulances as much as possible, and hitch up. The ambulances were lightened and we started up Black Canyon, over a rough road, which, however, was nothing in comparison to what we afterwards encountered … we started in climbing, and such climbing! Why, a California packer would not have attempted to drive his pack-train over such a mountain. But, it was the best we could do, and on we went, "slow like a snail," over great, rough trap boulders, some of which were as large as an ambulance. Now and then, the animals had to be unhitched, and the ambulances pulled up by means of ropes. Oh! It was trying on nerves. Our poor nerves gave out early in the day, and leaving men and officers to "do their duty, nobly," we crawled to camp, where we found Lieutenant King, Dr. Soule, and other friends, who gave us something to eat and drink and a good bed to shake in. It was about 5 o'clock in the afternoon, when we got over our shake and fever, and thinking our party ought to be near port, we started out to hail them, if within sight. They were in sight, and soon landed on the summit, tired and hungry, after their hard days work- a day that told fearfully on men and animals. Capt Brown having arrived from Camp Verde, during the afternoon, with a pretty fair escort, Colonel Stoneman thanked Captain Sanford and his men for well performed services, and, in the kindest manner possible, ordered the Captain to turn back to his post. We then started on over a ten-mile mesa, that would have been level, but for the great number of hard-hearted, nigger-head boulders, which made the ride very unpleasant. We made a dry camp, and all, save the sentinels, slept as soundly as ever tired men slept.

Three years later, following subjugation of the Indians, road work started in earnest on the east side of the Bradshaws. The Hellings Flour Mill, from Phoenix, had a large contract with Camp Verde and its associated Indian Reservation. Transportation of goods all the way to Prescott over the Wickenburg road and then on to Camp Verde would be far too expensive. It made a lot of sense to establish a more direct road through the Black Canyon.

A correspondent for the *Miner* posed this question in the issue of March 6, 1873:

There is one thing that appears strange to me, and that is, that the people both of Prescott and the Salt River Valley, don't open a good road direct from this post to Prescott, for I am informed by good authority, that the military road, partially opened via Black Canyon, the Lower Agua Fria and Bower's ranch, could be made an excellent road with a comparative small amount of work, and it would shorten the distance more than one half, over the usual route via Wickenburg, Date Creek, etc.

By September 27th of that year the *Miner* reported a meeting in Phoenix, called by Hellings & Co. for the purpose of raising funds to open a new road through Black Canyon to Prescott and the Verde. Captain Hancock of Phoenix was engaged to lay out and survey the route. Only a few years before he had surveyed the townsite of Phoenix.

Within days, over forty men were at work on the project. The *Miner* of November 8, 1873 declared that the completion of this new road was second in importance only to the arrival of the telegraph in Phoenix. The new distance from Prescott to Phoenix was ninety-five miles.

Only a week later, the first wagon train completed the trip from Phoenix to Prescott in just five days. Via the Wickenburg road it would have taken ten.

The *Miner* on January 16, 1874, described more activities in that part of the territory.

> Hellings and Co. have a gang of men at work repairing the new road from Phoenix to Camp Verde, which was badly washed in places by the late rains. Messrs. H. and Co. built the road, which is a public convenience, and as they can get no assistance from other parties in repairing it, they will probably apply to the Supervisors of Maricopa and Yavapai counties for permission to incorporate it as a toll road.

> We understand that Gen. Crook contemplates a further shortening of the military road to Camp Verde, by building a new piece of road from Aqua Fria valley by Maple Shades, and through Copper Canyon to the Verde valley. Should the General carry out the plan, the distance to Phoenix from Prescott by that route and Hellings and Co.'s road would be only about ninety miles.

As soon as his work on the Miller Cutoff road, from Prescott to Skull Valley, was complete, Lieutenant Thomas was soliciting men to work on the road to Camp McDowell. The *Miner*, November 19, 1875:

> Work for All—Engineer Officer, Lieut. Thomas, requests us to say to those seeking employment that he will hire as many as present themselves at Swilling's place at Black Canyon on the same terms, etc., as were observed in the building of the Skull Valley road. The road from Camp Verde to Camp McDowell is the one upon which he wants to put the laborers. "There is work and bread enough for all."

On another page of that same issue:

> The Hon. John Smith, yesterday received a communication from Lieut. Thomas stating that in case the people of this section of the country furnish some means he would make the new road from Prescott, direct from the Verde to Phoenix after having completed it to McDowell.

On May 29, 1877, the *Miner* commented that the Board of Supervisors for Yavapai County had let the contract for construction of the road from Prescott to Black Canyon to Mr. James Patterson for five thousand dollars. Patterson would, the following year, become a principal in the Patterson and Caldwell stage line running over that road.

Just two months after Patterson had started his work on the Black Canyon road, travelers reported it to be in good condition. Hope was voiced for Maricopa County to carry the road on in equal fashion to Phoenix.

Still, critics abounded. The *Miner* reported the following on November 30, 1877:

> The ox train of Hance and Graham arrived yesterday from the Salt River, with 40,000 lbs. of flour manufactured at the celebrated flouring mill of C. H. Veil, East Phoenix, consigned to C. P. Head & Co., of this place. Mr. Hance who superintended the train while in transit condemns the Black Canyon route in the bitterest terms and thinks he can haul with the same team and wagon at least one ton more freight over the route via Wickenburg and in less time with a great savings to his stock.

Captain Hancock—Surveyor of Phoenix and the Black Canyon Road

Stages for the Black Canyon Road

The key ingredient for the establishment of stages on the newly completed Black Canyon road was the opening of the Tip Top mine in 1877. Although the mine itself was nestled well back into the Bradshaw mountains, its associated mill was located at the town of Gillett, on the Agua Fria River, not too distant from the road connecting New River and Black Canyon City.

By early January of 1878, James D. Monihon of Phoenix was laying plans for a buckboard service between that town and Gillett. Within a couple of months the service was in place. Passengers paid $5.00 one-way or $8.00 round-trip. The buckboard left the Phoenix Post Office every other day at 8 a.m. Although Monihon did not provide service to the mine, reassurance was given that connecting service was available by saddle animals. Not much, but it was a start.

From the other end, at Prescott, service began in February with a stagecoach owned by Thomas Cusack and his partner, Murphy. The stage left Goldwater's store in Prescott every fourth day with a destination of Gillett. The one-way fare was $10.

Mail still traveled from Prescott to Phoenix via the Wickenburg road, but that would soon change. Tip Top and Gillett both needed mail service, and the day wasn't far off when the government would have to provide it. A trio of Arizona men probably had that in mind when they announced their new enterprise in March of 1878.

First the three purchased Cusack's line from Prescott to Gillett and only a week later added the buckboard line from Phoenix to Gillett, run by James Monihon. The Patterson and Caldwell Company was the proud new owner of a stage line running from Prescott to Phoenix through Agua Fria (Dewey), Big Bug, Cottonwoods, Bumblebee, Black Canyon, and Gillett.

Of the three, James Patterson was best known and probably the only one who could have afforded the sizable cash outlays. As previously noted, he was a builder on the Black Canyon road under contract from Yavapai County in 1877. Just prior to entering the stage business, Patterson purchased the Plaza Livery Stables on Goodwin street in Prescott from Gideon Brooke for $8,000.

Courtesy Sharlot Hall Museum

Plaza Stables in Prescott

William Caldwell had been engaged in other enterprises, such as lumber, before the stage line with little or no success. The third member, Alfred LeValley, was probably a laborer whose wife worked as a seamstress.

Alfred LeValley

Born in the state of New York in 1847, Alfred was the son of Sarah and Moreau LeValley, a wagon maker. At age fifteen he moved with his parents to Waverly, Iowa where he met and married Carrie Taylor in 1869. In 1873, Alfred and his wife moved to Kansas and from there to Arizona in 1876. Of their six children only one daughter, Minnie, was born in Arizona during their brief stay.

The *Miner* of March 15, 1878, after having announced the first departure of the new stage line, went to great lengths to belittle the U.S. Mail Agent for not ordering the establishment of mail service on the Black Canyon route.

> The first coach left the Plaza Stables this morning with six passengers and a heavy private mail, consisting of letters, papers, packages, etc., illustrating plainer than language can tell it, the urgent necessity for the establishment of a government mail on the route. We were informed a few days ago that Major Truman, U.S. Mail Agent, was at Los Angeles, en route for Prescott, and hoped to be able to make him see some of our wants in relation to mails, but much to our disappointment, in looking over the *Star* of that city, we discover that the Major had concluded not to leave the line of the railroad, but would return to his comfortable quarters in San Francisco, without giving Arizona any attention.

> The President, Post Master General, or who ever has the appointment of Postal Agents, always make mistakes when they appoint lymphatic and physically lazy gentlemen to the office of Postal agent, such men if they must have office, should be judges or placed in positions where the chief duties are to sit or lie down, and think. For instance, Frank Ganahl, would make but an indifferent Postal Agent though mentally he is qualified for almost any position. He likes to rest too well, and from what we hear of Major Truman, he is just such another. Swap him off and give us a wide awake man for Postal Agent, one who is not afraid to travel and see for himself what is needed. If such an agent could be induced to visit Central and Northern Arizona, we have faith to believe there would be mail ordered at once on the Prescott and Phoenix route, via Agua Fria, Black Canyon and Humbug as well as on half a dozen routes in Mohave and

Eastern Yavapai. Mail agents don't seem to realize that a want of mail facilities grows with the rapidly increasing growth of this country in population and mineral and business growth.

The *Miner* of the same date added a good plug for the new stage line as well as for its own circulation.

> The Tip Top stage line, of PC & Co., advertised today, is the institution which "we long have sought, and mourned because we found it not." It is a starter for the ultimate establishment of a U.S. Mail, Post Offices, Wells Fargo and Co.'s Express, and all the paraphernalia of a first class stage route. People should encourage the line, ride on it, send packages by it, correspond through it, subscribe for the *MINER*, and have it brought by it, etc.

A week later, the *Miner* was boasting of the success already attained by the line.

> Patterson and Caldwell & Co. were compelled, owing to the large number of passengers booked for Gillett, to send out an extra stage this morning, which speaks well for the enterprise the gentlemen have started.

> Patterson and Caldwell & Co. had to put on an extra stage to Gillett this morning, in order to accommodate the travelers, including about 1,000 pounds of extra baggage.

On April 12th, the *Miner* handed out more praise.

> Travel between Prescott and the Tip Top mines is increasing. Every stage that leaves either place is always loaded with passengers and baggage. Yesterday's stage brought in nine passengers and this morning's coach took out eight passengers and over 500 pounds of baggage.

Hindsight leads us to believe that the *Miner* thoroughly jinxed the operation. Two weeks later Patterson sold out his controlling interest to L. C. Palmer and, by the 10th of May, that interest moved again into the hands of the remaining partners, Caldwell and LeValley.

Patterson and Palmer were seasoned businessmen while Caldwell and LeValley still had a lot to learn. Nevertheless, the *Miner* conditionally continued its optimism. The last sentence in its article of May 10th concluded: "Close attention to its affairs will make the line one of the best in the Territory."

In spite of the inclusion of silver bars to its other cargo and an extension of the line to Maricopa Wells, trouble was on the horizon for the Caldwell and LeValley stage line.

First, there was a new competitor on the route by the name of Bennett. Next came along what should have been good news—the long awaited Postal contract to be let by July 31, 1878. Surely, this was the pot of gold at the end of the rainbow. They had the best operating stages on the route, but the government only considered the cost to provide the service, not who was there first or who had worked the hardest.

Caldwell and LeValley were underbid by Kerns and Griffith, operators of a line in Southern Arizona soon to be replaced by the Southern Pacific Railroad. Being the larger and better capitalized firm, Kerns and Griffith could easily bid a losing proposition, hoping to fare better once the route was expanded to other fledgling towns. For them the gamble paid off.

There may have been some foreboding thoughts in the minds of Caldwell and LeValley, as the latter moved his family to the more isolated Antelope Station (Cordes). From there he could more readily escape the onrush of creditors should they lose the mail contract and their gamble of the last few months.

Feigning a broken stage, one of the owners refused passengers or freight on his arrival at Gillett that last Friday in September, 1878. The driver with his empty coach drove quickly back to Antelope Station where he met the other owner and LeValley's family. All they could carry was loaded aboard one of the company's coaches, and with the extra horses in tow, a strange group moved quickly eastward, toward the New Mexico line.

The company's creditors were furious as the news traveled just as quickly from Prescott to Phoenix. Tom Cusack, owner of the original line, made the first effort to recover his property. The *Miner* of October 4, 1878 carried the story.

A Stage Company Skipped the Country

The Proprietors, Employees, Family, Coach Horses and the Whole Outfit Crossed the Mogollons

A Constable and Sundry Creditors in Hot Pursuit

The firm of Caldwell and LeValley, who have been running an independent stage line between Prescott and Phoenix, that is to say, a line without a mail contract, with the expectation of receiving the contract when a mail should be put on, were disappointed, Messrs. Kerns and Griffith having underbid them, and in the meantime having run largely into debt to station keepers, merchants, mechanics, etc., found themselves near the close of their career, when the mail was to be put on by the contractors on the first day of October, unable to liquidate, and, as appears by their action they concluded to "flee from, the wrath to come" and strike out with such property as they could easily move, and try to get beyond the jurisdiction of Arizona officials before their absence was observed. They accordingly announced that they had reduced their line from a semi-weekly to a weekly, this was to keep people from wondering why they were not making their regular trips twice a week, and on leaving Gillett last Saturday they refused to bring the regular shipment of bullion, saying that their coach was disabled, and that it would be fixed at Prescott, so that it could bring the bullion next trip.

Instead of making the trip to Prescott, however, they came as far as their own station on the Agua Fria, and there gathered up their loose stock, some twenty horses, put Le Valley's family in the coach and with a Mexican employee to drive the loose stock started for New Mexico, via Little Colorado.

It was some days before it became known that they were gone and they were well on their way across the Mogollons before a constable from Gillett, accompanied by Tom Cusack, a man from Session's ranch, and perhaps others started in pursuit. The constable we learn was armed with an attachment for the property but had no warrant for their arrest. So that if he overtakes them and they can satisfy the demands he has against them they will probably be allowed to go on with whatever else they may have.

So far as we can learn of their indebtedness it is as follows: James Patterson, between four and five hundred dollars, L. Bashford & Co. about the same, Tom Cusack, nearly the same, Howey and Patterson two or three hundred, Campbell and Parker, nearly the same, Sessions at Agua Fria, over three hundred, etc. In addition to these amounts there are several smaller bills here in Prescott, and they are said to owe nearly everybody at Gillett. Phoenix has not yet been heard from but it is presumed they owe considerable there.

Only a week later, news came back that Cusack and company had caught up with the fleeing party.

Tom Cusack, Mr. Sessions and the constable from Gillett who followed the absconding stage proprietors, Caldwell and LeValley, across the Mogollons with attachments, overtook them and received their pay in money and stock. The absconding party continued on their journey towards New Mexico, but on the return of Cusack and party, L. Bashford & Co. got out another attachment and warrant of arrest, which was telegraphed to a deputy sheriff at Apache [County], and the chances are that they will yet be brought back and caused to disgorge the remainder of their property to their creditors.

The next piece of news on the matter took five months to arrive in Prescott. When it did come, on February 21, 1879, many Victorian eyes must have opened wide.

Rumor— It is currently reported that W. H. Caldwell, formerly in the lumber business here, and afterwards of the Caldwell LeValley stage line, between Prescott and Gillett, has been killed somewhere in New Mexico. It will be remembered that Caldwell and LeValley became involved in debt last fall, and that the two partners, with LeValley's wife and children gathered up the stage stock, and with one stage struck out across the Mogollons, it is presumed for Kansas. Word was brought back that when they reached the railroad Mrs. LeValley and children took to the cars and left the two men to bring on the stock. Subsequent to this, we learn, letters have been received here from Mrs.

LeValley, saying her husband had arrived in Kansas, but had left Caldwell behind, and in the meantime a New Mexican or Colorado paper has an account of the finding of the body of W. H. Caldwell, shot through the heart. We are also informed that there was bitter jealousy existing between Caldwell and LeValley on account of Mrs. LeValley, and that Caldwell's relations with her were anything but agreeable to LeValley. This is the report as it comes to us and we give it for the benefit of those who, either from motives of curiosity, a morbid appetite for scandal or feelings of personal sollentude [?] for the welfare of the parties, who are all well known here, may desire to read it.

LeValley and Family Return to Kansas

LeValley and his family relocated to Liberty Township, Coffey County, Kansas where he farmed, planted a fine orchard, and added to the size of his family.

By 1900 Alfred had moved his family to Hutchinson, Kansas where they lived until Alfred passed away in 1909 and Carrie followed in 1910. Both are buried in Oak Hill Cemetery, Osage County, Kansas.

Kerns and Griffith lasted but a few years, being replaced in 1885 by the Arizona Stage Company belonging to Gilmer and Salisbury. That line was in turn supplanted in 1894 by the Black Canyon Stage Company owned by the Hocker brothers.

As recently as 1917, buckboards still carried mail and a few passengers from the terminus of the Prescott and Eastern Railroad as far south as Black Canyon. The stage station which still exists in that town was built after the turn of the century.

Opening stage lines in the early days of the Territory was risky at best. The type of man suitable for that work would have to be like Patterson, Caldwell, and LeValley, tough and relentless, willing to take chances even if it cost their reputation or their life.

Photo L. J. Hanchett Jr.

Staged Holdup at Pioneer Arizona Living History Museum—North of Phoenix

Photo L. J. Hanchett Jr.

Stage Robbery Site—North of Gillett

Whereas the forcible stopping of stages upon the public highway, for the purpose of rifling the mails and robbing the express and passengers by a certain class of lawless villains is becoming alarmingly frequent.

Introduction to acting Governor's proclamation August 12, 1879

Chapter Nine
More Knights of the Road

The Acting Governor's Proclamation

Acting Governor, John J. Gosper, issued the following proclamation concerning stage robberies on August 12, 1979.

> Therefore, I, John J. Gosper, Acting Governor of the Territory of Arizona, do hereby authorize the payment out of the Territorial Treasury, the sum of $500 to any individual who shall kill, by means of firearms, or otherwise, the highway robber while in the attempt of robbing the mail or express, or search of the passengers, and the sum of $300 shall be paid for the capture and conviction of anyone connected with the robbing of stage, express or passengers as above mentioned.

> This offer is to take effect from this date, and to continue in full force and effect until by proper authority the same may be rescinded.

Stage robbers were literally worth more dead than alive. The end of stage robbing should have been within sight, but some men didn't know the meaning of fear and so the courts would have to teach them. The *Miner* of December 19, 1879 reported yet another robbery and its result.

> Wm. Morgan, convicted for robbing the stage was brought in for sentence. In passing sentence, His Honor, Judge Silent, said: "It is the intention of this court to stop the practice of highway robbery, so far as it is in its power to do so. You have been found guilty of that crime, and this court will impose the full penalty of the law. The sentence of this court is that you be confined to the Territorial Prison for the term of your natural life."

In those days, life-long incarceration at the Territorial Prison in Yuma was worse than a sentence to hang.

Murder on the Stage Line

Simple robbery was not always the result when stages were stopped by desperate men. Although infrequent, sometimes passengers were killed. Such was the case when the Prescott to Phoenix stage was held up on November 26, 1879. According to the *Miner* of the following day:

> The Prescott and Phoenix stage via Gillett, which left Prescott yesterday, Thanksgiving morning, when within two miles of Gillett was stopped and robbed by three Mexicans. Billy Thomas, partner with Johnny Bostwick, at Gillett, was on board and was shot and mortally wounded. The mail was taken. The robbers before leaving Gillett on their mission of deviltry stole from Mr. Ayers [stage driver] three very fine horses, thus mounting themselves in good shape. More than likely, ere this, they are far on their way towards their native land, Sonora, where they will find protection and shelter from

their friends and relatives, who wink approvingly at any crime perpetuated on Americans. Several parties have left Prescott in pursuit of the tan-colored boys who committed this daring robbery on the public highway, and woe be unto the rascals if they are overtaken.

Following the trial of the suspected participants, the *Miner* of November 26, 1880, gave full details of the crime.

The particulars of the crime as developed by the trial, are about as follows: The Prescott stage was just entering a small canyon, about two miles outside Gillett, when three men were observed by the driver running toward the stage. Two of them ran along the right side of the stage, and one on the left. One of the two on the right side of the coach snatched the reins from the hands of the driver, at the same time firing a couple of shots at him. While he was doing this, his two companions placed themselves on the opposite side of the coach, and began to fire into the coach at William Thomas, a merchant of Tip Top, who was the only passenger. After having been wounded several times Thomas fell to the bottom of the coach, and his murderers then began another murderous attack on him with knives. When one would stab him on one side Thomas would spring to the other side of the coach, when he would be received with a murderous cut from a knife in the hands of the other Mexican, exhausted at last, he fell insensible, and, while he was in that condition Dominguis jumped into the stage and threw him out. This had the effect of reviving him somewhat, and he crawled ten or twelve feet from the stage, and laid down; and while in that position Dominguis placed a pistol to his temple, and would have fired, had it not been for the intercession of the other two Mexicans. The men then robbed the stage of the mail and made the driver, Wm. Ayres, get from Thomas his trunk keys and open his trunk, from which they took everything of value. After robbing Thomas and the driver they then forced the latter to aid them in unhitching from the stage, the horses, which they mounted and rode off. The man wounded by them was taken to Gillett and died at that place Nov. 26th—one year ago today. He had received nearly a half score of wounds, the most important being in the chest and abdomen.

In a lengthy written confession, Dominguis admitted to participation in the crime, but insisted that he had been coerced at gun-point and was by no means the actual murderer. That honor, he said, belonged to Fermin Frambes. Additionally, he noted that the other robber was Umecino Moraga. Both of these men, he claimed, could easily be found in Sonora, Mexico. Dominguis was hung in Phoenix on November 26, 1880, the first lawful hanging in that city.

A Favorite Place for Robbing Stages

In planning for the robbery of a stage, special attention was given to the best place for committing the crime. Unlike modern Hollywood versions, most robberies were done by men on foot. For that technique to be effective, the robber would pick a spot where the stage was moving very slowly if not nearly stopped. As a further precaution, the most remote spot was usually chosen to avoid interruption, or rapid pursuit during or after the crime.

Such places could be found in the hills between Bumble Bee and Gillett. There the horses would slow to a walk and, on occasion, the passengers would follow behind the stage to lighten the load when climbing a steep hill. Another reason for so many robberies occurring a couple of miles north of Gillett may have been because that area was in Maricopa County. Law enforcement was possibly not as successful there as it was to the north, in Yavapai County.

Under the title "Taken In," the following article appeared on September 1, 1882, in the *Phoenix Herald*, authored by Theron T. Widmen.

Two Black Canyon Stages Robbed

The highwaymen made a big haul. Eight or ten passengers are made to stand and deliver. Wells Fargo & Co. boxes are cleaned out. The most daring robbery ever perpetuated in the Territory. Two robbers successfully do the job. The robbers probably secure a large amount of money. Nobody hurt and the United States mail unmolested. On the arrival of the stage from Prescott on Sunday morning our town was thrown into considerable excitement by the sight of two smashed Wells Fargo boxes and the stories of the passengers of the robbery of the previous evening. A Herald reporter drew from the passengers the following account: Saturday night about eleven o'clock, when Stewarts' Black Canyon Stage coming down from Prescott had reached a point on the plain about two miles above Gillett, the driver and Capt. G. C. Gordon, of the Sixth Cavalry, Camp Bowie, who was seated on the box, discovered two horses secured to a tree a short distance ahead and a few yards from the road. The driver remarked "robbers," and almost immediately two men sprang from behind a mesquite bush and with shotguns leveled ordered the driver to halt. They rapidly approached, paying special attention to Capt. Gordon, whom they no doubt took for a Wells Fargo messenger. As they neared the stage the captain heard the order "Come down from there, come down from there." And without standing upon the points of ceremony he came down. "Throw up your hands," and the Captain's hands went up. Then one of them turning to the passengers remarked: "Come out from that," and out they came, their hands went up and they were ranged alongside the captain. The passengers in the coach were Dr. Lloyd and Mr. Solomon, of Graham county. One of the robbers, a very large and powerful man, now covered the passengers with his shotgun while the second, a medium sized stoop shouldered man, went through their pockets, taking from Mr. Solomon fifty-five dollars in cash, a gold watch and some bank checks for about $1,800, the latter of which, after careful examination the robber returned. He then turned his attention to Dr. Lloyd, from whom he secured thirty dollars, a fine gold watch and a check for $175 which he also returned, remarking to the doctor, when he found so little coin, "You are about as hard up as I am." He then paid his respects to the captain, when he met with better success, securing $364.50 and a valuable gold watch and chain. He then turned his attention to the Wells Fargo box, smashing it open with a large rock which had apparently been placed by the roadside for that purpose. These he coolly explored, tearing open letters, and getting in the coin as if it was an all night job. Before he had finished the boxes the up-going stage was heard approaching and the guard remarked, "hurry up, the other one's coming," but he coolly continued to open letters until the other stage had approached, within a few yards, when both robbers covered the driver with their guns, ordered him to halt also and ordered the passengers to, "come out of there," which they did with the greatest alacrity to the number of six or eight. "Put up your hands," and their hands

went up also. Again the short man began to explore the pockets of the passengers for arms, and valuables and when he had finished that job he proceeded to use the express box found on this stage as he had on the downward bound stage. One of the passengers on the upward bound stage was Dr. Ainsworth, of Prescott, and another a Deputy Sheriff of Tombstone. Our informant had no idea of how much he secured from these passengers but thought that Dr. Ainsworth lost between three and four hundred dollars. In the meantime Captain Gordon had been coaxing for his watch, as the robbers seemed to be good natured and inclined to talk, and finally it was returned to him, after some delay, the robbers carefully examining it and running his chain between his fingers in hesitation. Mr. Solomon followed the lead of the Captain, but the second stage approaching, he remarked, "Wait a bit," and proceeded with his work. When he had "done" the second crowd Mr. Solomon renewed his request, when the big man, who seemed to be the leader, said, "give it to him," and it was returned without further delay. Following up their good success the Captain requested the loan of a dollar to get some breakfast, and two were returned. Mr. Solomon also complained that he was "dead broke," and received three dollars. Dr. Lloyd asked for nothing and received nothing. He was evidently well satisfied to get off, as well as he did. Our informant states that the upward bound stage should have heard the smashing of the express boxes as he could distinctly hear the passengers talking some little time before the stage came in sight, while the highwayman was beating the express box with a rock and that they should have certainly seen that something was wrong, as their coach was in sight some two hundred yards before arriving upon the scene, the sky being unobscured, and a bright moon shining.

The highwaymen were perfectly cool and self possessed to the last degree, even to the utmost carelessness. They talked and joked with the passengers without reserve and in a natural tone of voice. Their features, however were carefully concealed by silk handkerchiefs which were well down upon their breast, and through which holes were cut for the eyes. The job took about an hour, and when completed, both men covered the crowd with their guns and commanded: "Now git out of here," and they got.

Of all the stage robberies that have taken place in the Territory, this takes the precedence for pure recklessness on the part of the highwaymen. The men were evidently old hands at the trick, and most desperate characters. Neither driver was molested, the robbers evidently taking them for impecunious individuals, not worthy of attention and only useful to have away the passengers when they had no more use for them. The mails were not disturbed in either stage. Sheriff Orme and Wells Fargo detectives left yesterday for the scene of the robbery and to endeavor to trace up the robbers.

Between June of 1883 and the same month in 1885, the stage was robbed no less than six times, all between Gillett and Black Canyon City. The first two are a story by themselves.

June 28, 1883

The north bound stage from Phoenix to Prescott was stopped about three miles from Gillett last evening by two masked highwaymen with rifles who demanded Wells Fargo's treasure box which was thrown off. Four passengers, including Miss Fleming and George Tinker [editor of the *Flagstaff Sun*,] were on the stage but were not molested. There is no knowledge here of the amount of money obtained by the robbers.

July 2, 1883

The stage from Phoenix to Prescott was stopped again last night by two masked men within one mile of the same place where it was stopped last Thursday night. The amount in the box is not known but it is thought to be considerable as large amounts of money are in route here. The opinion prevails that they are the same men who committed the robbery last Thursday night and that they have a personal knowledge when treasure of any amount is being shipped.

Wells Fargo had their reputation at stake and it wasn't long before a plan was in place. From an uncredited and undated news article:

The twelfth legislative assembly, of which the writer was a member, having adjourned, Pat Hamilton and the writer took the Black Canyon stage for Phoenix and thence to Tucson. One day at lunch—Pat had gone to Pueblo Vieja—George Martin and two strangers came in and took seats at a table on the opposite side of the hall; before seating, Mr. Martin leaned forward and spoke to the strangers, both glanced towards me and said something to Martin, who crossed the room and said: "Those two gentlemen are Well's Fargo special officers and they desire a few words with you after lunch." I was introduced, Martin returned to the office, Thacker began by saying: "You have heard of the Gillett robberies?" I nodded ascent. "We have been on these robberies for weeks, can't get a clue and are now at the end of our rope; our agent, Mr. Martin, tells us if there is anyone in the Territory capable of working the cases to a successful issue, you can. Will you help us out of this tangle?" I was en route to Missouri, but had stopped at the Pueblo to visit a few days. Considering the matter a few moments I decided to give it a trial, and Thacker and self immediately left for Phoenix, via old Maricopa Wells, Hume remaining in Tucson. Before going to Gillett, I learned from Thacker that the box contained $900 in $20 gold pieces and $35 in paper; that the holdups were always at one point of the road. This information suggested to me that there was a reason, and to find this reason was to locate the criminals. Mr. Thacker said: "You will investigate the agent, the company is suspicious, think the agent in collusion," but agent proved to my satisfaction to be innocent of the charge. I must go alone for Thacker to go would create suspicion, but if I had occasion to write him, to address the letter to John Lang. With letter from stage agent, directing drivers to allow the "bearer" make no mention of the fact. Arriving at Gillett about midnight; taking a seat where I could keep an eye on all persons and movements in the room, the first thing to attract attention was the agent's location of his little two and a half foot square table where he opened the express box; I also noted this table was railed off in front high enough for one to lean upon and take a look into the box. With an eye on this agent as he opened the box, I noticed two men enter the room. They were the blacksmiths, of Gillett, and well known by all, they walked up to the aforesaid railing, leaned upon it and the larger of the two men looked into the box; the agent being busy did not notice the movement, but the writer did. After joking with the agent a few moments, the larger man slightly nudged his companion and both left the room. Instantly the thought flashed through my mind; here is a clue. Those two blacksmiths are the robbers; if anything is in the box, they go up the road and when the stage comes along a few minutes later, the trick is turned and they return to Gillett unseen, laugh over the incident as easier than "shooting fish in the Panhandle." I had spotted the robbers within five minutes after reaching Gillett, a question of eyes and brains, and so it was in the Santa Fe case. Next morning I jocularly asked the agent if the stage was held up last night, he laughed and said, "nothing in the box last night." This I knew of course. Walking around I dropped into the blacksmith shop, chatted with the two men awhile; my object was to ascertain which of the two mentally dominated; an easy thing to do by any close observer. Sauntering over to the post office, the postmaster like everybody else in Gillett, talked of nothing else but the robberies and failure of the special officers. As all others he too had wild ideas of the matter. Deciding to put in another night, as a matter of "confirmation," and to pass away the time, I went down to the mesquite out of sight, smoked my pipe and thought over the situation. Later in the afternoon I gathered a few rocks, not particular to kind or quality, and returned to the saloon. Showing my find to the agent I remarked: "What do you think of that, good gold rock ain't it?" He looked at my samples, and smilingly said: "Nothing to it, if that is all you know about minerals better try something else." Several miners were in the room and one came over, glanced at the rocks smiled and returned to where the others were sitting. "What," says I, "do you mean there's nothing in that rock?" and I made a move in the direction of the miners, but one of them shook his head in the negative. The above was merely a play of mine, but it afforded much amusement to all the miners that night, and they had many guffaws at the expense of "that chump over in the corner; he don't know enough to go inside when it rains." The same scene was enacted that night and my suspicions were confirmed. The following day I went to Tip Top. I had learned the last payday at the mine had followed the robbery of the night before; also learned that the big blacksmith was a fiend for "bucking the tiger," therefore, my trip to the mine was to get a clue to the stolen money. Meeting with a miner who ran a faro game during paydays, I learned by some "round about questioning" that the two blacksmiths had a game there during payday; that they had "about $900 in gold twenties and thirty-five or forty dollars in paper all of which they lost during the day." Desiring to secure his name and address, as he had described the stolen money and what became of it, I pretended to wish to correspond with him prior to the next payday, and so obtained my wish. I returned to Gillett and that night to Phoenix. Thacker was surprised at my early return, and supposed I had given up the job as unsolvable, but when I gave him my notes with the two blacksmiths at the bottom, he slapped his leg, saying "Straight as a string, how did you do it so soon?" My reply was to the effect, "my first idea was to solve the

reason why the holdups were at one place, and why the stage was held up only when something was in the box, this was accomplished within five minutes after I arrived at Gillett. I told Thacker one was mentally the weaker, and if placed in separate cells, with judicious questioning, the weaker man would turn 'states evidence,' and this was so, the leader drew twenty-five years and the other one nine years."

Shades of Sherlock Holmes!

Within a month of the robberies, Joseph Chambers and James Larsen were named in a complaint initiated by Lyman Jilson, Wells Fargo agent from Phoenix. William Mulvenon, Under Sheriff for Yavapai County, arrested Joe Chambers on July 31, 1883, while James Larsen was being arrested at his blacksmith shop by H. C. McDonald, Deputy Sheriff for Maricopa County.

Larsen, being the "weaker of the two," had buried some of the loot, from the July 1st robbery, underground at his shop. Indeed, he did turn "states evidence" and during the trial for Chambers provided a complete account of the robbery on the 27th of June. That escapade had netted the thieves only $22.50. The robbery of July 1st was a little more successful with the proceeds amounting to almost $600. Larsen's testimony makes fascinating reading.

James Larsen being first duly sworn testified as follows:

My name is James Larsen, I am 31 years of age. I am a blacksmith by occupation and reside in Gillett. I know the defendant, Mr. Joe Chambers, I have known him for 8 or 9 months, somewhere about there. I know about the robbing of the stage between Prescott and Phoenix on about the 27th day of June last. About that time we both went out there and held up the stage. I mean the defendant, Joe Chambers. Mr. Chambers, the defendant, had a Winchester rifle and I had a shotgun. He held the rifle on the driver. I don't know the drivers name. Mr. Chambers and myself stopped the stage that was going to Prescott. That occurred on the 27th day of June last in Maricopa County where the stage was stopped. I think there was someone else besides the driver along side of the driver. That was the driver that was on the stage that night (witness pointing to Mr. Emas Nichol, in the court room). We both stood on the left side of the stage, on the farther side from the driver, when the stage was robbed that night.

Mr. Chambers, the defendant, had a handkerchief on his face that night, and had in his hand a rifle. He presented the rifle at the driver of the stage. He said "stop." The driver stopped. The defendant said "throw off the box." The driver threw off the box. That box was the Wells Fargo and Company box. The box was broken open when it was thrown off. It was broken afterwards. I think it was me that done it. Mr. Chambers, the defendant, in this case was with me when the box was broken open. After the box was thrown from the stage, we carried it a little distance, about 30 or 40 yards.

This was done between 10 and 12 o'clock at night about 2 _ miles from the town of Gillett, where myself and Mr. Chambers broke the box open. We found $22.50 and a shawl. Nothing else was found in it. The money we took home with us. I mean by home, the town of Gillett. Afterwards we divided the money between us, the defendant and myself. We left the shawl on the box. After the box was broken open we left there.

The boxes that Wells Fargo & Co. use to carry their funds on the roads are wooden boxes iron bound. That was the kind of box the driver threw off that night when Mr. Chambers asked the driver to throw off the box. When we opened the box we found a shawl in it. There was wrapping the shawl some kind of yellow or brown paper. I did not notice if there was any piece masked in it. We left the shawl in the box there. I do not remember any baby shoes. I don't remember what the defendant did say when we were going away from the box. After we got through with the box we went down to Gillett. We walked part of the way over the hills and part of the way over the road. After we got to Gillett, myself and the defendant slept in the same house. We divided the $22.50 we got out of the box some days afterward. During the time before the division was made, I kept the money.

I have known Mr. Chambers, the defendant, and first met him about last Christmas. There was not any United States mail bag thrown that night and no letters. The passengers were examined or searched. Before the 27th of June last, Mr. Chambers and myself had some conversations about robbing the stage. It was understood between Mr. Chambers and myself that on the 27th of June we should rob the stage. Mr. Chambers has been with me since about the 4th of April last, I think.

The defendant told me that he had been in Colorado and New Mexico a great deal. He never told me about the robbery of stages or Wells Fargo & Co. in Colorado or other places. He helped me in the shop, not under any regular wages, he was just there helping me whenever I had any work in the shop. Mr. Chambers, the defendant, first advanced the idea of robbing the stage. I have not shown any of the officers where any plunder from the stages has been concealed that was taken out of the stage on June 27th, 1883.

James Larsen

Clearly, Larsen had been well instructed to talk about his friend, Chambers, as, "Mr. Chambers, the defendant." Larsen not only got the lighter sentence, but was also pardoned by Governor Zulick within three years after his incarceration. Frontier justice worked in strange ways.

In spite of the capture and imprisonment of these two scalawags, the stage road north of Gillett continued to be a favorite spot for holdups.

January 14, 1884
More Stage Robbery

Last night as the south bound stage on the Black Canyon route reached a point between the Canyon and Gillett it was halted by a man with a shotgun. He immediately, on the driver holding up, gave the order "throw out that box," which was complied with and then came the order "throw out the mail," and that was complied with also. "Drive on," and the driver drove on and that was all the stage people knew about. There was one passenger on board, Mr. Frank Durand, and he was not molested. The driver was Mr. Chas. McCool, a new man. Mr. Chas. Charlebois who is in the butchering business at Tip Top and Tempe with Mr. Marlow was riding immediately behind the stage on horseback and halted with it and went on with it without being molested.

After halting the stage the robber seemed to hesitate for about a minute before the box and mail came out and probably at this time he first discovered Charlebois, but concluded as no demonstrations were made against him to "put it through" as he had begun. It is not known whether there was anything in the express box or not, but it is probable that it was very light as little express goes through by this route to or from Prescott now. What he got from the mails cannot be known for some time.

April 22, 1884
"Hold Up"

The south bound coach from Prescott to Phoenix, when about six miles north of Gillett, was stopped by another "lone highwayman," who demanded and received the Wells Fargo box and went on his way rejoicing, no doubt, though there was little or nothing in the box. There was but one passenger and he and the mails were undisturbed. The robbery took place about a mile from the old Swilling ranch. It is asserted that it is well known who does this business in that region of the country. If this be the fact it might be well enough to take in the gentleman, though no doubt he is poor, as the pickings from the express box on that line have for a number of months been very scarce. It might save him a great many disappointments, however if the officers would care for him, and it might also keep him from being shot by some excitable passenger.

June 3, 1884
Same Old Place

On the arrival of the stage from Prescott yesterday, it was learned that the mails and the passengers this time, had been subject to the usual freebooters' inspection on the Black Canyon route, some distance above Gillett. McCool, the driver, after being ordered to "halt," and while the robbers were going through the one passenger and the mails, was fired upon by the man who held the gun, probably through the agitation of the latter or some move on the part of McCool. The charge missed its object, however. The passenger lost his coat, vest, gold watch, and reports also $200 in cash. What was in Wells Fargo box is unknown.

On another page:

Jesse Robinson, the gentleman who was cleaned out in the Gillett stage robbery, arrived by this morning's coach. He lost $190 in money, two watches and most of his clothes. The robbers compelled him to break open the express box for them and were a burly couple of individuals generally that would not hesitate to shoot and did shoot at the slightest provocation.

In desperation, the *Daily Phoenix Herald* proclaimed on June 5, 1884; "Gillett stage 'robbers' is becoming a very common expression. It renews its existence in the public mind once a month or oftener."

Another Double Robbery

As seen before, sometimes the stage robbers could get two for the price of one, a good bargain any day. From the *Daily Phoenix Herald*, August 18, 1885:

Knights of the Road

Two More Stages Robbed—
Three Masked Men Take in Both Stages

Between New River and Gillett

They Take Both Teams but Get Little Coin

Somebody who does not read the public prints very much continues to try to get something out of Wells Fargo and Co.'s express boxes, on the route between Phoenix and Prescott, which ceased to carry coin and bullion over that route some months ago. An attempt was made last evening on both stages to squeeze something out of the boxes, but of course it was a failure.

As Charlie Hubbard, the driver of the south bound stage which reached Phoenix this morning, reached a point about three miles this side of Gillett at about 10:30 o'clock last night, he was stopped by three highwaymen and told to deliver up the express, which he did, as gracefully as circumstances would permit. On their first appearance two showed up from behind the bush, and disguised as they were, in masks and blankets wrapped around them, the driver thought they were Indians, about to attack him, especially as they came out mumbling unintelligibly, and drew his revolver, but on glancing down the side of the road near him, he found himself covered by a shot gun of a third party which changed his mind as to the shooting part of the business.

The express box was broken open by the use of a hatchet by one of the robbers but nothing was found in it more than a China letter. They then demanded the purse of the only passenger, Mr. A. Berchum of Gillett, who was on his way to Phoenix, he had but six dollars with him and the robbers divided it, taking three. They then took the team, two horses, forbid the driver to come down the road in this direction and started south as they said, to rob the north bound coach, which would be along in an hour or two. Charlie Hubbard went back to Gillett on foot and got another team for his wagon, and with his passengers, came on south.

The highway men had met the north bound coach about two miles beyond New River station. It had no passengers on board. They took the express box, broke it open and found nothing in it to amount to anything. They also broke open a box of fruit on board, scattering it around, helping their selves. The driver of the north bound coach was J. S. Hallabaugh and this was his first trip for the company. Finding nothing in the box they also appropriated his team, two horses, and came on south. Hallabaugh says as also does Hubbard that no horses were in sight when the robbery was being committed though Hubbard tracked one of his horses as he came south by a peculiarity of the hoof. The brunt of the transaction this time will fall on the Stage Company in the loss of the four horses should they not be recovered though the probabilities are that they will be found as they were probably brought immediately to the vicinity of this valley or left along the road. The tracks were followed along the road south to this side of Beechum's station and it is quite likely that the robbery was committed by the same parties who robbed the Maricopa stage beyond Gila on the 7th inst. In fact, two of the robbers tally in size with those who did that job. This time two of them were tall men about six feet in height and one a short heavy set man probably 5 ft. 4 in. In height. They were thoroughly masked, spoke good English without a brogue and talked freely.

The horses they took were a span of sorrels, one with stripe in face and has the heaves; the other a smaller sorrel sway backed and high head; the second span was a sorrel and a bay. All of the horses are shod all around and one of them has a very round hoof, so much so that it is quite noticeable.

The mails were not disturbed in either coach, the idea of the robbers seems to be to make a haul from the express boxes which for some months back have carried nothing but letters and packages a fact that has been well known among the newspaper reading public, an announcement to that effect having been made by the company some time since.

A day later two of the horses came walking down Washington street and a third was reported to be out on the Grand canal. From this it was concluded that the highwaymen must have returned to the valley and were still there. A huge effort was expended on the part of the highwaymen with not a lot to show for it.

Stage robbing, as described in the foregoing articles, would have to be called more of a sport than occupation. Certainly, none of these men made a living at it, yet the stages continued to be robbed. Possibly the challenge outweighed the risk, and the poor rewards!

Territory of Arizona
Executive Department
Office of the Governor

Whereas: I have been informed that on the night of the fourth instant, the stage from Prescott to Phoenix was stopped by two high-waymen near Bumble Bee on the Black Canyon Road and the United States mail rifled.

Now Therefore: I, C. Meyer Zulick Governor of Arizona, by virtue of the authority in me vested, do, hereby, offer a reward of two hundred and fifty dollars for the arrest and conviction of each of the Robbers.

In witness whereof I have hereunto set my hand and caused the Great seal of the Territory to be affixed Done at Prescott this fifth day of June A.D. 1886.

C. Meyer Zulick

By the Governor
J. E. Harish
Acting Secretary of Territory

Governor Zulick Offers a Reward for Yet Another Stage Robbery in 1886

Photo L. J. Hanchett Jr.

Black Canyon Station

Cordes, Arizona

All travelers are hereby notified that after July 1,1894, a new stage line will run between Phoenix, Black Canyon, and Prescott. This line will make the quickest time and yet give the passengers eight hours rest on the road during the night. Leave Prescott 8 a.m. Tuesday, Thursday, and Saturday. W. J. Mulvenon, agent.

Advertisement in *Miner,* June, 1894.

Chapter Ten
Stations on the Road

For those who have trouble sleeping on today's airplanes or in a modern automobile, the above statement is somewhat of a curiosity. How could anyone hope to sleep on a stage coach traveling at night over some of the roughest country to be found in the U.S.? Was this a joke, or were our pioneer ancestors really so tough that they could sleep under those conditions? What about the highwaymen who frequented those curves and grades, could they be ignored as well? Certainly, just as today, travelers would have to get off the road and pull into a stage station equipped with sleeping quarters if they wanted any chance for real relaxation.

Most stage stations were initially named for some nearby geographic feature such as Agua Fria—after the river of that name, or Black Canyon—after that creek. Many would eventually carry the name of the person who developed that spot such as Cordes, Goddard, or Gillett.

Unlike the Wickenburg route, the Black Canyon Road followed pretty much the same path until modern road construction methods came into use. Of course, that was long after the stage lines had breathed their last. Stage stations still came and went, but in this case it was mostly due to a fresh intersection with another road to reach some new destination taking precedence over a previous stopping point.

Much like the stations along the Wickenburg road, some became famous while others simply served their function of providing rest and sustenance for travelers. Of those on the Black Canyon Road, only Gillett, once a destination in itself, is well remembered and therefore deserving of its own chapter. The rest are covered briefly in this section including one station where nothing exciting ever happened. Bumble Bee would have to take the prize for being the dullest of stations.

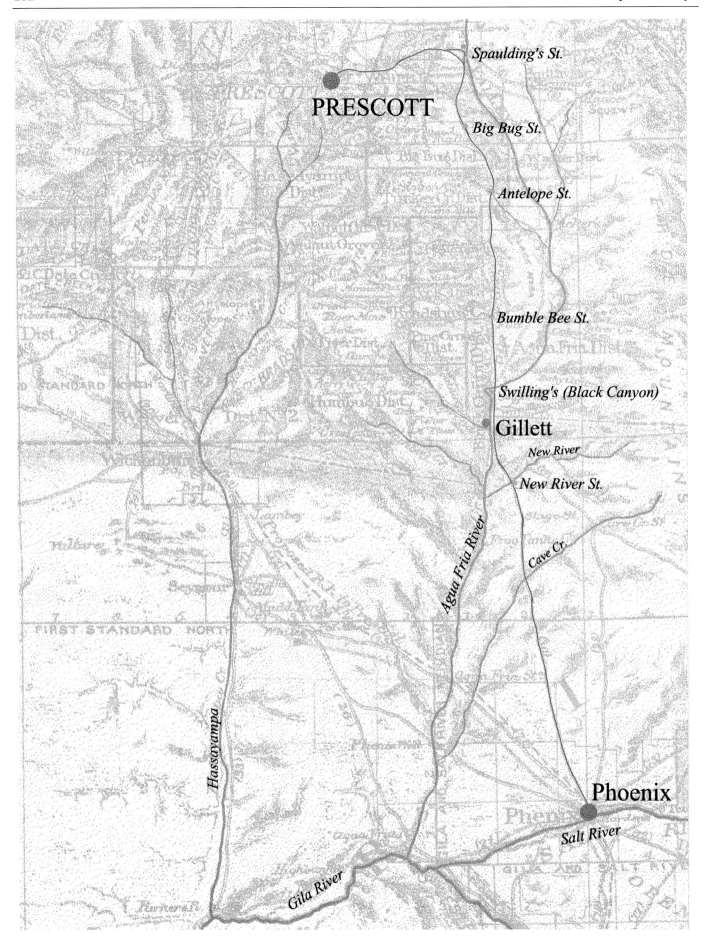

Spaulding's St.

PRESCOTT

Big Bug St.

Antelope St.

Bumble Bee St.

Swilling's (Black Canyon)

Gillett

New River

New River St.

Agua Fria River

Cave Cr.

Hassayampa

Phoenix

Salt River

Gila River

Stations Along the Black Canyon Road

Courtesy Sharlot Hall Museum

Agua Fria

The Agua Fria Station, located near what is now known as Dewey, was first established by Henry Spaulding sometime before 1876. Spaulding had purchased a one half interest in the ranch at this location belonging to Dennis Marr. Located just down the road towards Camp Verde, a few hundred yards beyond the intersection of that road and the Black Canyon route, Spaulding's station was simply a stopping point for travelers along those two roads. Stagecoach travel did not formally begin for another two years. According to the *Miner* of January 28, 1876, Spaulding's wife was already well known for, "steaming hot dinners of chicken, mushrooms and all other kinds of good things, such as nobody knows better how to prepare than Mrs. Spaulding."

As early as 1877, it was known as Spaulding's Station. By February 22, 1878, the *Miner* asked its readers to, "Notice the advertisement of Spaulding's Station on Agua Fria. It is hardly worthwhile to say a word about it, as nearly everybody knows that it is the best stopping place in the Territory, and we 'don't bar nobody, nor nothin.' The station is right on the road from Prescott to Verde, and but a few hundred yards out of the way for those going to Gillett, Tiptop, Big Bug, Kit Carson and Peck, via Agua Fria route."

It seems characteristic of station keepers, men who had daily contact with the traveling public, to occasionally have run-ins with some of the more unsavory individuals who came along. Sometimes the result was injury or death for the station keeper. In this case, Spaulding got the best of his opponent, who then filed a complaint with the local Justice of the Peace. Although Spaulding was made to appear before Justice Noyes in Prescott for the offense of pointing a double barreled shotgun at Jacob Armentrout, he was, according to the *Miner* of February 21, 1879, discharged, as the Territory had failed to make a case against him.

As early as 1870, this area, known as Agua Fria, sported a sophisticated flour mill. The mill serviced Woolsey and Lonesome Valleys which by then had, "over 2,000 acres planted in wheat, barley, corn, potatoes and tame grasses."

Grains were not the only thing processed in the area, as the Agua Fria Furnace was also located nearby. Ore was smelted from such mines as the Silver Prince, Black Warrior, Kit Carson, Silver Flake, and Mike Herman. The result of this operation was a base bullion worth over two thousand dollars per ton.

Life on the frontier could still have some glamour as shown in the following article from the *Miner* dated August 15, 1879.

> Perhaps the finest and most tastily arranged parlor, of its size, within a thousand miles of Prescott, is that one at the Agua Fria Station, arranged, fitted up, furnished and decorated by those two beautiful little Misses, Ida and Emma Spaulding. The room is detached from the station buildings, is about eight feet square with a portico in front and the interior is a perfect representation of a ladies parlor richly decorated with pictures hung about the walls, miniature furniture, house plants and everything necessary for convenience and elegance.

> Their three year old brother, Clarence, like many another and older brother of older sisters in larger establishments, is every ready to walk in, with his pants in his boots, and disarrange and muss up things generally, to the great annoyance of these little housekeepers, and apparent

mortification of the wax and China dolls that sit in the cushioned chairs or recline lazily or luxuriantly on the sofas and lounges; nevertheless they manage to keep their little parlor neat as a pin, and take great pride and pleasure in inviting their friends to call.

A traveler visiting the Spaulding Station in 1876 made the following observation on the children there.

> It is not every place one stops in traveling that the children are an attraction, but at the Agua Fria Station we are free to acknowledge a liking for the children, or a weakness if it be one, to wish one's self back again in cap and pinafore, to tread the rough path of the world anew, with all the trials, hardships and disappointments that an experience of a lifetime has taught us in store for those who are just setting out on a journey which we shall soon have accomplished.

On December 3, 1888, Spaulding sold his ranch to Robert DeLarge of New Mexico for $5,000. DeLarge was a stock raiser who intended to place a large number of cattle at the ranch. Spaulding agreed to run the operation for DeLarge during its first year of operation.

Courtesy Arizona Historical Society/Tucson

Big Bug

There were two separate locations and names for the station on Big Bug Creek. Originally it was called Cottonwood Station and was situated at the intersection of the Black Canyon and Peck mine roads. W. H. McMichael was the station keeper during 1879. In that same year the Big Bug station came into being and was located $2^1/_2$ miles south of the Cottonwood station. At that time Snider, Munsey and Company held possessory rights to 160 acres and the station.

By 1880, Snider had apparently sold out to his partner as William M. Muncy was then owner of the land and station. On July 13, 1882, Muncy sold his rights for $1,200 to Joseph Mayer who had previously owned a hotel and restaurant at Tip Top mine. Mayer paid

Munsey in gold carried by his wife Sadie in a little sewing bag underneath spools of thread, needles, scissors and socks to be darned.

Mayer went right to work building a new home and station. A central hallway divided the guest rooms from the family's quarters. A large dining room and kitchen were located next to the general merchandise store which had a small bar at one end. Long porches, front and back, completed the new setup.

Mayer soon became famous for his meals and hospitality. Sadie took on the job of first Postmistress for Mayer in the year 1884 and served in that capacity as well as "town doctor" for many years.

Joe Mayer clearly had a lock on the stage business in Mayer. By 1885, the station at Cottonwood had ceased to be although McMichael was still living at the same location.

Life wouldn't always run smoothly for the Mayers, for they too had some rough spots. In February, 1890, a large dam built six miles upstream by a placer mining company broke under the pressure of very heavy rains. Mayer hadn't bought into the words of the man in charge of the dam who insisted it was strong enough to hold back the worst of floods. Mayer moved his family and the majority of his household furnishings to high ground just in time to watch the roaring flood waters sweep everything else away.

Mayer of course rebuilt the stage station adding guest cottages, a livery operation, and eventually a powder house to store in-transit dynamite away from his buildings. Brick buildings followed until Joe Mayer had interests in much of what became downtown Mayer.

What had begun as a remote stage station turned into a bustling community with its namesake, Joe Mayer, the town father. In 1898 the railroad came to town and stagecoaches were no longer needed for transportation to Prescott. Mail for small communities to the south was still carried by horse drawn vehicles for many more years.

Antelope

Originally known as Antelope Station, taken from the stream that runs nearby, the first keeper for this station appears to have been William Powell, as we learn from an article in the *Miner* dated April 12, 1878. Later on, this location was renamed Cordes after the family that owned it beginning in 1882.

Letter From Antelope

We are camped for the night at the hospitable station of Wm. Powell, which by the way, is a credit to this section of what was once the stronghold of the Apaches. One mile west from this place the noble, brave Townsend was murdered by these fiends. Were all the Indian lives in the Territory sacrificed as a retribution for that of Townsend, the scout and frontiersman, it would fall short of accomplishing that end. From Spaulding station on the Agua Fria, the road to this place leads over a rolling country and is one of the best in Yavapai county. ... The descent from Prescott to this place is great, consequently, the difference in climate is perceptibly felt. The cottonwoods have donned their Spring apparel of green, and the contrast is great between those on Granite Creek and those which grace the bubbling streams in this more tropical clime. Grass is green, growing luxuriantly and no complaint is heard from stock growers on that score. Early on the morrow with

Earp [Virgil] as reinsman, we will be off for Gillett, the bullion producing camp of Yavapai, and until we reach there, adieu.

The *Miner* of June 25, 1878 reported that Alfred LeValley, of the Prescott and Gillett Stage Company (factually, Caldwell and LeValley Stage Company) had rented the station at Antelope and had moved his family to that location. LeValley told everyone that his reason for doing so was to lower his cost of boarding horses for the stage line. Later, circumstances convinced many that he was really setting the stage for a quick escape from creditors.

By February of 1879, Jack McAlister was the new keeper at Antelope Station. In November of that year, McAlister sold out to Otto Bolin and possibly his brother for $1,500.

The story of Ottto Bolin and his murder at Antelope station is typical of many unnecessary deaths on the Arizona frontier. Alcohol and its indiscriminant use resulted in many foolish killings.

The scene was Otto Bolin's house at Antelope Station. Present inside the house were John Grasse, a traveler who had stopped for a while due to muddy roads in the area, Otto Bolin, station proprietor, and Wesley Clanton, a stockman from Big Bug. Outside, just a few yards away, was hired hand, Adam Mannsmann, chopping wood. It was a cold winter day, January 21, 1882.

Bolin was serving whiskey to Grasse, who, by later accounts, was already very drunk. Grasse started to drink only a part of each shot, and throw the rest into the fire. Bolin, offended by Grasse's actions, asked why he was throwing whiskey into the fire. Grasse told Bolin it was none of his business what he did with it as he had already paid for it. Bolin then accused Grasse of saying that he would fix Bolin before night. Grasse denied having said that but Bolin became very excited and told Grasse to get his weapon as he was "ready" for him.

Both men went outside where Grasse had stashed a pistol. As they stepped out onto the front porch Grasse reached for his gun, but Bolin got to it first and then proceeded to push Grasse down on the floor of the porch. Bolin, according to witnesses, was sober at the time.

Bolin and Grasse made numerous threats to each other and then Bolin pushed him down again, only this time Grasse fell to the ground off the porch. Grasse next told Bolin that he would kill him.

Soon Bolin was being chased by Grasse who had a knife in his hand. Bolin suddenly stopped and grabbed Grasse by the coat while yelling at him, "You Goddamned fool, you're going to kill me."

Grasse stabbed Bolin in the left side of the chest inflicting a wound that was one and one-half inches wide and six inches deep. As he ran past the hired hand who was chopping wood, Bolin cried out, "I am stabbed." Bolin was still able to run another twenty feet into his house where, after locking the door, he laid down on his bed.

Bolin also passed by Clanton who, by then, was outside looking for his horse so that he could leave the premises. Bolin told Clanton,

"He has stabbed me right through the heart and I am going to die." After Bolin went inside, Grasse told Clanton that Bolin had kicked him. Grasse asked Clanton to go inside the house to see if Bolin was badly hurt.

Clanton entered the house and found Bolin stabbed in the left breast. He asked Bolin if he wanted a doctor but Bolin said it was no use, he could not get there in time. Bolin was then asked by Clanton if he wanted his brother at Tip Top notified. Again, Bolin exclaimed it would be of no use. Bolin asked Clanton to sew up his wound which Clanton obligingly did.

Clanton then left the house and went to Bumblebee to send word to Bolin's brother and notify the authorities. By evening Clanton returned to Bolin's side and advised him that his brother had been called for whereupon Bolin asked if he was told to come "quickly." Clanton said he had done that.

Bolin asked Clanton if he thought he might survive the wound. Clanton judiciously told Bolin that he was not too familiar with wounds of that type but thought he might live. Bolin died at 3 a.m. the next day.

Grasse was tried and sentenced to four years at the Yuma Prison for manslaughter. No doubt his drunkenness and Bolin's aggressiveness led the judge to the lesser sentence.

Nearly a year later, on January 25, 1883, John Henry Cordes purchased the station from Otto Bolin's brother, Augustus, for $769.43. Cordes had come to Antelope from Gillett where he had labored at the Tiptop mill for a couple of years. There he worked two shifts a day, night shift at the mill, and day shift tending bar at a local saloon, saving money to buy the station.

John Henry brought his wife, Lizzie, to Antelope with him and together they raised a large family. In 1886, Cordes applied for a post office using the name Antelope. Because of the confusion with Antelope Valley on the west side of the Bradshaws he was forced to reapply changing the name to Cordes, which stands today.

Bumble Bee

The *Miner* for December 12, 1879, tells us that Mr. Bobo was making improvements at Bumble Bee Station. The tax roles for Yavapai County show A. I. Bobo in possession of the station at Bumble Bee during 1880. The next year W. W. Snyder held 160 acres of land and the improvements known as, "Bumble Bee station on the Black Canyon road to Phoenix."

Snyder held onto the station until February 21, 1885 when he paid $1,000 to his wife Ida for all of her rights to the "Bumble Bee Ranch and Stage Station," as well as her interest in the brand 1A and all stock so branded. Later that year the property and stock were, according to the tax records, in the possession of Snyder and Ellis.

Surely Bumble Bee Flats, where the station was located, could have been called Peaceful Place as few violent deeds occurred there. Maybe we should be content with finding one spot in Arizona not known for its raucous behavior. Whatever it lacks in exciting history, this location certainly makes up in beautiful scenery.

Located just below Sunset Point on the modern Black Canyon Highway, tens of thousands of Arizona visitors look down on its peaceful beauty each year. If they were to close their eyes for a moment, and listen to the sounds which fill the wind, they might still catch an echo of stage driver McCool shouting to his horses on the old stage road a thousand feet below.

Black Canyon

Jack Swilling was probably the first official station keeper at Black Canyon. Arriving in the area during the early 1870s, Jack did much to develop mining, farming, ranching, and road construction there.

The *Miner* of June 18, 1875 provided some reasonable predictions concerning the Black Canyon location.

Black Canyon and Below—H. G. Ballou, the Express man, has recently been on a prospect to the lower Agua Fria, where he found some immense gravel beds that in time, he says, will pay and afford work for a large number of miners, but, at the present high rate for transportation, it does not offer sufficient inducement for a company to take hold and bring in water, which, although in abundance is to be had, will cost more, in proportion to the pay, than the diggings will warrant. Mitchell is running two arrastas on the mine he recently bought from Swilling and Swilling has established a ranch below the Canyon, where he has in a crop of corn, quite a large field of sorghum and an extensive vineyard. This will be the favorite Station on the New or Helling's road to Phoenix when travel springs up on that route as it is bound to do on account of the great savings in distance. A mail route is much needed on that route in order to assist in the development of the country. Prescott is now their nearest P.O., and forty or fifty miles is too far for a community to have to send for their mail.

Swilling's arrest in early 1878 and subsequent death later that year precluded his ever running a full blown stage station. Nonetheless, his popularity with the traveling public and his hospitality at his ranch should earn him the title of Black Canyon's first station keeper.

Charles E. Goddard took over the job of station keeper at a location north and east of Swilling's ranch in 1895. On the south bank of the Agua Fria river, Goddard maintained his station for the next eight years with little or no problems, until the station keeper's greatest fear came true for him in 1903.

It was the first day of February in that year, and around the dinner table at Canon or Goddard Station five adults were busy consuming the evening meal. Those present were C. E. Goddard, station keeper, his wife, Frank Goddard, the station keeper's brother, Frank Cox, an assistant to Mr. Goddard, and Milton Turnbull, a local resident. The events of that night could well be classified as some of the most hideous to have occurred in the Arizona Territory. The testimony of Milton Turnbull at the Coroner's inquest for Mr. C. E. Goddard best describes what took place.

... we had just started to eat when two Mexicans came into the dining room without knocking at the door. Mr. Goddard arose from his place at the table and walking toward them inquired in Spanish what they wanted. One of them replied "supper." Mr. Goddard replied as soon as the family gets through eating my wife will get you some supper. The Mexican replied, "We want supper right now." Mr. Goddard replied, "Excuse us; the family is eating and you will get your supper just as soon as we are through." The Mexican that was doing the talking took a few steps toward Mr. Goddard, looked at the other Mexican and said "Bueno," which was apparently a signal to commence shooting and he at once pulled a gun and fired at Mr. Goddard who fell to his knees and said, "Oh my God." The Mexican at the time of the shooting was within an arms length of Mr. Goddard. I think that Mexican fired three shots. After the first shot Mr. Goddard crawled to the front room. Frank Goddard got out of the dining room into the front room which was dark and looked for a gun. Mrs. Goddard rushed out of doors through the kitchen, ran around the house and went into the front room through the front door. At the first shot I slid off my chair and went under the table. The second shot, the light on the dinning room table went out. I remained under the table 'till the Mexicans went out, a period I should say of three minutes. Mrs. Goddard called to me from the front room, "Milton, if you are not hurt come in here and get a gun." I went into the front room, she handed me a gun and I watched at one of the doors leading into the dining room thinking the Mexicans would come back in as soon as they had loaded their guns which I could hear them doing on the outside. They did not come in however, but went to the store which was by the side of the house. The light was burning in the store, I heard them open the store door, and a few minutes later close it. I thought they must be in the store so we closed the doors leading into the dining room, and I took a position at the window of the front bedroom expecting to get a shot at them when they came out of the store. I remained at the window the balance of the night 'till broad daylight but did not again catch sight of the Mexicans. Frank Goddard and Mrs. Goddard were in the front room guarding and nursing Mr. Goddard.

I did not take particular notice of the Mexicans when they came into the room—I had seen them earlier in the afternoon at a distance. They both appeared to be the same height and about the same size and were dressed alike. They wore light colored duck coats, blue overalls, light shirts, cotton I think, black hats medium sized, straight brimmed and one of them at least wore a moustache, but I am not certain about the other. I did not see any belts. I think thy carried their guns in the top of their pants. I am pretty certain Mr. Goddard thought the Mexican was feeling in his pocket for money to pay for his supper when the Mexican pulled his gun. I should judge the Mexicans to have been each about thirty years old.

A separate inquest was held for Mr. Cox and again, Turnbull's testimony was the most revealing.

Without any warning the Mexicans pulled guns and began to shoot. One Mexican stood at the side of the table and the other one at the end of the table and close to the side of the table where Mr. Cox and I were seated. Mr. Cox was to my right therefore between this Mexican and me. This Mexican shot at Mr. Cox at the same second that the other Mexican shot Mr. Goddard. The next shot was fired at me and I fell out of the chair and under the table, where I lay as if dead until the Mexicans left the room when I got up and ran into the front room. In the excitement, I was under the impression that Mr. Cox was not hit and that he had got out of the room through the door by which the Mexicans came in. I thought Cox would be back with help and several times during the night said to Mrs. Goddard, "It is funny Cox don't come with help." I did not know he was dead until the next morning after day light. Cox never spoke to the Mexicans during the time they were in the house.

Turnbull was apparently the man who took the news to Phoenix and the Sheriff's office there. Throughout February suspects were apprehended and Mrs. Goddard traveled many miles in an attempt to identify the right men. Not until a pair of Mexicans fitting the description furnished by the survivors were located in Naco, Old Mexico, would Mrs. Goddard positively recognize the men who had killed her husband and Frank Cox.

Mexican officials were still reluctant to turn the murderers over to U.S. Justice. Only a clever ruse, carried out with help from the railroad authorities, would get the two wanted men into U.S. Territory where they could be arrested. On the very next railroad payday, the two were given paychecks drawn on a bank in Douglas, Arizona. Having been told that those checks could only be cashed at that bank, both men hurried across the border to collect their pay.

Arizona lawmen were, of course, waiting for them and whisked them off to Prescott to stand trial as soon as they were apprehended. Hilario Hidalgo and Francisco Renteria were tried and found guilty of murder on March 25, 1903. By July 31st of that year they were both swinging from the hangman's scaffold in Prescott.

New River

The earliest reference to New River occurred in the *Arizona Sentinel* dated September 25, 1875. Mr. Griffith, state agent for Kerens and Mitchell, informed the editor that the New River station would be abandoned immediately. The editor then concurred stating, "This is a good move as that station has been so infested with Mexican robbers and border outlaws that it has been impossible to find a reliable man who will stay there."

Two years later, a traveler from Prescott to Camp McDowell noted in the *Miner*:

I arrived here after a very pleasant trip from Prescott, by way of Black Canyon, New River, and Cave Creek. Patterson's improvements on the Black Canyon road are noticeable everywhere along the line of march, and in some places are of such a nature as to call down upon him eternal blessings from the lips of the traveler. The road being somewhat new, the late rains have washed it out in several places, but a couple of good, strong Hiberians, with a shovel apiece, would repair them in a few hours. The trip from Prescott to New River is too well known to be described over. It has been "set up" so often that I suppose you have it standing in the galleys, and in case you are short of copy, just sandwich it in this letter, and I will take a fresh start from New River.

New River is a little settlement with a population of two inhabitants; but these same two inhabitants are just at present very enthusiastic on the future prosperity of their embryo village. They see in the dim vista of the future the tide of immigration pouring into their little valley, and only hear the dull thump of the lumberman's axe felling the pines preparatory to their being used in the erection of comfortable dwellings. In fact, if such and such a thing happens, they would not take any odds from any town in the Territory; nay, not even Prescott. You have already asked yourself, what can be the cause of this sudden exultation, and I will satisfy your curiosity by informing you that it is no less than the erection of the Tip Top mill in the vicinity of New River. One of the aforesaid two inhabitants informed me that the mill will be situated at the mouth of Grand Wash, about three and a half miles from New River Station, and Jack Swilling had the contract for cutting the wood. The mill is coming by way of Phoenix, as will all the freight for the mine and mill, and this will necessarily make quite a lively little station out of New River.

Once again, development of a new location was dependent on mining and the labor force and materials upon which it in turn thrived.

A *Miner* notice dated April 12, 1878 stated that J. L. Lamlin, formerly of the Barnard stables in Prescott, had rented the New River Station in connection with W. H. Caldwell of the Patterson and Caldwell Stage Line. They planned to keep an A-1 station and dairy.

Charles Mullen may have been the first station owner in New River as the Maricopa County Tax Rolls for 1879 mention a Mullen's Station there. That was probably the station discussed in a *Miner* article dated April 18, 1879, which noted that John Taylor, in company with R. Gillespie and Charles Spring, burned down the New River Station south of Gillett and committed highway robbery. The three were captured in Pinal County but subsequently escaped.

Between 1881 and 1883, George Hall was in possession of the New River Station. In 1883, the *Daily Phoenix Herald* noted:

> The Black Canyon Stage this morning brought information of the destruction of the barn of the stage company by fire at the New River Station yesterday at 2 o'clock. All the hay, grain, harnesses, etc. stored there and six head of stage horses were burned. There was no insurance and the loss is estimated at about $1,500.

By 1892, a new stage route was in place between Prescott and Phoenix. This one was called the Castle Creek route and came through Copper Basin, Walnut Grove Dam, and Castle Hot Springs.

New routes of course meant new stations and such was the case on the Castle Creek route. Another New River station popped up again on New River but this time some nine miles southeast of Frog Tanks (now Lake Pleasant).

Five weeks after taking possession of that station in late April 1900, Anton Olsen and a man named Stewart were murdered by four Mexicans. The *Arizona Republican* for June 9 and 10, 1900, revealed the following under the title, "A Station Slaughter." The murders were compared to that of Vulture Mine Superintendent, Gribble, in 1888.

Olsen and Stewart were both found shot, lying outside the station house. The murders had been followed by robbery, as beds were torn apart and cigars and other merchandise was scattered throughout. The murders were said to have been committed by four Mexicans who had tried to murder a prospector by the name of W. H. Rice the night before.

Rice and Dan Nelson, a Deputy from Yavapai County, started in pursuit of the murders after noting the condition of the bodies and effects of the men at the station. Sadly, a picture of what was thought to be Stewart's wife, from Minnesota, was found in the debris.

A peddler named Van Kirk and a woman living near the Arizona Canal crossing just north of Phoenix gave the following descriptions of the four. "Two rode bay horses, one a sorrel and one a buckskin horse. All were armed with revolvers and two carried Winchesters. One of them wore a sombrero."

The murderers were believed to be members of a gang of nine desperate Chihuahua Mexicans who operated around Clifton for several years. Five were killed in one way or another and the leader was captured, tried at Solomonville, convicted, and sentenced to be hanged. On the night before the execution he broke out of jail. He had killed three women and is said to have a record of twenty killings in this territory and Sonora. It was supposed that he was the short, stout man with the long mustache and stubby black beard described by Van Kirk and others.

The last word received was that the outlaws had led their pursuers to Mesa, doubled back, and were looking for an outlet into the Tonto country. How many outlaws, both red and white, had chosen that path for their escape?

Courtesy Arizona Historical Society/Tucson

The Stage to Castle Hot Springs

Courtesy Arizona Historical Foundation

Frog Tanks

Rothrock Photo of Gillett, Arizona Territory—1882

Photo L. J. Hanchett Jr.

Gillett, Arizona 1998

Photo L. J. Hanchett Jr.

Ruins of Burfind Hotel, Gillett

Gillett—This, we learn, is the name of the new town now in course of erection, near the Tip-top Co.'s mill on the Aqua Fria. It is named in honor of Mr. Gillett, one of the Company's best men and miners. The location of the town is said to be all that could be desired.

The Enterprise, January 30, 1878

Chapter Eleven
Gillett

Courtesy Arizona Historical Society/Tucson

Dan B. Gillett—Mine Superintendent

A lot of hope and a multi-million dollar silver mine was all it took to start a new town in the Arizona Territory. *The Enterprise* went on to say:

Mr. Seely, who arrived from Gillett today, is our authority for the foregoing statements. He further informs us that the Tip-top Mining Company is going to supply the town with water, by means of pipes, from a point $1^1/_2$ miles above, on the creek [Agua Fria] where the water runs the whole year round.

Anders and Rowe are erecting a large warehouse.

Mr. Seely brought with him some fine looking specimens of Tip-top silver ore, which may be seen and admired at the office of Mr. C. C. Bean, upstairs, in the bank building.

L. Levy, who also came in today, and who is about to start a business in Gillett, says the place is one of the liveliest he has ever been in. Buildings going up in every direction, and hope, sweet hope, written upon every man's countenance. T. J. Drum, W. W. Hutchinson and several other Prescotites are down there. Drum is a lawyer, who, like most lawyers, likes to have his fun. Knowing this, the "boys" of Gilllette kept saying to one another, upon Drum's arrival there, "Let's fire him out, we want no lawyers here," etc. When Drum was about ready to leave, several gents volunteered to saddle his horse; he didn't object, so they fixed his saddle on in a way it shouldn't have been-pummel to tail and 'tother end foremost; covered it nicely, with his overcoat, when Drum, after an ineffectual attempt to mount, fixed things in proper shape and "fired himself out" amid the cheers of his friends.

Just two weeks earlier, a team had been sent to the area to survey the townsite and lay off lots, etc. The mill itself had come from California through Maricopa Wells. An army of mechanics was forming at what would be Gillett for the purpose of erecting the mill which was estimated to be complete around March 1,1878.

A letter to T. C. Bray, a merchant in Prescott, reveals much of what was going on in Gillett.

Dear sir: I arrived at the Tip-top mill site, after a long and tedious journey. Tender smiles greeted me from the corner of every saloon, and they are growing numerous I assure you. Messrs. Ganz and Co. have opened out their liquor department, but only temporarily, which will answer the purpose until their store is completed, where in a couple of weeks, the choicest wines and liquors will be lavishly dealt out to lovers of the "critter." The town-site has been located, surveyed and lots are being rapidly disposed of. They vary from $100 to $250 each, according to location. Your friend, "Kentuck," has taken unto himself a lot as near a corner as possible: but you know he doesn't like to deal in real estate. The principal streets in this city are, viz: California, Mill, Main, Pine and Market: if there are any more I can't see them for the brush. I think California Street will be the most popular because my lot is on it. Three buildings are in the course of construction. Anders and Rowe are hauling in lumber by the thousands. As the old darky says, "you can't prognosticate the future." The place bids fare to be lively, at least for the next four months. The real estate men held a grand mass-meeting yesterday, Jack Swilling acting as chairman. After several hours of mental demonstration it was decided to christen the new born city "Gillett," in honor of one of the most affable gentlemen of the place. We take great pride in our grand prize, yet we extend our hospitality to the weary fortune-hunter.

The very existence of Gillett seemed to hinge on the sale and consumption of alcoholic beverages. The *Miner* for February 1 and 15, 1878, described a new saloon built by Messrs. Keading and Wright. The article mentioned the fact that Moss, the post office man, dispensed

fluids from his log house, adding that they supposed the Postmaster-General wouldn't object.

The *Arizona Sentinel* for February 9, 1878, noted: "The place possesses many natural advantages, and in a few years we may expect to see shade trees growing in the streets as in Florence and Phoenix." Not withstanding all the opportunities for success, treachery was following close at hand.

The *Miner* of March 8, 1878 reported harsh happenings in one of the four Gillett saloons.

I am under the painful necessity of recording the first case of utter cowardice that has been perpetrated at the new town of Gillett. Last night, two men, by the names of Grindell and Calhoun engaged in hard words over a game of cards, in Levy's saloon, and Calhoun went out to the north side of the house, and taking deliberate aim, fired through a window and shot Grindle through the body, the ball penetrating vital parts. There can be no excuse tendered in palliation of this deed. Calhoun gave Grindle no opportunity to defend himself, but acted the dastardly and cowardly ruffian. I do not wish to advocate lynch law, but the repetition of such outrages of this character will render it essential. Calhoun cleared the country after making the remark, "Sam we have a man for breakfast, but I swear I did not shoot him!" Grindle cannot live.

On March 15, 1878, a follow up story in the *Miner* fully demonstrates how complicated a simple murder can get.

Wm. H. Edwards came in today from Gillett, bringing word that Ed Grindell, who was shot there several days ago, is dead. He brought up Samuel Calhoun and J. J. Jones, accused of being either principal or accessory to the shooting and Sam [sic] Kennedy, for an assault on Calhoun, while a prisoner, and also for assaulting the minister while on the way to Grindell's funeral. Jones is accused of robbing Grindell, after he was shot, of sixty-five dollars, forty of which he has delivered to Grindell's friends.

Records for the hearings in front of H. H. Cartter, J. P., for Kennedy and Jones, were preserved by Yavapai County. Unfortunately, there is no hearing record for Calhoun. Jack Kennedy was fined several hundred dollars for his attack on Calhoun made three days after the murder. Admittedly, Kennedy was intoxicated at the time and claimed that the gun he brandished wasn't even loaded. Kennedy had known Grindle since the latter was five years old, and they had been the best of friends during that time.

Jones' case was dismissed as Cartter found that no crime had been committed. It seems that John Jones had cleaned out Grindell's pockets as he and others placed the wounded Grindell on a table. Jones too was intoxicated, as were many residents of Gillett much of the time. Feeling ashamed of what he had done, Jones, once he sobered up, shared his new found wealth with other acquaintances of Grindell. One of those acquaintances was the Deputy Sheriff, Burnett.

By April 12, 1878, the news from Gillett was good and a letter to the *Miner* gives valuable insight into conditions there.

Gillett and Its Outlook—Thousands of Dollars Daily

At 2 p.m. We arrived at the new and thriving town of Gillett, which although not three months old contains several stores carrying large stocks of goods that will compare favorably with the mercantile houses of our own town, Prescott. Anders and Rowe, C. P. Head & Co., and C. T. Hayden are the owners of these mammoth establishments. A brewery has been established by Mr. Peter Arnold, and the people will be furnished with a beverage healthy and agreeable through the exertions and enterprise of this gentleman. Saloons dot the town in many places and seem to be doing a prosperous business. Mr. Edwards has erected at quite an expense a meat market which supplies mill and mine, together with the populace, fat roasts and steaks. Building is progressing all over town and the place presents a lively appearance. Town lots are worth $50 and $250 each. J. W. Swilling has valuable farming lands surrounding the new Dorado, a fine young orchard already shows thrifty signs of progress. Wood choppers and haulers are numerous and help to fill the place with an industrious class of people. Corrals are going up and being filled with hay for the accommodation of freighters and others who are arriving continually from the Capital and other

points throughout the Territory. Messrs. Clark and Crooks have a wagon and blacksmith establishment in full blast and are putting up a small dwelling house from adobes, with Mr. Allen, the Prescott bricklayer as master of ceremonies. C. T. Hayden has in course of erection a storeroom, which, when completed, would not be a discredit to the new County buildings of Yavapai were it situated adjacent thereto. The motive power that keeps the machinery of this new and lively burg alive is the Tiptop Company's ten stamp mill, which in every particular and form seems to be perfect. The building is substantially built, having for a foundation the solid rock, therefore, such a thing as the machinery settling and getting out of line is entirely out of the question. The engine that propels the whole apparatus of the institution is a 76-horsepower. The mill, besides the ore crusher, dry kiln and one of Howell's improvements on White's roasters, have four combination pans and two 9-foot settlers, which enables the company to work their ore up to $94\frac{1}{3}$ per cent of the assay which probably is not excelled by any mill in the United States. The whole amount of bullion produced at the mill during the month of March, with a great delay on account of incomplete belting, etc., during the first thirteen days of the month, aggregated $47,309.69 the average of all ore worked at the mill since it started, shows that it has yielded exactly $185.60 battery assay per ton. The only ore worked as custom thus far has been about twenty tons, however the company has purchased considerable ore from outside mines as an accommodation to miners and prospectors throughout Humbug district.

There is sufficient ore on the dump at the mill just now, to keep it running steady for thirty days, which amount is not likely to diminish, as the amount arriving daily is in excess of the amount being worked.

Mr. Hoffman has departed for new fields and his place is to be filled by an experienced millman from California, Mr. G. H. Weber. At present the management of the whole business rests with Mr. Gillett and H. C. Cushwiler, two affable and good businessmen. The company have in their employ at present in mill and mine 136 men, who receive their stamps punctually at the end of each month, therefore, from this source there are no complaints. The average bullion yield from all ores that have been worked since the mill started up in the latter part of February to the present time, is $172.09 [per ton]. There are now piled up for use at the mill over one thousand cords of wood and the supply is continually kept up by numerous persons who have contracts for furnishing fuel. The company boards the mill men in the company's boarding house which is judiciously and carefully managed by Mrs. J. E. Brown, assisted by her accomplished daughter, Miss Annie, late of San Francisco. It is the opinion of the honest, conscientious mining men that the Tip-top stock will, on its merits, go up to $8 or $10 per share in a few months. The mine is developing finely and no lack of rich ore. The whole cost of milling and mining per month is $15,000, and with a yield of sixty thousand every thirty days, which it will not be difficult to accomplish, hereafter dividends of 40 or 45 cents per share will be declared, which of itself, will bring the stock up on its own merits, and if those who own stock in the Tip-top lack faith in its future outcome, we would advise them to cast it to the winds, as the substantiality of the mine is beyond question, notwithstanding slanderous reports to the contrary. The people are jubilant over having the prospect of mail service put on between Prescott and Phoenix, two very important points in connection with this section. The road at several points between Antelope and Gillett requires some work to make it safe for travel and our Board of Supervisors should see that a small sum of money be used in repairing same. Good restaurants are one of the things that make life pleasant in this section. Messrs. Smith and Levy furnish all the delicacies to be found in the market, and sufficient to satisfy the most fastidious. Mrs. Brown, also accommodates many who visit the new city, and taking everything throughout the camp in connection, it would be difficult to find a more jovial, happy people, or better conducted town in any frontier country. Tomorrow we intend to make a through examination of the mine and until then, adieu.

More glowing reports followed as stage after stage hauled thousands of dollars in gold and silver from the mill at Gillett to Prescott and ultimately San Francisco. Even well known Virgil Earp of Tombstone fame got into the act as a stage driver for Patterson and Caldwell's line. On March 29, 1878, Earp reported to the *Miner* that, "the mill works better and better as the machinery wears smooth, and the operators become better acquainted with its management."

On June 12, 1878, the prediction of lynchings in Gillett came true. It wasn't the typical Hollywood version either. The lawman didn't succeed in holding off a lynch mob using sheer fortitude and determination. Three men died, all outside the law and accepted practices of civilization.

On June 14, 1878, Alfred LeValley, driver and partner in the P & C stage line, gave a brief report of the happenings in Gillett. On June 21, 1878, the *Miner* was provided with a full report from Deputy Sheriff, Burnett.

The Homicides at Gillett

75 Citizens Aroused

Mr. James C. Burnett has furnished us with the following statement of the serious difficulty that took place at the new town of Gillett, on the 12th of this month, in which three men lost their lives. He says: "I was standing near the saloon door of Frank Smith, in the town of Gillett on the 12th day of June 1878, and while there standing heard a row inside the saloon. I immediately stepped in and found the now deceased Setwright engaged in a quarrel with a man named Farrell, and that he had struck Farrell over the head twice with a bottle, breaking same. I arrested Setwright and disarmed him, finding a small pistol on his person which carried a large ball. I kept the prisoner during the afternoon, and about sunset Mr. Weir came to me and asked me to deliver the prisoner over to him, promising that he would take him out of town to his camp, about six miles distant. I consulted with Setwright and he agreed to go with Weir, and the next day would accompany Weir to Prescott and deliver himself up to the authorities for the offense committed on Farrell. I consented to this arrangement and turned Setwright over to Weir. I then went with Setwright and Weir to the store of C. T. Hayden, where Setwright wished to arrange for the packing and working of some silver ore. Arrangements were perfected with Hill, agent of Mr. Hayden, for the packing of ore, etc., who was to hold the receipt for the same until Setwright returned from Prescott. Weir and Setwright then mounted their mules, rode to the store of C. P. Head & Co., and Anders and Rowe, transacted some business and took the trail leading up the canyon in the direction of Weir's camp. In a short time, about 15 minutes, Setwright returned to Smith's saloon, remarking 'they thought to murder me but I got my man.' I asked Setwright why he had returned, he stated that he did not intend to be murdered. At this time Tom Farrell made his appearance and was in the act of assaulting Setwright. I arrested Mr. Farrell and gave him in charge of Mr. Ayers and turned to arrest Setwright who jumped on his mule and started at a fast gait from town. At this juncture, Messrs. Cusack, Mann and Taylor, came up from he feed yard of Messrs. Cusack and Mann, and stated that Weir's mule came up without a rider. We immediately started out on the trail taken by Setwright and Weir, and at a distance of some two hundred yards, found Weir dead, shot through the head. I ordered all the horses available to be saddled and summoned several men to accompany me for the purpose of capturing Setwright who had gone on the Phoenix road. After riding $1^1/_2$ miles and upon arriving at Moore's station we found Setwright's mule, we asked parties at the station where Setwright was and were answered by someone that he had fell from the mule and had then gone down the road. Taylor and myself went out on the road but could not find him, we then returned and met a man by the name of Rodgers at the station, who told me that the man Setwright had run into the willows. I ordered Mr. Rice, clerk of C. P. Head & Co., to go with Taylor and myself and search the willow patch—we failed to find him—returned to the house and heard a cough in the brush immediately in the rear of the house, we searched and found Setwright, who exclaimed he was dying. I arrested him and returned with him to Gillett, upon our arrival at Gillett we found that the Coroner had held an inquest on the body of Weir, who had been brought to town and placed in a house. I placed the prisoner, Setwright in the same room and summoned C. P. Raines and Col. Taylor, to assist in guarding the prisoner. It was now about 9 o'clock in the evening and I found the whole populace very much excited and bent on dealing some summary punishment, and I found it necessary to clear the house of all persons except those selected by me to guard the prisoner, E. P. Raines and Col. Taylor, being those selected by me to guard and keep the prisoner safe.

From nine o'clock in the evening until three o'clock in the morning, the citizens who had formed themselves into a company intent on punishing the murderer of Weir, made numerous demands for the prisoner. At each time they made a demand I warned them to desist, promising to take the man safely to Prescott where he could be dealt with in accordance to law and justice. At about three o'clock in the morning the crowd, about 75 in number, made a general demand for our surrender and the prisoner. We had broken the windows sufficiently to allow the free use of our arms, which we pointed at the mob and called on them to halt. They then split and formed on each side of the house, threatening to blow or burn up the house if we still further refused to deliver up the murderer. About this time Mr. Raines took station at the back window and Col. Taylor at the front door, remarking that he had got enough of this, turned the key, opened the door and stepped out, saying to the crowd, 'I have a double barreled shot-gun and this thing has got to stop.' I heard three shots fired and saw Taylor fall. I called to the crowd that they had murdered Taylor and to desist. They again demanded that we surrender; and finding it impossible longer to withstand the excited numbers, I told Mr. Raines to tell them that we would surrender if promised no harm. He called out that 'The Sheriff surrenders;' and myself and Raines walked away from the building, leaving Setwright within, safely bound. He was taken by the crowd and executed."

This is a true and fair statement of the affair from beginning to end, and it is my wish, Mr. Editor, that you publish the same.

Jas. C. Burnett

Clearly, there was no sympathy for Weir's killer, Setwright. On the other hand, whoever pulled the trigger on Col. Taylor would have to answer for his deed, or would he? Remember, this was the West, and people were judged by a somewhat looser standard then they would have been back East. The *Miner* of the same date put it very succinctly.

The shooting of Taylor was quite another matter, and, although he was evidently seeking the reputation of a "Chief," and endeavoring to make people believe that he was a great detective, and sought to impress upon the people of Gillett the idea that he was a terror, a master mind, and that a wave of his hand was enough to quiet almost any kind of a tumult, yet he had been guilty of no overt act, was acting within the sanction of the law, and the taking of his life if, done intentionally, was certainly murder.

If, however, during a time of great excitement, when nearly the whole population was enraged, and exasperated at the killing of their friend without cause, Taylor stepped out and defied them all with a shot-gun in his hand, as represented by some, then the case assumes a different phase and partakes more of the character of a riot and the death of Taylor one of its casualties.

The editor of the *Miner* might have recalled that just a few weeks earlier Col. Taylor had sent, by his testimony, a good man, Jack Swilling, off to prison in Yuma. One has to wonder how many of Swilling's friends were present in that mob of seventy-five who demanded Setwright's life.

As so often was the case with vigilante justice, no one was brought to trial for Taylor's death. Gillett settled back to being a mill town, but the tranquility would only last for a while.

With Jack Swilling and D. B. Gillett no longer in the picture, the Tip Top Mine Co. had second thoughts about the location of its mill. The *Miner* of December 27, 1878 carried news of the worst kind.

> Col. Biddle, Inspector General of the Military Department, who is on a tour of inspection, went by the Tiptop, and telegraphs from Phoenix, that everything is looking splendidly at the mine. The mill he says is to be moved from Gillett to the mine, and five or six more stamps added. This will, of course, save the expense of transporting the ore five or six miles, and be handy to wood, etc., which will be good for the Company, but a little tough on those who have invested in real estate and improvements in the town of Gillett. That hitherto, promising young city, has lived upon the mill and the business which it attracted to the place, and this movement seems to be calculated to knock its underpinning out.

Although the mill in Gillett shipped $21,000 in mid April, 1879, eight months later the *Miner* reported that the mill was shut down and only one store was open there. It also noted that a boarding house kept by Curtis, and a brewery and feed yard run by Pete Arnold, were still in operation.

The census taken in Gillett in early June of 1880 reveals that only two men out of the one-hundred persons recorded could definitely be associated with the mill. J. H. Cordes,

millworker, and J. G. Trotter, assayer, were no doubt on the mill's payroll. Additionally, twenty two men gave there occupation as miners, four were laborers and three were wood cutters. Any or all of these could have been employed by the mill.

Nearly a dozen persons from Gillett were working in hotels or at the stage station. There were, of course, a couple of professional gamblers, one brewer, several packers, ranchers, farmers, and also a lot of women and children staying at home.

Fortunately for the residents of Gillett, the mill stayed put through 1882, as John Henry Cordes remained employed there until the end of that year. In January, 1883, Cordes moved up to what was then called Antelope Station, purchasing it from the Bolin brothers at that time. Eventually that station would become known as Cordes, and the town is still called that today.

Otto Bolin who had been recorded in 1880 as station keeper at Gillett, apparently moved up to Antelope before November of 1880 as he is listed as proprietor at that location in a *Miner* advertisement dated November 29, 1880. Bolin was murdered at Antelope in January, 1882.

Once the mill was moved to the Tip Top mine location in 1884, Gillett depended on the stage lines to keep it going. It made very little sense to have a stage stop located so that you would have to cross the Agua Fria River twice in order to make use of the facility. Nonetheless, Gillett survived until nearly the end of the century as a stage stop on the Black Canyon line.

An article appeared in the April, 1935 issue of the *Arizona Historical Review*, authored by that famous storyteller Will Barnes. The complete text of Barnes' work is included herein, as nobody could have told it better.

THE BLACK CANYON STAGE

By WILL. C. BARNES

"Forty Years Ago, November 15, 1892." The old timer scanned the "forty years ago" column in his Arizona paper. Two of the items caught his eye.

"Hon. William O. O'Neill, Chairman of the Territorial Worlds Fair Commission arrived in the city last night by stage from Prescott."

Just below this another.

"Hon. Will C. Barnes of Apache County is in the city from his cattle ranch near Holbrook. He will be a visitor to the Territorial Grand Lodge of Masons during the coming week. He came down from Prescott via the Black Canyon Stage."

As he read the items the old timer smiled. He recalled the day very well. Six o'clock in the morning, dark and cold, a foot of snow on the ground. The huge Concord "thorough brace" stage stood in front of the hotel at Prescott. The passengers were already climbing into its dark depths. He recalled them all as if it had been but yesterday: two women of middle age, Sisters of Charity, dressed in their distinctive garb; William O. O'Neill alias "Bucky," tall, dark and handsome, politician, sheriff, outlaw hunter (a few years later as captain of Rough Riders he was the first soldier to fall at San Juan hill in the Spanish war); Price Behan, politician and ex-sheriff; a young commercial traveler from San Francisco, making his first visit to Arizona, and the writer, range cattleman of that day; together with the stage driver, a typical character of the old stage days.

Every nook and corner of the lumbering vehicle was filled with U.S. mail sacks and Wells Fargo express matter. The passengers stowed themselves away inside the coach as best they could. For the first five or six miles the road was decidedly up grade. The snow made progress very slow. Under the weather conditions the driver had the seat on top all to himself. At the top of the grade, six miles from Prescott, the driver pulled up the team and clambered from his high seat. Daylight had come, but the sun did not penetrate the heavy clouds. Muttering and cursing to himself, the driver stumbled through the deep snow to the heads of the leaders. O'Neill, watching him from the "swing" seat of the coach, saw him pull a bottle from his overcoat pocket and take a long drink. A minute later the driver took his seat on top, gathered up his reins,

threw the brake off, and gave a wild Apache yell. The team started off down the steep grade at a keen trot, the coach swaying and rocking like a ship in a heavy sea. It took but a few minutes to convince the men inside the coach that the driver was drunk and could not or would not control his team.

The heavy coach rocked and plunged along the rough road, skidded recklessly around the curves, and dropped into deep chuck holes covered by the snow. The driver with shrill yells even encouraged his team to increase their speed. The long lash curled over their backs as they tore down the rough grade. Drunk as he was, he wielded the whip with skill and accuracy.

Inside the coach, the four men hastily decided on a plan of action. No time was to be lost. Prompt action alone could avert a bad accident. On the back seat the two Sisters of Charity clung, one to the other, as the coach rushed along.

Behan, a deputy United States Marshal at the time, sat inside on the left or near side. The drunken driver on top was clear over on the other side, half hidden by the top of the coach. Behan opened the door carefully, stood on the iron step, reached up and grasped the iron railing that ran around the top. Before doing this both he and O'Neill took their heavy six shooters from the leather holsters at their sides and shoved the weapons inside their trousers waistband for quick action. They also took off their heavy overcoats. Standing on the iron step Behan gave a foot to O'Neill like a woman mounting a saddle horse, a lusty boost landed him on top the stage directly back of the driver's seat. Behan's left arm shot round that worthy's neck with a choking grip while his right hand grabbed the reins from his clutching fingers. O'Neill, closely behind, pulled the jehu from his seat and back onto the top of the stage. A clout on the side of his head from O'Neill's heavy six shooter cured all desire on his part to fight back.

A pair of handcuffs was snapped onto his wrists. Then as the team was stopped he was dragged unceremoniously to the ground, the big leather "boot" behind the stage was unstraped, and with his hands still in the brace of the steel shackles the gentleman was bundled into the boot, the cover pulled back into place and strapped down tightly. He made no further trouble.

At noon, under Behan's expert driving, the stage reached the regular mail station [probably Big Bug] where always a new driver and team were furnished. The drunken driver, not yet sobered up, was turned over to the station keeper to be sent back to Prescott as a prisoner on the "up" stage.

No other driver being available, Behan agreed to drive the team down to the next station, Gillett, some thirty-five miles south. The new team was a notable one in that region. Four fine mules, each as white as snow, perfectly matched as to size and gait; one of the most picturesque and unusual stage teams in all the far west. Young, lively and full of pep they were "just rarin' to go," when hitched up. The road now ran down the mountain side on a narrow shelf cut from the rocky walls. There was a mass of sharp curves and dangerous corners. As the stage dropped down into the lower altitudes it grew milder. The snow disappeared, deep mud took its place. Rain also began to fall in torrents. Progress was very slow. Darkness found the stage at the head of a long, narrow grade which ran for fifteen miles down the Black Canyon.

The "down" and "up" stages usually met on this stretch. At every turn each driver stopped his team and "stopped, looked and listened." Each peered into the stygian darkness, seeking the dim blinking lights of the other stage, a two-candle power lighting system that didn't shed its beams very far ahead. Each driver carried a long tin horn such as New England fishing smacks use in fogs. These were blown at regular intervals. A long blast was a warning; two short "toots" an acknowledgment. The system called for the "up" stage to crawl into the first wide place in the road and wait for the "down" stage.

Crude as it was the method worked fairly well for years. Occasionally a crash of thunder or some other noise would kill the sound of the horn. Then the two stages met perhaps at some point where passing was not possible. Then the "up" team was unhitched and with two men at the tongue of the stage to guide it the heavy vehicle was rolled carefully back down the grade until a place was reached where it could be snuggled into a corner and allow the other to pass. There was plenty of adventure and excitement traveling in those days.

Where the Black Canyon came out into the vast open valley in which lay the Salt River and the city of Phoenix, a lively mountain stream, the Agua Fria (Cold Water) must be forded to reach the stage station on the southern side. The "up" driver warned his side partner that this stream "was running banks full and more."

It was nearly midnight when the stage rolled out of the dark canyon onto the gravelly bank of the Agua Fria. The river was surely booming. O'Neill had taken turns driving and both men were soaked through and through and half frozen. The night air was keen and raw. Behan stopped the stage a few yards from the water's edge. Across the boiling, turbulent river they could see the lights of the station. They blinked and glowed in the dark like will-o'-the wisps. Over there warmth and food awaited the weary, chilled travelers.

The four men stood at the water's edge in the pelting rain studying the situation. Adventurers all, used to meeting difficult situations, they personally were willing to risk the crossing. But the two Sisters. What of them? The men went to the stage door. The two women were huddled together in the dark stage shivering with cold. O'Neill told them briefly of the situation, of the danger in crossing under such conditions. They could wait for morning and hope for a drop in the stream's flow.

It was a scene for a word painter. The pouring rain, an occasional flash of lightning, a sound of thunder, the stage with its dim candles only emphasizing the darkness the more, the four white mules like great ghosts, and the dripping men. Behind them were the dark walls of the Black Canyon. Ahead were the swift waters of the stream; across from them, the station lights, food, shelter, and warmth.

Clear eyed and unafraid, the elder of the two women spoke. "Gentlemen," she said, "we are but two frail women. You men must decide. We leave it all to your good judgement. All of us are in the hands of our heavenly Father. He will surely answer our prayers for guidance and success."

Thus encouraged the four men stood on the gravelly bank and made their plans for the crossing. Just below the crossing, the stream entered the canyon again. No one knew how deep the water was on the crossing. If deep enough to float the heavy stage the whole affair might be swept down stream into the canyon and all be lost.

Cold and numbed as they were, no one could possibly hope to swim in such a swift current. It was agreed that Behan was to drive. A water bucket hung under the boot at the rear of the stage. O'Neill was to fill it with small stones with which to hasten the movements of the mules, should they need any action of that sort. The other two men, each with a Sister of Charity at his side, were to stand on the upstream side of the vehicle. There, holding tightly to the rail on top they were to lean far back and act as a sort of counter balance against the tremendous pressure of the swift stream against the side of the stage. They hoped the combined weight of the four would meet any tendency of the stage to overturn. In the event it did happen, it was agreed that each of the two men was to grab a Sister and devote his very best efforts to get her safely to shore.

Behan and O'Neill climbed to the driver's seat. "All ready?" queried O'Neill, looking back at the four figures clinging precariously to the side. The two men looked inquiringly into the faces of the women. "All ready, gentlemen. The good God has us all in His protecting arms. He will not forsake us in the time of need." Behan loosed the brake and with a wild yell the mules lunged into the whirling water of the stream. O'Neill did his best by pelting the animals with rocks, aimed with fine precision. Both men yelled like wild Indians. Behan lashed at them with his whip.

As the gallant little leaders struck deep water and began to swim, they were swept around with the current and down stream. The longer legged "wheelers" kept their feet a little while then they too were forced to swim. Finally the huge stage itself floated free. The water was up to the knees of the four clinging to the side. Each was leaning back just as far as their arms would allow to keep the stage from overturning. Behan, cool and collected, did his best to keep the team headed towards the farther bank and also from becoming entangled in the harness and draft rigging. As the stage swung around in the stream the wheels on the lower side struck a submerged rock. The stage began to rise slowly, due to the tremendous pressure against the upper side. For one or two dreadfully agonizing minutes it seemed as if it would be turned over in the water and all be lost. Just at this critical moment, however, when it looked as if nothing could save them, the two little lead mules touched the bottom with the points of their front feet. How those little fellows did claw and tear at the steep bank. Gradually they got the stage to move ahead. The long legged wheelers also touched bottom and they clawed and dug at it as if they realized the need of using every ounce of power available.

Inch by inch, second by second, the heavy stage began to move through the water towards the bank. Gradually it settled back onto an even keel, The going out was very steep and it took the last rock in O'Neill's water bucket, plus much yelling and slashing of the whip, to get the whole outfit safely out onto the solid land. Three minutes later Behan drove the team through the grove of cottonwoods to the station. The door flew open, a flood of light was in their eyes. Once inside, the two Sisters, wet and cold as they were, dropped to their knees, the men standing uncovered beside them in silent prayer.

Gillett was simply an expediency of its day. In spite of all the hope that surrounded its founding it was only a temporary business necessity, a mill to serve a mine.

Little remains today but the foundation of the mill, a few scraps of tin roofing, and the carcass of a hotel that was supposedly called the Burfind. Eventually the hotel was turned into a dude ranch, but its position on the west bank of the Aqua Fria ensured it a short life. No one could cross the raging river during a rainy spring or summer. There simply was not a bridge for miles in either direction.

FALLS ·ON·
ARIZONA CANAL.

OFFICE OF THE
DAILY PHOENIX HERALD
A. MORFORD
EDITOR AND
PROP'R.

DAILY PHOENIX HERALD

BILLIARD HALL

PHOENIX HOTEL

REFERENCES.

1 County Court House.
2 Baptist Church.
3 Washington St. Methodist Church.
4 Public School House.
5 Centre St. Methodist Church.
6 Salt River Valley Canal.
7 Residence of J. T. Simms.
8 Gazette Printing Office.
9 Kales & Lewis' Bank.
10 Valley Bank.
11 Herald Printing Office.
12 J. Y. T. Smith's Flour Mill.
13 Public Plaza.
14 Irvine Building.
15 Phoenix Swimming Baths.

16 Phoenix Hotel, Chas. Salari, Prop.
17 Gregory House & Lumber Yard.
18 Hotel Lemon.
19 Catholic Church.
20 Dutch Ditch.
21 Maricopa Canal.
22 Grand Canal.
23 Arizona Canal.
24 Residence of H. H. McNeil.
25 Residence of M. W. Kales.
26 Property of E. B. Kirkland.
27 Loust Bros.' Ice Factory.
28 P. Minor's Lumber Yard.
29 H. W. Ryder's Lumber Yard.

Courtesy Phoenix History Museum

BIRD'S EYE VIEW OF
PHŒNIX

HEAD OF ARIZONA CANAL.

IRVINES BL

RES. OF
H.H. McK

22
21

COPA CO. VIEW LOOKING NORTH-EAST.

ARIZONA.

SKETCHED BY
C. J. DYER,
PHŒNIX, A.T.

PUBLIC SCHOOL HOUSE.

GREGORY HOUSE.

PHŒNIX, The county seat of Maricopa County, is situated in the Salt River Valley, 28 miles north of M——
Station, on the Southern Pacific Railroad. The town is embowered in shade trees and shrubbery, has streams ——
water through every street, is surrounded by orchards, gardens and vineyards, and is one of the handsomest in th——
The streets face the cardinal points, are broad and spacious and lined with trees. The County Courthouse, in th——
of a square and surrounded by trees, is a handsome two-story brick, surmounted by a tower. The School H——
large and commodious brick structure, of two stories, almost hidden in a cottonwood grove. The Methodist——
and Catholics have tasteful places of worship. There are several large mercantile establishments, a steam flo——
with daily capacity of 180 barrels, two ice factories and a planing mill. The Odd Fellows, Masons Workmen, Kn——
Pythias, Good Templars and Chosen Friends have flourishing organizations. Two newspapers, the *Herald* and ——
have daily and weekly editions. The altitude is 1800 feet above the sea level and the climate is one of the health——
the world. Snow never falls and roses are in bloom in December. Phoenix is the center of an extensive and fertil——
almost 50 miles in length by 18 in width, and containing over 300,000 acres. Every variety of grain, grasses, fru——
vegetables give a prolific yield. For fruits, grape culture and wine making the soil and climate are especially a——
Everything is grown by irrigation. Eight canals convey the water from the Salt river over the land. The Ariz——
is one of the largest works of the kind in the United States; it is over 40 miles in length, 56 feet wide on the botto——
58 feet on top, is 7 feet deep and has a capacity of 40,000 miner's inches. It has reclaimed and made valua——
100,000 acres of rich land. The office of the company is at Phoenix; the President is Hon. Clark Churchill and th——
Engineer is Charles A. Marriner. The Territorial Insane Asylum is situated near the town, also the extensive an——
tiful grounds of the Arizona Industrial exposition. The Normal school is situated nine miles up the river. A——
road from the Southern Pacific will be completed to Phoenix by January 1, 1886. The town is rapidly growing——
charming situation will yet make it the leading city of Arizona. Population about 3,500.

SCHMIDT LABEL & LITHO. CO. PRINT. S.F.

Swilling House at Black Canyon

Jack Swilling, to whom Arizona owes a great deal for his zeal and perseverance in opening up rural districts, has moved from his ranch to the new town of Gillett, where he is busy selling town property, etc., and is said to be making money. He deserves all the good luck imaginable for his big heart, indomitable energy and go-ahead-ativeness.

Weekly Miner, February 1, 1878

Chapter Twelve
Jack Swilling

Jack Swilling was always busy. He was busy mining, ranching, farming, developing land, siring children, helping friends, fighting Indians, drinking, and bragging. A man who was already bigger than life nevertheless found it necessary to embellish stories about himself and others. As with many other men of his day the outcome was inevitable, he paid with his life.

Without Swilling we might have had to wait a while for Phoenix to become a reality. Someone would have eventually done what Swilling did, but he did it first, and probably better.

Jack W. Swilling

In his first thirty-four years, we know that Jack Swilling did a lot more than most men in their lifetime. Born in South Carolina in 1830, Swilling fought in the Mexican–American War, married a young lady from Alabama who had his first child, left to mine at Gila City, Arizona, moved back to New Mexico and became a Southern sympathizer. His next step was to desert the Confederate Army, going to work as a messenger for the Union side. By 1864, he was organizing groups of men to search out and destroy bands of Apaches, and eventually ended up in

Tucson where he joined Charles Hayden in establishing a grist mill. Following more mining endeavors in the Wickenburg and Rich Hill areas, Swilling returned to Tucson to carry the mail from the Pima Villages, south of today's Phoenix, to Prescott.

While in Tucson, in 1864, Swilling met and married Trinidad Escalantes Mejia, a young Spanish woman. It is not clear what became of his marriage in Alabama, but in that day it was not uncommon for a man in love with the West to leave a wife back in the States only to marry a woman of Indian or Spanish origin.

We can only guess at Swilling's wonderment as he rode through the Salt River Valley on his mail carrying trips. No doubt the ruins of canals and villages stuck firmly in his mind as he took his wife to their new home in the Walnut Grove area of the Bradshaws.

The Swilling Irrigating and Canal Company

Swilling left Walnut Grove and such friends as Pauline Weaver after having been there just a year. His next stop, according to Trinidad, was Wickenburg where they stayed for two to three years. It was during their stay in Wickenburg that Swilling and sixteen others founded the Swilling Irrigating and Canal Company to bring water to that land known today as the Valley of the Sun. Of course, Swilling had other accomplishments during his time in Wickenburg. In 1867 he was appointed an election Judge for the Wickenburg precinct. By the fall of that year Swilling had done something unheard of even in Arizona's early years. The *Miner* of October 12, 1867, told the story:

> On Sunday evening last, in this place, Jack Swilling killed a Chileno with a double-barreled shot-gun and then scalped him. The circumstances were these: Last May Jack was on a spree, and the Mexicans generally fearing him when on a bender, kept out of his way; but this Chileno, to show his bravery, got a double-barreled shot-gun and dodged around corners after him. Jack was too drunk to know anything about it, and the fellow would have killed him had it not been for myself and others—that, too, without any cause whatever, Jack not knowing him even by sight, and never a word passed between them. The Chileno had been gone from here nearly all summer, and returned only a few days since from Weaver. Last Saturday evening a Portuguese came to Jack and told him that he had better be on his guard, as this Chileno swore he would kill him before another day. Jack started to hunt and kill him then, but some of his friends disarmed him. The next morning Jack was in town again and in a fit of intoxication got hold of a double-barreled shot-gun provided by some inebriated friends, hailed the Chileno in the street, and fired both charges into him killing him instantly; then in his drunken frenzy scalped him. There seems to be little sympathy felt here for the deceased by Mexicans or anyone else. He was known as a thief and desperado, and undoubtedly deserved his fate.

Bringing the waters of the Salt River to the fields of the Valley was no doubt Swilling's greatest accomplishment. Without this achievement there would be no need to, "Catch the Stage to Phoenix."

The *Miner* of February 8, 1868 had a lot to say about that new place called Phoenix.

Phoenix, A.T., Jan. 1st, 1868

The above place, perhaps is new to you, and to many readers of the *Miner*, notwithstanding it is settled principally by old Arizona pioneers, who do not intend it to remain a stranger long, as it will certainly be one of the most important settlements in Arizona, and like the bird it derives its name from, will rise like smoke from a tar-kiln.

Phoenix is situated on the west bank of Salt River, about thirty-five miles from its mouth, and about the same distance below Fort McDowell; it is seventy miles from Wickenburg, and about eighteen miles from the Pimas; with good roads to all the above named places. About two months since, Jack Swilling and a small party of men came here, looked at the country, liked it, and located the water right; went back to Wickenburg, organized a company, and returned here with the men and means to bring out a ditch, or rather canal on which there are at present some eighteen or twenty men at work. The ditch will be large enough to irrigate some ten or twelve miles, which is only a small portion of the rich and fertile land in this valley, and a great part of which looks as if recently cultivated. The cotton, tobacco, castor bean, and other plants, are still growing spontaneously over the apparently ancient fields of *Quien Sabe*, whose ruins, in the shape of high mounds of slate rock and adobes, are left along the borders of old acequias or canals, the latter being built on the ground, and from thirty-five to fifty feet in width. The banks, in places, are still from five to eight feet high and run out ten to twelve miles from the river, and, I believe, the whole length of the valley. The ruins are from one half to three and four miles apart, and from fifteen to twenty feet high. The river here is quite large, (rather too much so, at present, having taken a rise), and has lots of good fish, with plenty of ducks, geese, beaver, and other game along the stream; also plenty of timber for building and other purposes. The climate is the mildest I have ever experienced. There has been no frost yet sufficient to kill anything, and every thing looks green. The summer birds still remain. The mountains in the vicinity are full of gold quartz and burro deer; and up this same Salt River is where all the old Montezuma maps point as the head and source of all the gold that has been scattered so profusely over this country. So, if you wish a good farm or mine to get rid of your fever, or to spend a happy and prosperous New Year, come up Salt River. Don't be afraid.

A second correspondence dated April 5 showed up in the *Miner* issue of April 18, 1868.

Having read the *Miner* from time to time, and seeing letters therein from every portion of the Territory except these Salt River settlements, I have this day constituted myself your special correspondent, and will, therefore, endeavor to act in that capacity until you have cause to punish me for my presumption in thus crowding this little scrawl upon you.

On the 18th day of November last at the town of Wickenburg, in this county, a joint stock company was formed under the name of the Swilling Irrigating and Canal Company, of Salt River, with a capital stock of $10,000 divided into fifty shares.

The stock selling very readily, business was soon commenced, and on the 12th day of March, 1868, a ditch, or rather, a small canal, was completed and in the short space of two hours time, a large body of water was turned in. The ditch carries enough water to irrigate at least 4,000 acres of land. This enterprise has but commenced, and is of the utmost importance to the miners in and around Wickenburg, particularly those engaged in hauling quartz from the mines to the mills. There are but few persons who would credit it, unless they were personally acquainted with the fact that the two Companies, viz.; Inger and Chapman, who have been engaged in hauling quartz for the Vulture Mining Co., have consumed $6,000 worth of corn and barley per month, the money always being paid in gold bullion, upon its delivery. Produce of all kinds can, and will be delivered at that point, at lower rates than from any other point (known to the writer) in the Territory.

In order to give you a description of the country I would have to consume more time than the person waiting for this letter (we have no mail as yet) will permit. Yet if I were permitted to do so I could give you but a slight idea of the real value and extent of the lands that are susceptible of irrigation and practical culture. This valley is estimated to be 15 miles wide, and 20 miles long; that is to say, the distance from Salt River to the Agua Fria is twenty miles, and between that stream and Salt River, the width of the valley is fifteen miles, a perfectly level plain of the finest soil I have ever seen in this or any other country.

It was the intent of the Company to take the water out in the old *acequia* or canal, which was used many years ago by a people whom we know, or can learn, but little. Suffice it to say that they were enterprising and truly industrious, as we have many proofs thereof, in the shape of ruins of what were once massive structures, the most colossal of which, can be traced for twenty miles (that is the old *acequias* mentioned). The Company, seeing the importance of putting in big crops this year, to supply the immense demand for grain and hay at Wickenburg and Vulture City, suspended work on the large canal and have succeeded in completing a ditch which will be more than sufficient to supply the wants of those who are engaged in farming at present.

The Directors inform me that but seven shares remain to be sold, all of which are to be reserved for men of families, and old bachelors need not apply. We have but five families here at present, and as soon as Chaplin Blake, of Fort McDowell, shall have finished a little ceremony that is now progressing rapidly, one more will be added to this number, I hope ere this year closes, we will have a baker's dozen, and then we have room for more.

Since the settlement was started, we have not been troubled by the Apaches. We often receive a visit from the Pima and Maricopa Indians, whose friendly relations toward the whites cannot be questioned. They sometimes make themselves very useful in crossing animals over the river, which, of late, has been very high.

When they are around, one can feel a degree of safety not otherwise felt, as they are ever vigilant. I am one of those timid beings whose constant fear and dread of the Apaches has made very cautious. Having read but little of Longfellow's works, I can look upon the "noble red man" only in the light of a dastardly, murderous whelp, whose very existence has been the bane of Arizona. But for them, no doubt, this beautiful valley would now be populated by the progeny of the prosperous people destroyed by the hands of the Apaches.

If General Halleck will be allowed to put his ideas into practice, we will soon have an influx of people from the States, and we can extend the right hand of fellowship to them. The following gentlemen, some of whom are no doubt personally known to you, are putting in crops, and thus far have had no backsets: Jack Swilling is cultivating 100 acres of wheat, barley and corn; George F. Freeman, 100 acres; J. Burns, 50 acres; Thomas Hogue, formerly of Walnut Grove, 80 acres; Messrs. Duppa and Vandermark, 100 acres; Mr Adams, 50 acres; S. Sawyer, 50 acres;

Mr. Rowe, 50 acres; F. S. Johnson, 25 acres; and last, but by no means least, our old friend Davis, will put in 100 acres of sorghum sugarcane.

We will be able to muster about one hundred and twenty good, large sized Democratic votes for the regular nominee of the Democratic party for Delegate to Congress, Samuel Adams, Gov. McCormick, or any other man, to the contrary notwithstanding.

Several significant concepts are pointed out in the letter. First, Phoenix came into existence to feed the men and animals of the Vulture mine and mill. Interestingly, location near the Pimas and Maricopas guaranteed these pioneers minimal interference from the Apaches.

More significant to today's inhabitants, fast development for the Valley has been its sustenance for 129 years. Hawking the virtues of the Valley of the Sun is not a concept invented by the present day inhabitants.

The Swillings Settle in the Valley

Upon completion of the Swilling Ditch, Swilling took up a claim on what is now the southeast corner of 32nd street and Van Buren in Phoenix. Trinidad, in her later years, claimed that she lived for a while with her chickens in the chicken house waiting for Jack to build her a home.

What a home it would be! 96,000 adobes went into the construction of what was probably the largest house in the Territory. Swilling's interest in politics and people in general, helped to make their home a general rendezvous for all who were passing through the Valley. July of 1869 saw Swilling in the position of Justice of the Peace for the Phoenix Precinct, then still part of Yavapai County.

A letter to the Editor of the *Miner* from Swilling, dated October 20, 1870 reveals much about his political standing.

An old pioneer of Arizona desires to say a few words to his friends in reference to the election of a Delegate to Congress. My vote and influence goes for P. R. Brady, just because he is an Arizonan, and because I think that it is the

duty of every Arizonan to vote against Mr. McCormick.

Like many others I voted for Mr. McCormick before, but I cannot do so now. He has done nothing for us, except to make fine promises; and if he has tried something, as he says he has, he has failed. We have less troops—less mails—and less protection. The Surveyor-General is a carpet back editor sent here with public money to maintain a blackguard newspaper, but with not a dollar to survey our lands. The "Little Governor," whose business is to attend to the affairs of the Territory, drives with Mr. McCormick over the country in a carriage paid for by a government contractor. At this place he has lost the respect of men of all parties by his course. During his recent speech here McCormick tired everybody out with his long twaddle about getting a money order office in Tucson and many post offices throughout the Territory, but failed to explain why he wanted naked savages to vote, or the charges brought against him of working only for money paid by contractors.

If you see fit, you can print this over my signature to let my friends know how I feel.

Salt River is for Brady by a great vote, and an honest one—no frauds will be permitted here.

In spite of Swilling's logic, McCormick won easily.

The *Miner* of December 17, 1870, reported that Jack Swilling was then helping to build the Hayden Ditch on the south side of the river. By February, 1871, an important issue had been settled. Maricopa County had been carved out of Yavapai County by the Territorial Legislature.

Of course, another question was soon raised. Where would the Phoenix townsite be located and what would it be called? Swilling's preference, that it be located in Mill city, which surrounded his home, was denied. His selection of the name Phoenix, a word probably suggested by his learned friend Darrel Duppa and confirmed by Swilling from a dictionary he owned, was granted.

The original townsite was located in the half section south of Van Buren between Seventh Street and Seventh Avenue some four miles west of Swilling's home. Swilling's plan called for his home to be used as government offices if the city had been located around his house.

By April of 1871, Swilling was out prospecting again, this time in the Bradshaw mountains northwest of Phoenix. The *Miner* of April 1, 1871, stated:

> Many persons have left McDowell and Phoenix for Bradshaw, among them John Smith, of the former place, and J. W. Swilling, founder and promoter of civilization on Salt River. Mr. Swilling, and party, were laying out a road to the diggings.

Only a few days later, April 15, 1871, the *Miner* reported the death and subsequent burial of Colonel Jacob Snively a close friend of the Swillings. Snively had been living with them in Phoenix from the fall of 1870 until his departure for the White Picacho mountain where he was killed by Apaches and buried at the site. His mission was to lay out a road to newly discovered mines in the area. Just as Snively played an important role in Swilling's life, so would he provide an ironic twist to the events leading up to Swilling's death.

No doubt Swilling had a perfect location in what seemed to those early pioneers a veritable paradise. In November, 1872, a friend, Edward Irvine described Swilling's place for the *Miner* of November 23rd.

> On Saturday, November 9th, Granville Oury, J. B. Hartt and myself started out afoot, on a little excursion. Avoiding the roads we followed up the Dutch Ditch, a branch of the Swilling Canal; crossed the Extension, another branch of the same, and came upon a neat little artificial pond in a clump of willows and cottonwoods which was covered with tame ducks, the property of J. W. Swilling, whose house, a comfortably large one, 59 × 80 feet, stood nearby. Mr. Swilling's ranch is conveniently situated near the head of the main ditch, on which he has a vineyard and an orchard containing apple, peach, plum, pear, cherry, fig, walnut and orange trees, all of which looked thrifty and promising, except the latter, which were injured by the frost. A patch of fine large cane close by gave indications of the future production of sugar.

A 4720 square foot house when most folks were living in one room cabins! Irvine added that: "Mr. Swilling has an Apache boy—Gabilan Pollero (Chicken Hawk)—and a girl, Mariana, who are gentle and obedient and make good servants."

At forty-two years of age most men would have been content to settle down and spend the rest of their lives on that 160 acre homestead in heaven, but not Swilling. By spring of the following year, after having led a winter expedition of settlers to the Pueblo Viejo Valley on the upper Gila River near present day Safford, Swilling was splitting his time between laying out new canals in the Valley and mining in the Black Canyon area.

Moving Up to the Black Canyon

Swilling sold his possessory rights and improvements on his 160 acre ranch in Phoenix on August 28, 1873. The buyer was Hellings and Company, owners of a flour mill nearby. Swilling sold out for $3,000, no paltry sum for that day.

The *Miner*, April 24, 1874, reported his progress at mining on the Black Canyon.

> Mr. J. W. Swilling is working an arrastra, on ore from his recent discovery, in the Black Canyon. Persons who know, say that he has the richest gold lode ever discovered in Arizona.

A man by the name of Chipman reported to the *Miner* on March 2, 1875, that Swilling was recovering from a "long spell of sickness." Swilling's "sickness" was apparently related to alcoholism, as it was with so many pioneers of that day. As an added complication, Swilling was addicted to morphine. The two proved a deadly combination.

A personal report from Swilling was printed in the *Miner* of March 26, 1875.

> Jack Swilling called upon us on Saturday and gave us some items concerning Black Canyon, and the wants of the people of Agua Fria. Mr. S. is one of those who assisted in conquering the Arizona wilderness and adding it to the domain of civilization.

Jack Swilling and His Adopted Son, Gabilan Pollero, in a Humorous Pose

He represents quite a population of settlers along the Agua Fria and its tributaries who are currently cut off from all mail facilities and desire the establishment of a post-route along what is known as the new Helling's road from Prescott to Phoenix. A mail on this route would accommodate those living about Bowers' ranch, Bogg's ranch, Black Canyon and, in fact, a number of large settlements now entirely cut off from the outer world. This route he assures us shortens the distance from here to Phoenix some 30 miles.

Mr. S. is putting out a vineyard and opening a farm on the Agua Fria below the mouth of the Canyon, and is the proprietor of the Valenciana mine. He, with his family is settled permanently on the Agua Fria, and has heard with some apprehension the reports of Indians wandering in that direction, supposed to have escaped from Col. Dudley's outfit though upon further inquiry he feels as if it may be a mistake, and that the tracks and Indians reported to have been seen were those known to have been in that neighborhood for several months and have thus far proven harmless. They consist of only a few families and have managed to keep away from the white settlers.

Later that year the *Miner* reported that Jack and Trinidad's daughter Matilda, age 8, as well as Swilling's father, then living in Alabama, had died. Matilda was buried in a little graveyard on the ranch.

In a lighter vein, the *Miner* of June 30, 1876, carried an article about a troop of visiting dignitaries touring the mines recently discovered by Jack Swilling.

In Soak—Ralph H. Rodgers, Col. C. P. Head and W. W. Hutchinson made a trip to Black Canyon last week to look at the new discoveries made there by Jack Moore, J. W. Swilling and others, and as the weather was excessively hot, in that country, they left their coats at Swilling's ranch and rode to the mines, twelve miles distant, in their shirt- sleeves, intending to return to the ranch the same evening, but were detained in their examinations longer than they calculated on, and night found them still at the mines without tent, blanket or bush to shelter them; but as they were all accustomed to shift for themselves under such circumstances, they each took, what S. S. Fenn, the Idaho Delegate, would call a Missouri blanket, and settled themselves in the sand for a comfortable nap. During the night there came up such a rain-storm as they all declare has rarely, if ever, been known to visit this rain-blessed region in its rainiest season. It rained and poured down in cataracts and floods, until, not only our mine hunting friends, but the whole earth thereabouts was perfectly saturated with it. To get up and run, was only to make matters worse, as there was not a bush nor a rock in many miles of them to break the force of the storm, and they each lay, like Enoch Arden, "prone upon the ground, dug their fingers into the wet earth and prayed" Rogers, who is accused by his companions of being the Jonah of the party, inasmuch as his going out to look at mines is generally a signal for rain, was frequently heard during the storm to mutter to himself something that sounded like swearing, which was no doubt an invocation to the rain-god to let up, but in the meantime his want of faith in the efficacy of prayer was manifested in an effort to dig himself deeper into the sand, so as to husband all the warmth his body had to communicate to the ground, as if he expected a protracted siege. Col. Head says, if he owned a dry ranch, and the corn was suffering for want of rain, he would stake Rogers out in the middle of the field and confidently expect a rain-storm inside of six hours.

Jack Swilling's new ranch on the Aqua Fria aroused as much interest as his old place in Phoenix. A stop at Swilling's place was a "must do" for the traveling public. Of course, letters to the editor of the *Miner* almost always resulted from those stops. On December 29, 1876, the *Miner* published one of many glowing reports.

Swilling has a nice place on the Aqua Fria, almost opposite the mouth of Black Canyon Creek. He was not at home, but his wife and children, and a nephew—recently from the States—were. He has abundance of land, water, wood and mining claims. Several tons of rich looking silver and gold ores, from mines nearby, in Bradshaw mountain, were here sacked, awaiting shipment to Smith's Mill at Wickenburg. There are about fifty miners in the district, all of whom are hopeful of success. They are praying for the erection of a mill at some point in the district. One should be put up there, right away, by some of our Prescott capitalists. It is too far to haul ores to Wickenburg via Phoenix.

Just two miles distant from the Tip Top was the Swilling Mine. The *Miner* of April 6, 1877, carried a good description.

Next we proceeded about two miles distant to the Swilling Mine owned by Jack Swilling. The superintendent, Mike O'Donnell, an old Comstocker, is here showing his early training in developing mines. They are now engaged in sinking a shaft on this mine, and have got down about thirty feet. A solid, well defined ledge of thirty inches of rich ore encourages them in this work, and the evidence is convincing that the ledge will widen. They are now preparing to run a tunnel in under the mountain to strike the ledge. Mr. Swilling has also two other first class mines in course of development, the Cricket and the Basin mines: on both of which there is a ledge equal to that of the Swilling. There is a drift in course of progress on these two mines, running in at present about twenty feet each. Ore is being extracted steadily from all of these, of which the Cricket is the richest, assaying about $2,000, the Basin $1,500, and the Swilling about $1,000. Eight men are now employed, but a larger force is in contemplation to prospect the Swilling on the eastern line. There has been extracted from these mines about $10,000 worth of ore, and about 25 tons still remain on the dumps.

The same issue carried a small piece entitled, "Jack's Garden."

..... an enclosure of about six acres, this waving with vegetation of various kinds, together with the shady trees which line so thickly the margin of the stream, and the birds of various plumage singing merrily in the branches, brings to memory those fond recollections of the groves, brooks and hills with which our boyhood days were spent.

By July 13, 1877, the *Miner* noted that Louis Stevens and C. F. Cate had left Prescott for Black Canyon to purchase Swilling's ranch. Stevens at that time had cattle grazing there. There is, however, no record of such a purchase taking place. Cate did purchase an interest in the Swilling Mine early in July.

On July 29, 1877, a homicide took place at Swilling's ranch. Thomas Mallon and Henry Randall, two packers, argued over a pack-saddle whereupon Randall killed Mallon using a double barreled shot-gun. Mallon had killed another man the previous March and apparently Randall felt he was dealing with a dangerous man to whom he should give no

advantage. Within ten days Jack Swilling appeared in Prescott to testify in Randall's behalf. Randall was easily acquitted.

Swilling's wife, Trinidad, was growing ever more concerned over Jack's drinking habit. Swilling would stay drunk for days or even weeks at a time. Trinidad, along with her six children were probably still provided for as Swilling sold off portions of mines, land, and even a mill site during the last half of 1877. Nevertheless, Swilling would sober up when he traveled out into the mountains on hunting or prospecting trips.

To Gillett and Beyond

Sometime during 1877, Swilling laid claim to 160 acres near the town of Gillett. By early February, 1878, the Swillings had moved to the Gillett area, while keeping the ranch at Black Canyon. As noted in the *Miner*, Swilling was involved in selling lots and providing wood for the mill which was just starting to produce silver.

The *Miner* of April 12, 1878, reported that the Swillings had moved on to a new settlement on the Verde River, about forty miles north of Fort McDowell. It then added that, "Mr. S. has taken up a ranch with a view of engaging in farming, stock raising, etc., the facilities for doing so being advantageous." Swilling could never be far from his mountains and that possible "rich strike." The confusion may have arisen when he and his family visited that area in March of 1878. Meanwhile, the Swilling family stayed at Gillett even as his health was steadily failing. Swilling lost nearly one hundred pounds over a four year period.

About the middle of April, 1878, Trinidad Swilling and a couple of Swilling's friends concocted a trip to get Swilling away from the bottle and the drugs for at least a few days. The *Miner* of May 3, 1878 carried a report of that excursion as written by L. G. Taylor for Swilling after his return.

Col. Snively's Remains.

Black Canyon, A. T., April 25, 1878

Editor *Miner*. A few days since, Jack Swilling, Thomas Barnum, George Monroe and Andy Kirby went out to the White Peak mountain for the purpose of bringing the remains of the lamented Col. Jacob Snively, who was murdered by the Apaches, at that mountain in March 1872, while prospecting with others, for a rich silver lead said to exist in that section.

Here, permit me to state that this makes six of the "old timers" that Mr. Monroe has assisted in burying in Christian graveyards, and seven for Mr. Swilling.

They arrived here today, and the remains were interred in the Swilling family cemetery. As there was no minister present, Judge Handy, of Gillett, read the usual Protestant funeral services, in a solemn, earnest manner.

While Swilling and friends were searching for the bones of Col. Snively, a stage was being robbed just outside Wickenburg. According to the *Miner* of April 26, rewards totaling over two thousand dollars would go to the captors of the highwaymen. You can bet that everyone from Prescott to Phoenix was looking under each rock and bush with hopes of getting a share of that reward. The *Miner* reported one such attempt to capture the outlaws in the April 26th issue.

Deputy U.S. Marshal and detective for the Stage Company, J. W. Evans, has returned from Signal City, whither he went in search of the men who robbed the mail and express below Wickenburg last Friday night. He found no trace of them and thinks they did not go in that direction. This, he says, is the worse case he has had, the rain obliterated the tracks so that he found it impossible to follow them. The only clue they have is that two of the men made large tracks, and one made small ones, therefore, the only show is to arrest two large men and one small one until they find the right ones.

Evans followed one footman who made large tracks and lots of them, nearly a hundred miles; and after making him exhibit the contents of his pack, turn his pockets wrong side out, etc., he found that he had no money and let him go about his business.

It is a difficult case, and one we fear, that will baffle the officers and detectives. U.S. Marshal Standefer is still out somewhere in the direction of Wickenburg.

By coincidence, or possibly by design, a man who was known to brag about having committed every conceivable atrocity, at least when under the influence, was poised and ready to give his best yarn ever to the first man ready to listen. Jack Swilling was notorious at making up stories about how he had robbed a stage coach, even on a night when the whole town knew he was sleeping off another drunk at the local saloon.

This time the gullible listener was working as an assistant to Deputy Sheriff H. H. McCall from Yavapai County. L. G. Taylor, also known as Col. Taylor, from Kentucky, the man who sent the article about Snively to the *Miner*, took every opportunity to pump Swilling for details which Taylor hoped would be sufficient to put Swilling away and provide Taylor with a tidy sum of money.

Swilling, in his best form ever, provided Taylor with more than enough fabrications to do the job. First, Swilling told Taylor about their expedition to find Snively's remains and how, while they were camped out one night, three men had passed within yards of their camp without waking up even one of them. Swilling seemed concerned because, as he pointed out, the tracks looked so much like the tracks he and his two friends had made. Swilling stated that he was afraid some "devilment" was going on and that he and his friends would be accused of it due to the similarity of the tracks.

Next, he related to Taylor the problems he was having with his family. He was sorry he had treated them so badly but nevertheless was intent on sending two of the youngsters to school at Cape Girardeau, Missouri. Swilling wondered if Taylor would act as an intermediary in getting his children away from his wife, Trinidad, so that his friend Andy Kirby could escort them to school.

Taylor questioned whether Swilling had the funds to carry out such a plan, but Swilling assured him he did. When pressed about the money, Swilling confessed that it was in the form of gold obtained from the stage robbed near Wickenburg. Taylor had all he needed, but Swilling wasn't through with him yet.

His next story was that he had sent George Monroe to the Hot Springs (Castle Hot Springs) to purchase that place as headquarters for a stage robbing operation to be headed up by none other than Swilling, himself. He assured Taylor that they would be advised when anything of value was moving on the road and added that Taylor should quit his dairy business, which Swilling had set him up in, and join the "gang."

On May 15, 1878, Taylor met Swilling and Kirby at Shingles and Anders saloon for a drink. McCall and Deputy Sheriff Jim Burnett followed him there and arrested the two. Then, McCall swore in Taylor to assist in transporting them to Prescott. McCall and Taylor, along with their two prisoners, spent the night at Gillett waiting for the stage to Prescott. The next morning McCall stayed with Swilling and Kirby at Gillett while Taylor proceeded to his dairy farm, formerly known as the Jack Swilling ranch, to prepare himself for the trip to Prescott. The stage picked him up there.

Upon arriving at the foot of Arrastra Hill, where Arrastra Creek crossed the road, the men got out of the stage to walk up the hill. Taylor, Kirby, and a man named Calhoun were walking ahead of the stage. Taylor asked Kirby why he had been so bold as to think he could escape the night before. Kirby replied that he had been planning to get a shotgun from Billy Moore's saloon and take the town with it. He then said he would escape and take Swilling with him.

Kirby made more incriminating statements during an overnight stop at Sessions ranch. According to Taylor, Kirby was concerned as to the whereabouts of Jack Swilling, adding that he was concerned that the S....B would say something that would give him away.

Shortly after their arrival in Prescott, the case was heard before U.S. Commissioner H. H. Cartter, acting as Justice of the Peace. Fortunately, for students of Arizona history, that hearing was well documented.

Attorney for the plaintiff was Murat Masterson while Fitch and Churchill represented the defendants. Interestingly, almost everyone on the government side carried two titles. Masterson was also representing the U.S. District Attorney.

On March 27, 1878, testimony began with William Reed, stage driver, the first witness called for the plaintiff. Reed carefully described the robbery as occurring on the Four Mile Hog Back about four miles out of Wickenburg. The driver admitted that he was not sure if the point where the robbery took place was in Yavapai or Maricopa County.

The three robbers he described as short, medium, and tall, armed with a shotgun, rifle, and six-shooter, respectively. On completion of the robbery, the bandits told Reed to drive on and not turn back to Wickenburg. To this they added that they would, "tie him up for the night" if he did not obey. Reed took this as a threat on his life.

The second witness on behalf of the plaintiff was none other than L. G. Taylor, the victim of Swilling's practical joke. In addition to relating all the stories Swilling had told him, Taylor added that on the day of their arrest Swilling told Kirby, in a voice loud enough for all to hear, that they better get word to Monroe in Wickenburg so that he could "get away." The issue of rewards came up. Taylor tried to convince the court that his real concern was that the guilty parties, Swilling and Kirby, be convicted. He also noted that he had learned detective Evans would be unhappy if someone else should get the reward after having chased the would be bandits all the way to the Colorado River. In magnanimous fashion, Taylor offered to add to the reward rather than claim a part of it if Swilling and Kirby were sent to prison. Taylor had another agenda, not yet known to the court.

Next, Taylor's boss, H. H. McCall, also known as General McCall, from Texas, took the stand. His testimony centered around the fact that he had gone to Gillett to meet with Taylor and find out more about the stage robbery. After that meeting he knew Swilling and Kirby were the men he was after. McCall also noted that Swilling had yelled out, while being held prisoner, that, "he would be damned if he wouldn't turn states evidence before he would go to Yuma for robbing that mail." McCall took that to mean that Swilling would turn on his fellow bandits before going to prison for the offense. Swilling actually had something else in mind. McCall felt that if a reward was offered it should go to him.

A passenger who had been on the stage as Kirby and Swilling were brought to Prescott was the next witness called for the plaintiff. This gentleman, Charles Calhoun, merely co-roberated Taylor's testimony about Kirby's comments concerning getting a shotgun and taking out the town of Gillett.

The prosecution then called Messrs. Levy and Smith, saloon owners, to the stand. Frank Smith testified first, stating that Swilling said over and over, "I am arrested for robbing the stage." Under cross examination by Fitch, Smith said that he did not know Swilling's condition on the morning of his arrest, but he had been drinking for the last three or four months!

Levy, in his testimony, added that Swilling and Kirby also said during their day of confinement at the saloon that they did not know anything about the stage robbery. Swilling, Levy said, was sober in the morning but drunk by the evening each day for the last three to four months.

A store keeper, Mr. J. J. Hill, was next to take the stand. He had been keeping store for C. T. Hayden at Gillett. Hill had only known Kirby for a few months, but knew Swilling since 1872 at Salt River. Hill stated that he had furnished the provisions for Swilling's trip into the mountains.

Hill testified that Swilling had told him on returning to Gillett from his expedition to recover Colonel Snively's remains that in observing the trail of the three men who had passed near to their camp during the night and then hearing about the stage robbery he figured out who the robbers must be. Specifically, he named Jim Rhodes, another man named Lewis and a small man, Charley Bennett. Furthermore, Swilling told Hill that Rhodes had stolen his shotgun during Swilling's absence from the ranch. Swilling was certain that it was Rhodes' trail that had passed near his camp.

On the day of his arrest, Swilling asked McCall to procure some Perry-Davis Pain Killer from Hill's store. While there, Swilling told Hill that General McCall had come all the way from Washington to arrest them and added, "of course we did it, by God we did it."

Hill then proceeded to explain the story concerning George Monroe going to Hot Springs to buy the place. It seems that Swilling was interested in moving himself and his family there if Monroe could convince the existing occupant to sell out. We need to keep in mind Swilling's health situation at that time. He was down to 105, pounds which was terribly slight for a six foot frame. Additionally, he was having severe problems with his "bowels," enough to require narcotics for the pain. Hot Springs was well known for its healing qualities.

The next witness was Jessie Jackson, currently a resident at Hot Springs. Masterson asked him about conversations with Swilling but found that there were none. When asked about a letter from Monroe, Jackson said he had left it at home and it would take twenty-five to thirty days to find it. Jackson never produced the letter. Seemingly, Masterson simply wanted to introduce the letter to help support Taylor's testimony, but never intended for the defense or court to see it.

The owner of yet another saloon in Gillett as well as part of the Swilling Mine, was then brought to the stand. C. F. Cate had passage on the same conveyance from Gillett to Prescott.

Cate's purpose as a witness was to confirm Kirby's remark to Taylor when stopping over at Sessions' ranch on the road to Prescott. Under cross-examination, Cate stated that Kirby was, "considerably under the influence of liquor," in fact, he had been all day.

Following Cate, F. W. Otis, Post Master at Prescott, and Robert Dubond, Assistant Post Master, were called to the stand. Prosecutor Masterson and Defense Attorney Fitch spent most of an afternoon arguing about how to prove that the U.S. Mail was indeed robbed at the time the stage was held up. The question to be resolved was whether the lack of a return receipt on a registered parcel sent to San Francisco did indeed prove that the parcel never got there. Neither of the witnesses were particularly convincing concerning the issue of that particular package being put on the stage at Prescott the night before. John Bullock, another driver for the C & A Stage Co. was called.

Bullock testified that he, "ran out the mail to Mr. Reed at Wickenburg," meaning that he took the mail from Prescott to Wickenburg who, in turn, would take it on the stage to California. Bullock, however, was not able to state positively that he had turned over any sacks of mail to Reed that particular time when the stage was robbed.

When court resumed at 9 a.m. on May 29th, Masterson declared that he was ready to close the case on the part of the government. Defense Attorney, Fitch, moved for a dismissal of the case stating that neither had the prosecution proved that a crime was committed nor had they shown that Swilling and Kirby were guilty of the crime charged. In fact, the only thing the prosecution had to hang their hat on was a suggestion by the defendants that they might have done so, but that suggestion came only when both were quite inebriated.

On the fourth day of examination, the defense began its parade of witnesses, the first being James Burnett, Deputy Sheriff for Gillett and the Tip Top mine. Burnett first stated that he, personally, had relieved Jack Swilling of all of his firearms before he had left on his trip to the mountains to retrieve Snively's remains. Burnett had done this so that Swilling, in his drunken state, could not hurt himself or anyone else. Secondly, Burnett declared that, when under the influence of alcohol, Swilling would claim to be the author of any mischief that took place. Next, Burnett related that Swilling had said many times, in a joking way, that he, Kirby, and Monroe had committed the robbery. On each of those occasions, when present, Kirby, would tell Swilling that he was being very foolish in talking that way.

On further questioning, Burnett claimed that most of the town thought that Rhodes and Bennett were the guilty parties. He felt that Rhodes was the leader and Bennett had been led into the deed by Rhodes. This information had been conveyed to McCall when he arrived in Gillett to arrest Swilling and Kirby. Nevertheless, Burnett agreed to help in arresting Kirby and Swilling even though he kept telling McCall that Rhodes was the man he should go after.

Another interesting point that came up during Burnett's testimony was that a letter had been written by Marshal Evans to Swilling seeking information about the stage robbery. Swilling had asked Burnett to respond, since he knew more about Rhodes. Eventually the letter was given to Judge Handy of Gillett to make a response. Strangely, Burnett never felt the need to pursue the matter any further in behalf of his so-called friend, Jack Swilling.

In the re-direct examination, Burnett was asked by Fitch, "you say that Rhodes stopped at Mr. Swilling's place. Was not Mr. Swilling's place generally a free ranch for anyone who was broke? His door was always open to receive any person who was hard up. It did not require certificate of character for them if they were hungry and broke." Burnett responded, "if he knew they were in need they could go there and get something to eat."

The next to testify was C. F. Cate. In cross-examination, Cate told Masterson in no uncertain terms that he did not consider Swilling a dangerous man and that his bragging while under the influence was no more than idle talk. He did, however, consider Rhodes to be dangerous and on one occasion had armed himself out of concern for a possible attack from Rhodes.

Andrew Kirby was called to the stand. He stated that he had accompanied Swilling on his trip to get Snively's remains but that they did not go to Wickenburg. In fact, he said he had never been to Wickenburg. Additionally, Kirby swore that there was only one gun in the party. Certainly, he claimed there was no shotgun, as reported by stage driver Reed, to have been used in the holdup.

After much debate on the question of whether Jack Swilling could testify on his own behalf, it was finally allowed by the court and Swilling took the stand. His testimony follows:

Mr. Fitch: State your name, residence, age and occupation.

Swilling: Residence Agua Fria, age 47, occupation rancher and miner.

Mr. Fitch: Without asking a great number of questions, I will request you, Mr. Swilling, to go on and make a full statement to the Commissioner of your expedition in search of Col. Snively's remains, and all the particulars connected therewith.

Mr. Masterson: We object.

The Court: Answer the question.

Swilling: We left, I think, on Thursday and camped out two or three hours and from there we went to Hot Springs. We got there sometime in the night, I don't recollect what time it was, I had been drinking pretty heavy and don't remember much about the road. The whiskey gave out there and I had some narcotic with me. We then followed up Arrastra Creek, George Monroe said six miles, and from there about four miles to the South Picacho where the remains were buried. We got there in the evening sometime about three or four o'clock and took up

the remains that evening, and camped. It commenced raining just before day. We got up and started before morning, I could not tell what time. It was cloudy and raining and it rained very hard on us. We then went another route back, further south, as I told George it was a desert country, and he told me he could show me three or four live springs where the lilies and cane were growing if I wanted to prospect there, and that was the reason we took that route. We went that way and the storm broke off. In the evening we stopped and cooked some dinner and camped, perhaps two or three hours, and dried our clothes. It had rained very hard, and we started again and come across Casa [Castle] Creek. Before that it had been raining very hard and since the rain there was one track that went down. It was very small only a few tracks, number five or six, and we then crossed Casa [Castle] Creek and went almost on the bank of Humbug and camped again, where we found some water in some tanks. It had been raining. In the middle of the day it rained again. After we left this camp it rained some again. We stayed there that night and the next morning we went on down the Humbug a piece and crossed over onto the Agua Fria across the hill, and went along the Agua Fria until we met the water coming down from the storm the night before, and came so deep that the little pack mule we had and horse I was riding, we thought couldn't cross it and I told them we would go across the hill and we got into my place on Sunday. I didn't go up to town that day, nor Monday. Tuesday I went to town. We brought in the remains and buried them a few days afterwards.

Fitch: Who was in the party?

Swilling: George Monroe and Andy Kirby.

Fitch: What weapons did you have with you?

Swilling: We had a Winchester rifle, is all I know of. I don't know of any other. I had none.

Fitch: Whose rifle was this?

Swilling: It belongs to Mr. Kirby.

Fitch: Do you recollect making any statements to Mr. Taylor—You heard Mr. Taylor's testimony here?

Swilling: Yes sir. I did not drink anything and I did not go to town on that day or on Monday. I wanted to keep away from whiskey, but I was taking narcotics at that time. I went up town

Tuesday morning and there was a report that the mail had been robbed near Wickenburg. That was Tuesday morning. It was on Sunday when I got in. I don't know what day of the month.

Fitch: When did you start out?

Swilling: It must have been the 18th we started out. It was Thursday. We got in on Sunday and was gone four days. That is we started the middle of the day one day and it was the middle of the day when we got back, that made three days.

Fitch: Do you recollect meeting Taylor at this saloon?

Swilling: Yes I recollect meeting him there. I was sober as I am now, and remember telling him about the mail being robbed, and telling him about the shoe track, and that it looked a lot like Charley Bennet's, and that Bennet had run off owing me some money and I wanted to follow, and Kirby and Monroe objected to it thinking they was camped down there, he and Rhodes amongst them. Says I, I am satisfied that Rhodes and that party has done it, and Rhodes has my gun, he took it while I was out to Cave Creek, and took it without my permission, and has my horse, the best horse I got, and says I would like to go and catch him. Says I, they should come right through the same mountains, and they might follow me and George Monroe. I recollect telling that but as to telling him anything about showing him the money, I recollect nothing about it.

Fitch: Do you recollect telling Mr. Hill about the stage being robbed?

Swilling: I recollect telling him I heard it up in town. It was the talk there in town, but nobody seemed to know the particulars, but the next mail they did. I don't know whether the mail brought the news or not.

Fitch: In regard to your statement that you had robbed the stage, what sort of talk was that?

Swilling: I don't never recollect talking any such talk as that.

Fitch: If you did talk it, were you under the influence of opiates and liquor?

Swilling: Well, whiskey alone never does it, but taking whiskey and narcotics together makes me do things—I suppose I do, my wife tells me I do—which is very bad, that I know I wouldn't do if I was sensible.

Fitch: You talk and do things you don't know?

Swilling: I do.

Fitch: You are acquainted with the country down there pretty well?

Swilling: Yes sir.

Fitch: You are a mountaineer and prospector?

Swilling: Yes sir.

Fitch: In which direction from Gillett is this place where you exhumed the remains of Col. Snively?

Swilling: I think it was about Southwest, or a little West of Southwest. It ain't due West.

Fitch: How far from Wickenburg?

Swilling: I think it is about fourteen miles from Wickenburg to White Picacho. I was out there twice, and I intended to prospect, but I could not find water.

Fitch: Was this expedition of yours to take up the remains of Col. Snively the only expedition of that kind you have been engaged in this country?

Masterson: We will admit Swilling has removed several remains.

Fitch: It is important in this case. I desire to show that Mr. Swilling has been in the habit of doing that sort of thing for years. That he has given of his time and labors to digging up the remains of old pioneers, mountaineers and friends who have been killed by Indians and placing them where he could give them a decent burial.

Masterson: Go on. That neither hurts nor assists the case.

Swilling: I have assisted in a good many cases of the same kind. I have assisted with means, and I have went myself, both in New Mexico and Arizona.

Fitch: You have done that frequently?

Swilling: Yes sir, and assisted in others.

Fitch: Have you and Mr. Taylor had any controversy?

Swilling: None whatsoever sir.

Fitch: Is there any clashing of interest between you respecting a ranch?

Swilling: I have been told that he has jumped a ranch of mine.

Fitch: Since your arrest?

Swilling: No sir , before.

Fitch: You don't know whether he has or not?

Swilling: No sir.

Fitch: Did you request Taylor at any time to go and jump a ranch in order to defeat Col. Head who had a mortgage on it, from collecting it?

Swilling: I don't recollect of it. If so, it was sometime when I was senseless and didn't know what I was doing. I was owing Col. Head a week before I was arrested. There is timber enough on the ranch to pay the debt.

Fitch: Do you remember the conversation he speaks of, in which you were anxious to secure his assistance in sending your children to Cape Girardeau?

Swilling: No sir, I don't recollect Taylor being in my house since I have been at Gillett.

Fitch: It might have occurred though when you were unconscious?

Swilling: It might have occurred.

Fitch: What is the effect of these narcotics upon your mind in this particular—that is, do you remember after the effect of the narcotic has passed away, what took place when you were under its influence?

Masterson: That is not evidence, and further, witness is not an expert.

Fitch: I will ask the question in another form. When you are not under the influence of these narcotics and are entirely conscious, do you then remember what you said and did when under the influence?

Masterson: The same objection. That is only stating the same question in a different form.

The Court: Witness can answer the question.

Fitch: When your mind is free from narcotics do you recollect what you did or said when you were under the influence?

Swilling: I know nothing about it, only what is told to me. I have done things at home I had no idea of, and there is and affidavit of mine now in my trunk, that if I do any more such things as that, to have me arrested and have me sent to an asylum. It is an affidavit I made long before I was arrested.

Fitch: Was it only your supposition that Rhodes and others had robbed the stage? You did not know anything about it yourself did you?

Swilling: Nothing in the world, but it was generally supposed that Rhodes and others were up to something. They were figuring around there, and Rhodes had got this gun of mine and he was armed. I knew Rhodes some ten or twelve years ago, but I knew nothing about him being a bad man, but I have heard bad tales about him. He stayed at my house helping around about the cattle and driving up horses and doing various things around. But as for knowing anything about it, I don't know it. Taylor was there and they camped right there close to my house.

Fitch: When did you receive this letter from the United States Marshal with reference to Rhodes and why did you go to Burnett with it?

Swilling: Because he was an officer and he told me he knowed Rhodes for 15 years. He told me Rhodes had been in the pennetentiary. He and Rhodes had some words at my house when Rhodes was stopping at my house and after I heard about him being at the pennetentiary, I requested Rhodes to leave my house. I told him that I would go and get his grub if he wanted it, but that as for his staying there, I though he was not doing me any good nor himself. When I went to Burnett with the letter, I did so because he could describe him and knew him longer than I did, and could tell about his being in the pennetentiary, what for and so on, and he promised to do it. Says I "If you don't I will, but you can do it better than I can and you are an officer."

Fitch: If there is any other matter or thing in explanation of your case that you desire to make a statement about, you may do so.

Swilling: About this narcotic I have been taking, I have been taking it 22 years. It is not a habit, and

I have been taking morphine for four years, putting it in liquor. Nearly four years. The doctors advised me to drink it. I got away from morphine and commenced taking laudanum and chloral, still worse, and has reduced me a great deal. I used to be a heavy man but just a few days before I was arrested I weighed 105 pounds. When I take laudanum and whiskey mixed together, I know nothing about when these things come upon me or goes off me. Wanted to see Mr. Cate on business and I was in town several days looking for him, and when I did see him, I was in a fix, that is I didn't know anything about it. I haven't got an enemy in the world, as I know of, and always looked on him as a friend, and he has always treated me so, and I don't know why I should have made any break on him.

Masterson: I have no questions to ask.

As might be expected, the court ruled the next day that there was no probable cause to believe the defendant J. W. Swilling guilty of the crime charged. U.S. Commissioner Cartter dismissed Swilling on that date.

That should have ended the matter, but somehow the Grand Jury, convening in Prescott on June 6th, for the Third Judicial District, using the same witnesses plus Henry Wickenburg, and John Pierson, managed to indict the three for stage robbery. Their attorneys, Fitch and Campbell, entered a motion to set aside the indictment stating, "The defendants have never been held to answer to a charge for any public offense whatever," and, "the Grand Jury was improperly impaneled."

On July 22, 1878, District Attorney, Paul Weber, disposed of the indictments by entering *nolle prosequi*. His argument was that the robbery really had taken place in Maricopa County. The defense objected and asked that the case go to trial, but that motion was overruled by the court and the case was struck from the docket.

A week earlier, on June 16, 1878, Marshall Evans whisked Swilling and Kirby off to Yuma, allegedly to provide them with a "speedy trial." The *Miner* reported on July 26, 1878 that the over zealous prosecution had failed to find the

right kind of evidence, but an examination was to take place on July 27, 1878.

The *Miner* of August 2, 1878, provided another blistering account of the activities in Yuma.

> Swilling and Kirby: These gentlemen accused of robbing the stage near Wickenburg on the 19th of April have had an examination at Yuma and not contrary to expectations of friends, are held over to answer at the October term of the Court with bail set at $3,000. These men were taken from Prescott without the privilege of consulting their lawyers or friends and cast into prison in a far off corner of the Territory where they were unable to procure legal counsel, being quite without money. The strong hand of the government however, with great magniminity procured all kinds of evidence and have, as above stated, been able to hold them until October.

A week later the *Miner* gave more details of what had happened at the examination.

> The examinations of Swilling and Kirby for robbing the United States mail was concluded on Saturday night at about 12 o'clock. The accused were held over to appear before the Grand Jury with bail fixed at $3,000 each. There were no witnesses for the defense, and certain depositions taken in Prescott and offered by counsel for the accused were ruled out on the grounds that Murat Masterson, whose name was signed to the stipulations as Assistant U.S. District Attorney, had no authority to act as such. The examination lasted two days and the better part of one night without intermission.

In fact, Masterson had received authorization from E. B. Pomeroy, United States District Attorney, but Evans, possibly still looking for his reward, had sworn that it was not so. To Swilling it made little difference as he died in prison on August 12, 1878.

On September 13, 1878, the *Miner* printed the following statement made by Swilling during his last few days on earth.

Yuma Prison, 1878

To the Public:
    Jack Swilling, whose doors have always been open to the poor alike with those of the rich and plenty, looks forth from the prison cell to the blue

heavens where reigns the Supreme Being who will judge of my innocence of the crime which has been brought against me by adventurers and unprincipled reward hunters. I have no remorse of conscience for anything I have ever done while in my sane mind. In 1854, I was struck on the head with a heavy revolver and my skull broken, and also shot in the left side, and to the present time carry the bullet in my body. No one knows what I have suffered from these wounds. At times they render me almost crazy. Doctors prescribed, years ago, morphine which seemed to give relief, but the use of which, together with strong drink, has at times—as I have been told by my noble wife and good friends, made me mad, and during these spells I have been cruel to her, at all other times I have been a kind husband. During these periods of debauch, caused by the mixture of morphine and liquor, I have insulted my best friends, but never when I was Jack Swilling free from these poisonous influences. I have tried hard to cure myself of the growing appetite for morphine but the craving of it was greater than my will could resist. I have gone to the rescue of my fellow men when they were surrounded by Indians—I have given to those who needed—I have furnished shelter to the sick. From the Governors down to the lowest Mexican in the land I extended my hospitality, and oh, my God, how am I paid for it all? Thrown into prison, accused of a crime I would rather suffer crucifixion than commit, taken from my wife and little children who are left out in this cold, cold world all alone. Is this my reward for the kindness I have done to my fellow man and the pay I must receive for having done a Christian act with Monroe and Kirby, that of going after bones of my poor old friend Snively and taking them to Gillett and burying them at the side of my dear child? George Monroe, Andy Kirby and myself are as innocent of the charge brought against us of robbing the stage as an infant babe. We went out to do a Christian act— oh God, is it possible that poor old Jack Swilling should be accused of such a crime? But the trouble has been brought on by crazy drunken talk. I am willing to give up life to save Monroe and Kirby, as God knows they are innocent. Oh, I think of my poor babies and you know that I would not leave them for millions of money. I am persecuted and prosecuted until I can bear it no longer. Look at me and look at them. This cruel charge has brought me for the first time in my life under a jailor's key. Poor L. G. Taylor, whom I liked and tried to help, has been one of those who have wrought my ruin, and for what I cannot conceive unless it was the reward money or to rob my family out of the old ranch. The reason I

write this is because I may be found dead any morning in my cell. I may drop off the same as poor Tom McWilliams did at Fort Goodwin. My persecutors will remember me. And my God help my poor family through this cold world is my prayer.

John W. Swilling

Considering Swillings reduced weight and complaints about his "bowels," death could have been due to liver failure. Certainly, much of his problem was self-induced, but one can't help wondering if monetary reward was the sole inducement for those who prosecuted him so relentlessly.

Soon after Swilling's death, those responsible for upholding the law, got busy trying to find the parties who really were culpable of the crime. By November 22, 1878, James Rhodes was found guilty and sentenced to nine years of imprisonment at States Prison in Michigan. Probably not a bad deal considering Swilling was held in Yuma, Arizona during the summer of 1878.

Meanwhile, warrants went out for Rhodes' accomplices Lewis Rondepoach and John Mullens. Governor John C. Fremont even offered a $500 reward for their capture. They were finally arrested at Olympia, Washington on December 16, 1878. Territorial records do not record their fate, as mail robbery was a federal offense.

Swilling's wife, Trinidad, remarried H. Shumaker who, in 1892, applied for the position of administrator for Swilling's estate. True to Swilling's words, his estate consisted of nothing but a claim of $5,000 against the U.S. Government for Indian depredations. Few, if any, claimants for that kind of loss ever saw restitution.

Phoenix Street Scene—1880s

A. D. Lemon Law Office—Phoenix

Courtesy Sharlot Hall Museum

Waterfalls on the Arizona Canal

Courtesy Sharlot Hall Museum

An Arizona Canal Scene

Arizona Canal

Ford Hotel Outing

Epilogue

It wasn't the human suffering element of stage travel that ultimately led to its demise, it was the fabled iron horse. Railroad tracks carried people and goods faster and in far greater comfort than any stage could hope to. But the railroad too had its shortcomings. Just as today, rails only work if you are going from point "A" to point "B." Tracks were not laid to every little town in the Territory.

As a supplement to rail travel, the stagecoach was still in use until the advent of automobiles. Stagecoaches or their equivalent horse drawn conveyance carried passengers, mail, and light freight from railheads to the smallest of towns well into the twentieth century.

Stage line owners survived in the 1800s only by continually changing their point of connection to the end of the railroad line. James Grant, owner of the California and Arizona Line, was a master at making connections with the then farthest east point on the Southern Pacific Railroad in Southern California. By the time that rail line was completed across Arizona in 1878, only stages running to Central Arizona served any purpose. The connection point had by then become Maricopa Wells and even stage schedules were set to match the arrival and departure of the trains.

Across the north of the Territory, the Atlantic and Pacific Railroad completed its tracks in 1882. At first this had minimal effect on the stagecoach lines of Central Arizona. By the early 1890s, plans were being made to service the burgeoning Phoenix market from the Atlantic and Pacific Line just as the Southern Pacific had done in 1887. The same year a new line entitled the Prescott and Arizona Central made its first run from Seligman to Prescott. By April 24, 1893 the Santa Fe, now owner of the Atlantic and Pacific, had completed its track from Ash Fork to Prescott. Three months later the Prescott and Arizona Central closed its doors.

By March, 1895, the Santa Fe line was extended to Phoenix and became known as the Peavine. The hills and twists were so extreme that the Santa Fe would later test its new diesel engines on this route. If they could handle those grades and curves, they would work anywhere.

The overall distance was farther than the old stage road, but the ride was sure improved. The trip from Prescott to Phoenix was so swift that folks could take weekend trips and still have time to enjoy the "big city." The stagecoach was through for the long haul, but continued on short runs until about 1910.

The *Arizona Republican* dated September 13, 1911 carried an article entitled, "Historic Wheels Have Rolled away."

> Buffalo Bill is making his last stand. The Indians have been subdued and are only heard of in real life when some white man is arrested for imposing on them, or they are jailed for fooling with the white man's fire water. The bandit caves of the Rockies are undermined by the gold seekers, the western deserts have given way to kine covered meadows and the iron horse pants at wayside stations and on the rocky precipices where the mountain sheep clung in days agone. The mule team has been supplanted by the automobile and the bray of the restive burro more seldom echos from the canyon walls than the neighing of miladies Arabian mount. The picturesque figures of the activity of a former day have vanished from the great west, save in the moving picture show. Last to survive the changing environment of the frontier was the old Concord thorough brace stage coach, but it too has gone. It went yesterday.
>
> Perhaps not all the Concord coaches are gone, for it is known that there are one or two left in Arizona, but they are of a latter vintage, built in imitation of those of an earlier time, to satisfy the demand of some resort still keeping alive the romance of the past. But the last of the really genuine, old wagons that did business in Arizona, when the stage coach was the pulse of western civilization, as the railroad is today, was sold yesterday by Ezra W. Thayer of this city, loaded on a train at sundown and ere daybreak this morning will be whirling away to Los Angeles.

But the work of this old stage coach is not yet finished. It is only entering the final chapter under the ownership of the Benham Curio company, to pose along with Bill and the Indians, before the moving picture machine.

The very idea that a noble stage coach should be carried off on the back of the same iron monster that forced it out of business just fifteen years before! And now it was to be nothing more than a bit player in another shameless western movie.

If only the stage coach could have authored and directed those movies, we might have learned how the West really was and not, as John Ford always said, the way it should have been.

Chronology

1846–Mormon Battalion broke first wagon road across Southern Arizona.

1857–Wagon road along 35th parallel (Northern Arizona) established by Lt. E. Beale.

1858–Butterfield Overland Stage ran across Southern Arizona with major stops at Tucson and Yuma.

1861–Civil war began.

1862–Arizona's only Civil war battle took place at Picacho Peak.

1863–Gold was discovered at several points along the Colorado River.

•Arizona Territory established by "Organic Act of 1863."

•Walker and Peeples' parties explore Central Arizona, looking for gold.

•James Grant establishes express service from San Bernardino, California to Prescott, Arizona.

•Vulture mine, south of Wickenburg, discovered by Henry Wickenburg.

1864–First territorial Government established near Fort Whipple.

1865–The Civil War ends.

•Three pioneers, Cunningham, Bell, and Sage massacred in Bell's Canyon.

1866–Freight wagons held up by La Paz and Tonto Apaches in Skull Valley.

1867–Capital moved from Prescott to Tucson.

•James Grant, Arizona's pioneer stage man, awarded contracts to carry mail from San Bernardino to Prescott.

1868–Arizona Stage Company began runs from La Paz to Prescott, through Wickenburg.

•Phoenix settled after water from Salt River was diverted by Swilling Irrigation Company.

•Stage line extended from Wickenburg to Maricopa Wells, southwest of Phoenix.

1869–Two soldiers carrying mail from Date Creek to Prescott killed by Indians.

1870–Declared to be worst year for Indian depredations.

•Military District of Arizona created in response to Indian menace.

•First diggings began at Nigger Wells, notorious for mysterious murders.

1871–Indians attacked west bound stage outside Wickenburg killing five passengers and driver. Event known as "Wickenburg Massacre."

•General George Crook sent to Arizona as Commander of the Department of Arizona.

1872–Peeples Valley cutoff road completed thus allowing avoidance of route through treacherous Bell's Canyon.

•Smiths Mill founded to process ore from Vulture Mine.

•Stagecoach road from Prescott to Phoenix rerouted through Vulture Mine and Smith's Mill.

1873–Threat to Central Arizona ends as Western Apache Indian tribes are placed on Verde River Reservation.

•New road is completed from Black Canyon to Prescott—hailed as second in importance only to Phoenix getting the telegraph.

•Wagon train completes trip from Phoenix to Prescott on new road in just five days.

1875–James Grant dies in California.

1877–Tip Top mine opened with accompanying mill in Gillett.

•Capital moved from Tucson back to Prescott.

1878–Patterson and Caldwell Stage line began on Black Canyon Route from Prescott to Phoenix.

•U.S. Postal contract for Black Canyon Route awarded to Kerns and Griffith.

•California and Arizona Stage Line sold to Gilmer and Salisbury.

•Jack Swilling dies in territorial prison at Yuma.

1879–Bounty money out of Territory Treasury set up for killing stagecoach robbers.

•New Vulture mill established at Seymour.

1884–Gillett's future in doubt as mill is moved to Tip Top Mine.

1886–Barney Martin family robbed and murdered at Nigger Wells.

•Charles P. Stanton murdered at Stanton, Arizona Territory.

1888–Vulture Mine Superintendent, Cyrus Gribble, and two armed guards robbed and murdered near Nigger Wells.

1889–Capital moved from Prescott to Phoenix.

•Vulture mine sold at Sheriff's Sale.

1895–Santa Fe line completed from Prescott to Phoenix.

1911–Last genuine Arizona stagecoach removed to California on railroad flatcar.

Acknowledgments

First, to my best side-kick, Walt Jayroe, without whose dedicated effort this book would never have gotten off the ground. Helping me search for Nigger Wells on Friday the thirteenth was only one example of his "beyond the call" effort. One proofreader declared, "Thank Heaven for good researchers." Walt is, without doubt, the best in Arizona.

Next, to a very special sister-in-law, Karen Brown, who spent countless hours editing and proofing.

Then, to Liz Hutton, a very talented artist whose work should be on every art lover's wall.

And, to Kris Karalius, a highly skilled designer and drafts-person.

Last, but most importantly, I must thank Wendy, my wife of almost forty years for her patience, encouragement, and love.

Of course, many others gave much of their time and skills to this project. Many thanks to each of them.

Elizabeth Coffin	Judi McLeod
Ecee Coffin	Patricia Moorhead
Regina Croly	Cindy Myers
Barbara Dunn	Curtis Ritter
James D. Hofer	Jennifer Robertson
Francis Johnson	Nancy Sawyer
Pearl Kehrer	Bobby Troop
Sheila Kollasch	The Staff of InfoType, Inc.
Paul LeValley	Chloe Woods
Mona McCroskey	Elizabeth Wright

Index

Bibliography

Alsap, T. J., *Memorial and Affidavits Showing Outrages Perpetuated by the Apache Indians in the Territory of Arizona During the Years 1869 and 1870.* Published by authority of the Legislature of the Territory of Arizona. San Francisco, California: Frances and Valentine, 1871.

Barnes, Will C., *Arizona Place Names*, revised and enlarged by Byrd H. Granger. Tucson, Arizona: The University of Arizona Press, 1960.

——, "The Black Canyon Stage." *Arizona Historical Review* (April 1935): 49–55. Arizona Historical Society/Tucson.

Barney, James M., Unpublished manuscript. Vols. I–III. Arizona Department of Library, Archives and Public Records.

——, "Forgotten Towns of Arizona: Seymour." *Arizona Municipalities*, (April, 1940): 15, 18.

Bechtel, Robert B. and Mynne Cordes Jarman, "Cordes and Cordes Junction." *The Journal of Arizona History* (*Winter* 1985) 429–449.

Botts, Gene with John and Marge Osborne, *The Vulture, Gold Mine of the Century.* Phoenix, Arizona: Quest Publishing Group, 1995.

Bourke, John G., *On the Border with Crook.* Lincoln, Nebraska: University of Nebraska Press, 1971.

Bowman, Eldon G. and Jack Smith, *Beales Road Through Arizona.* Flagstaff, Arizona: Flagstaff Corral of Westerners International, 1879.

Brinckerhoff, Sidney B., *Camp Date Creek, Arizona Territory: Infantry Outpost in the Yavapai Wars, 1867–1873.* Tucson, Arizona: The Tucson Corral of the Westerners, Fall 1964.

Butterfield Overland Mail Across Arizona 1858–1861. Tucson, Arizona: Arizona Silhouettes, 1958.

Calhoun, Kenneth M., Ed. "Yavapai County Memories, 1863–1894," by Charles Genung. *The Smoke Signal* 43, 44 (Spring and Fall, 1982). The Tucson Corral of the Westerners.

Conner, Daniel E., "The Walker Expedition in Arizona," Arizona Department of Library, Archives and Public Records, unpublished manuscript.

Cordes, Claire Champie, *Ranch Trails and Short Tales.* Crown King, Arizona: Crown King Press, 1991.

Crook, George, *General George Crook, His Autobiography*, Martin F. Schmitt, Ed. Norman, Oklahoma: University of Oklahoma Press, 1946.

Evans, Elwyn, *Hollingbourne and the Duppa Family.* Hollingbourne, Maidstone, Kent, England: All Saints' Church, Hollingbourne and the Hollingbourne Society, 1995.

Farish, Thomas Edwin, *History of Arizona, I–VIII.* Phoenix, Arizona: c. By Thomas Edwin Farish, 1915.

Fish, Joseph, *History of Arizona*, Arizona Department of Library, Archives and Public Records, unpublished manuscript, Parts I and II.

Gall, John, *The Black Canyon Stage Lines.* Arizona Historical Foundation, unpublished manuscript.

Genung, Dan B., *Death in His Saddlebags: Charles Baldwin Genung, Arizona Pioneer.* Manhattan, Kansas: Sunflower University Press, 1992.

Goff, John S., *Arizona Territorial Officials, Vol. II, The Governors 1863–1912.* Cave Creek, Arizona: Black Mountain Press, 1978.

——, *Arizona Territorial Delegates to Congress, 1863–1912.* Cave Creek, Arizona: Black Mountain Press, 1985.

——, *King S. Woolsey, Vol. I, Arizona Biographical Series.* Cave Creek, Arizona: Black Mountain Press, 1981.

Goodson, Rose Mary, *The Story of Congress, Arizona's Premier Gold Camp.* Stickney, South Dakota: Argus Publishing Company, 1995.

Grimes, Pauline, *Land of Our Own.* New River, Arizona: Self Published, 1987.

Hawkins, Helen B., "A History of Wickenburg to 1875," Master thesis, Arizona State College, 1950.

Heatwole, Thelma, *Ghost Towns and Historical Haunts in Arizona.* Phoenix, Arizona: Golden West Publishers, 1981.

Henson, Pauline, *Founding a Wilderness Capital, Prescott, Arizona, 1864.* Flagstaff, Arizona: Northland Press, 1965.

Illustrated Road Maps and Tour Book. Prescott, Arizona: Arizona Good Roads Association, 1913.

Jack of All Trades: J. W. Swilling in the Arizona Territory. Phoenix, Arizona: The Salt River Project, 1992.

Johnston, Francis J., *The Bradshaw Trail.* 1977. Riverside, California: Riverside Historical Press, 1987, revised edition.

——, *Stagecoach to Disaster.* Authors Collection, Unpublished manuscript.

Kleese, William C., "Obscure Towns of Nineteenth-Century Arizona: Gillett," *Copper State Bulletin* (Fall 1991): 103–106.

——, "Obscure Towns of Nineteenth-Century Arizona: Stanton." *Copper State Bulletin* (Summer 1993): 55–63.

Korwin, Alan, *Wickenburg, The Ultimate Guide to the Ultimate Western Town.* Phoenix, Arizona: Bloomfield Press, 1994.

Lauer, Charles D., *Tales of Arizona Territory.* Phoenix, Arizona: Golden West Publishers, 1990.

Luckingham, Bradford, *Phoenix, The History of a Southwestern Metropolis.* Tucson, Arizona: The University of Arizona Press, 1989.

Marion, J. H., *Notes of Travel Through the Territory of Arizona,* D. M. Powell, Ed. Tucson, Arizona: University of Arizona Press, 1965.

McClintock, James H., *Arizona: Prehistoric; Aboriginal; Pioneer; Modern. I–III.* Chicago, Illinois: Clarke Publishing Company, 1916.

McCroskey, Mona Lange, *Summer Sojourn to the Grand Canyon, The 1898 Diary of Zella Dysart.* Prescott, Arizona: HollyBear Press, 1996.

Miller, Joseph, *Arizona Story.* New York, New York: Hasting House, 1952.

——, Ed., *Arizona Cavalcade: The Turbulent Times.* New York, New York: Hasting House, 1962.

Morgan, Learah Cooper, Ed., *Echos of the Past: Tales of Old Yavapai*. Prescott, Arizona: Yavapai Cow Belles, 1955.

Nicholson, John, Ed., *The Arizona of Joseph Pratt Allyn: Letters from a Pioneer Judge*. Tucson, Arizona: The University of Arizona Press, 1974.

Peterson, Thomas H., "Cash Up or No Go: The Stagecoach Era in Arizona," *Arizona Journal of History* (Autumn 1973): 206–222.

Pry, Mark E., *The Town on the Hassayampa, A History of Wickenburg, Arizona*. Wickenburg, Arizona: Desert Caballeros Western Museum, 1997.

The Right Side Up Town on the Upside Down River. Wickenburg, Arizona: Las Senoras de Socorro, 1975.

Rosebrook, Jeb J. and Jeb S., "The Old Black Canyon Highway," *Arizona Highways* 70 (August 1994): 4–11.

Rozum, Fred A., "Buckboards and Stagecoaches: Establishing Public Transportation on the Black Canyon Route," *The Journal of Arizona History* 30 (Summer 1989): 165–180.

Sayre, John W., *The Santa Fe, Prescott and Phoenix Railway: The Scenic Line of Arizona*. Boulder, Colorado: Pruett Publishing Company, 1990.

Sherman, James E. and Barbara H., *Ghost Towns of Arizona*. Norman, Oklahoma: University of Oklahoma Press, 1969.

Smith, Dean, *The Goldwaters of Arizona*. Flagstaff, Arizona: Northland Press, 1986.

Soloman, I. E., "Stages Held Up," *Arizona Historical Review* 1 (October, 1928): 50–53.

Spude, Robert L. and Stanley W. Paher, *Central Arizona Ghost Towns*. Las Vegas, Nevada: Nevada Publications, 1978.

Stevens, Robert C., *Echos of the Past: Tales of Old Yavapai*, Vol. II. Prescott, Arizona: The Yavapai Cowbelles, Incorporated, 1964.

Summerhayes, Martha, *Vanished Arizona: Recollections of My Army Life*. Chicago, Illinois: The Lakeside Press, 1939.

Swilling, Trinidad, *Unpublished 1923 Statement Authors Collection*.

Theobald, John and Lillian, *Arizona Territory: Post Offices and Postmasters*. Tempe, Arizona: The Arizona Historical Foundation, 1961.

———, *Wells Fargo in Arizona Territory*. Tempe, Arizona: The Arizona Historical Foundation, 1978.

Thompson, George A., *Throw Down the Box: Treasure Tales from Gilmer and Salisbury, the Western Stagecoach King*. Salt Lake City, Utah: Dream Garden Press, 1989.

Thorpe, Winifred L., "Joe Mayer and His Town." Notes by Robert l. Spude. *The Journal of Arizona History* 19 (Summer 1978): 131–168.

Truman, Ben C., *Occidental Sketches*. San Francisco, California: San Francisco News, 1881.

Wampler, Vance, *Arizona, Years of Courage, 1832–1910: Based on the Life and Times of William H. Kirkland*. Phoenix, Arizona: Quail Run, 1984.

Weiner, Melissa Ruffner, *Prescott: A Pictorial History*. Virginia Beach, Virginia: The Donning Company, 1981.

Wilson, Bruce M., *Crown King and the Southern Bradshaws: A Complete History*. Mesa, Arizona: Crown King Press, 1990.

Yoder, Phillip D., "The History of Fort Whipple." Masters thesis, University of Arizona, 1951.